JOURNEY
Route 66

Ryan Ver Berkmoes, Margot Bigg, Andrew Bender
George R Joe, Mark Johanson, Nneka M Okona, Karla Zimmerman

It's the defining American road trip: Route 66. Dubbed the 'Mother Road' by John Steinbeck, this string of small-town main streets and country byways first connected Chicago and its big ambitions with the waving palm trees of Los Angeles and the blue Pacific in 1926. Once an escape to a better life, today it offers a nostalgic escape to the past, a window on natural beauty and wide-open spaces, an introduction to characterful small towns and even some very good pie.

Contents

Plan Your Trip

- My Route 66 4
- The Road to Authenticity 8
- Magical Open Spaces 14
- Fabulous Road Food 18
- Weird & Wonderful 22
- A History of Route 66 26
- 6 Ways to do Route 66 30

Go to p32 for the full route map

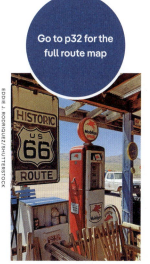

Hackberry General Store (p198), Arizona

Previous page: Stretch of Route 66, Amboy, California
JRTWYNAM/SHUTTERSTOCK

The Drive

THE MIDWEST
- City Guide: Chicago 36
- Chicago to St Louis 44
- St Louis to Joplin 62

THE GREAT PLAINS
- Galena to Tulsa 86
- Tulsa to Texola 104
- Texola to Glenrio 122

THE SOUTHWEST
- Glenrio to Albuquerque 148
- Albuquerque to Lupton 168
- Lupton to Topock 184

INSIGHT ESSAYS
- Rhythm of the Road 60
- The Neon Road 80
- Labor & Strife in Kansas 91
- A 'Green Book' Journey 100
- Cars & Route 66 119
- Route 66 in Film & TV 120
- The Dust Bowl 131

CALIFORNIA
- Needles to Barstow 206
- Barstow to Santa Monica 220
- City Guide: Los Angeles 232

Toolkit

- First Time 242
- Money 243
- On the Road 244
- Driving Problem-Buster 246
- How to Rent More than a Car 247
- Where to Stay 248
- Access, Attitudes & Safety 249
- Responsible Travel 250

- Route 66's Motel Evolution 137
- Vintage Gas Stations 140
- That Ain't Us: A Navajo Perspective 164
- The Guardian Angel of Route 66 182
- My Life & Route 66 202
- Finding Freedom on the Open Road 218

3

My Route 66

Ryan Ver Berkmoes @ryanverberkmoes

I'm not a morning person but when I'm on a Route 66 trip, I can't help but not be. At first light, I wake up in some wonderful old motel – the kind where you park right outside your door – and I hear vehicles going by and they are all saying, 'Come on Bub, join us!' And I do! I love a cafe breakfast but sometimes the wanderlust is too strong; the road trip is calling. It's coffee to go and I go. Surprises, pleasures and adventures await. It's always, 'This is pretty cool, but what's around that next bend?'

Ryan wrote the front and back chapters, the journey chapters from Chicago through Arizona, plus essays on film and his personal recollections. He's written over 160 guidebooks for Lonely Planet and has driven Route 66 at least 25 times.

Ryan Ver Berkmoes and one of Route 66's many Giant Muffler Man statues (p23)

MY FAVORITE STRETCHES

South of Springfield, Illinois
Century-old concrete roadway bends around even older farms in a flat landscape of stark beauty. p57

West of Mesita, New Mexico
Nearly 70 miles of delight through rolling hills and jutting mesas. p172

Road to Oatman, Arizona
The first time I drove this corkscrew and found a burro blocking my way, I started laughing. I still am. p199

MY ROUTE 66

Margot Bigg at Elmer Long's Bottle Tree Ranch, Oro Grande (p224)

Margot Bigg @margotbigg

I must confess: before I started researching this book, I thought of Route 66 as one long stretch of adorable roadside attractions. I'd driven stretches of the route more than once, but always viewed it as a relic of the past, failing to recognize its significance in shaping the landscape of American motor travel – and American mobility. It took slowing down and talking to the people who live along the route to truly understand its importance. And while some segments have turned into ghost towns, and others have been lined with strip malls, the love that so many have for Route 66 has not wavered.

Margot Bigg writes about experiential travel, especially in India and the Western US, for publications around the world. She's a huge fan of road tripping and loves taking the scenic route whenever possible. Margot wrote the Needles to Barstow (p206) and Barstow to Santa Monica (p220) chapters.

MY BEST CURIOSITIES

Liberty Sculpture Park
Anti-communism art installation. p214

Calico Ghost Town
Chukar partridges and fortune-telling machines. p216

Fair Oaks
Phosphoric acid-laced soda. p228

Andrew Bender @wheresandynow

As a kid in New England, Route 66 was a song; moving to Los Angeles, a mile from the Mother Road, it became my life. I've since been enchanted by Chicago's lakefront, onion burgers in OKC, and wide open spaces, but my heart always skips at the road's end in Santa Monica. My work has appeared in the *Los Angeles Times, Forbes* and more, and when not writing I'm often leading tours in Japan.

Andrew wrote the Los Angeles chapter (p232) and Finding Freedom on the Open Road (p218).

George R Joe @navajoguide

I grew up in Dilkon on the southwest edge of the Navajo reservation in northeastern Arizona. In Northern Arizona, for the best food and shopping, you must visit La Posada (pxxx) in Winslow. I'm fluent in Navajo and have worked as an educator, filmmaker, and communications professional. My travel site, *navajoguide.com*, covers travel in the Navajo nation, and I'm currently developing a travel app.

George wrote 'That Ain't Us': A Navajo Perspective (p164).

Mark Johanson @markonthemap

As an American who's lived outside of the US the majority of my adult life, I'm often nostalgic for places like Route 66, which seems to embody all the wonder and extravagance of the American experience. To me, it's a place built for the kind of serendipity many of us lost in the age of smartphones. A regular writer for NatGeo, *Travel + Leisure* and Lonely Planet, my first book, *Mars on Earth*, was released in 2024.

Mark wrote The Guardian Angel of Route 66 (p182).

Nneka M Okona @afrosypaella

Travel by car is my favorite mode of travel. In particular, I'm taken by the stunning, often otherworldly sunsets in Albuquerque along Route 66 and stargazing at Chaco Canyon. My work has been published by *Condé Nast Traveler, Travel + Leisure,* National Geographic and Lonely Planet. I'm also the author of two self-help books on grief and everyday healing.

Nneka wrote A 'Green Book' Journey (p100).

Karla Zimmerman @karlazimmerman

I've traveled Route 66 on its slowpoke path through Illinois multiple times over the past few decades. Atlanta, IL, delights me most. Who doesn't admire a town with a towering statue of Paul Bunyan clutching a hot dog? A contributor to more than 80 Lonely Planet books, I write about travel and oddball sights when I'm not eating doughnuts and yelling at the Cubs at home in Chicago.

Karla wrote the Chicago chapter (p36), A History of Route 66 (p26) and Rhythm of the Road (p60).

James Gulliver Hancock @gulliverhancock

I'm Australian but I spent a long period living in the US, where the pull of the road trip was always strong. I've worked on many amazing projects with Lonely Planet, each one a thrill for my younger self who loved to make drawings that explain things. *My How Things Work* series spans subjects from space stations to trains.

James drew the illustrated map (gatefold).

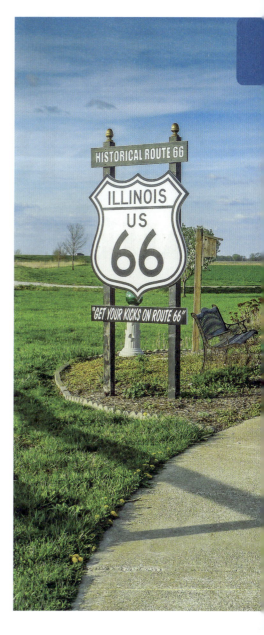

Route 66 sign, Illinois
PHOTO. ECCLES/SHUTTERSTOCK

The Road to Authenticity

With businesses at freeway interchanges stripped bare of originality, travel on Route 66 grows more popular each year for its authenticity.

WITH THE T-SHIRT you're wearing unlikely to survive more than a few washes before the seams unravel and the vehicle you're driving prone to crumple at the slightest contact with another, the durability of Route 66 offers a bedrock of delight when much of life seems ephemeral.

The mere idea that you can set off on a 2400-mile journey and encounter a constant stream of surprises, beauty, creativity, idiosyncrasy, wonder and so much more is a delight and even a source of wonder in today's world. You just never know what you'll find around the next bend. It could be a beloved old diner, a curio shop run with heart or a vista so magnificent, it takes your breath away.

Hello America

Driving 'America's Main St' is a roller-coaster ride of real-world adventure, without the queasiness in your stomach – except maybe on the way to Oatman in Arizona! But it's not all fun times and feel-good fluff either. Just under the surface of your experience is an awareness of the legions of travelers during Route 66's heyday, when, from the 1930s to the 1960s, this was an escape from despair, a route of hopes and dreams.

Dig deeper and you'll find every complexity of American history, from the Trail of Tears to segregation to the Tulsa Massacre to the range wars of the Old West and much more, because the Mother Road is a real road that spans two-thirds of a country with a turbulent past. After all, the beloved moniker, 'Mother Road,' comes from John Steinbeck's *The Grapes of Wrath,* a novel about class, poverty, the Dust Bowl and Route 66.

Route 66 souvenir shop, Tulsa (p96)
ABOVE: BILL CHIZEK/SHUTTERSTOCK. RIGHT: SUSAN VINEYARD/GETTY IMAGES

Timeless Design

One discovery you'll make on Route 66 is generational shifts in attitudes that strike wistful chords today. In the many restored gas stations found in all eight states, the buildings were designed as pieces of architecture bordering on the exquisite (see Shamrock, p126). Even the gas pumps were crafted with artistic flair. This craftsmanship extends to other mundane structures such as roadhouses, where weary travelers could stock up on groceries and refreshments. Built solidly from local materials like rocks and adobe, even the abandoned ones still stand proudly, decades after the last block of ice left the premises. Popular oddities like the giant 'Muffler Men' (p56), used for promotional purposes, have weathered the decades well. Compare them to today's equivalent: an unctuous inflatable figure flopping around until the plug is pulled on its blower.

The question of where to spend the night inspired hundreds of owner-operators to build motels that showed a pride of place and catered to the needs of newly mobile Route 66 travelers (p137). In Missouri, beautiful auto courts (collections of units usually arranged in a U-shape) were created from the local river stone by talented local stonemasons. In the Southwest, designers drew on local architecture traditions to craft tiny flat-roofed palaces in adobe.

As always, promotional considerations inspired visual artistry. Flashy neon signs are found all along Route 66, starting in Chicago, and are so popular that the National Park Service

THE JOY OF TWO LANES

America's interstate freeways are marvels of efficient transportation, binding together a vast country, but they are rarely themselves reasons for the journey. Wherever you find yourself in the USA, there are inevitably older, more scenic alternatives nearby. Whenever possible, hit the exit and take the two-laner (try US 40, US 50 or US 95), passing through small towns, along railroad tracks and winding through beautiful scenery.

ROUTE 66 IN MEDIA

Cars (2006)
Pixar creatives prowled the road getting inspiration for the mega-hit about a town trying to survive using its wits after being bypassed by the freeway.

Bagdad Cafe (1987)
Captures everything weird and dangerous about Route 66 in the scorched depths of the Mojave Desert.

(Get Your Kicks on) Route 66!
Driving to LA, Bobby Troup wrote this song and sold it to Nat King Cole in 1946, making music history.

Old Texaco gas station, Dwight (p50)

BUILDING GAS BRANDS

Gas stations were once seen by oil companies as the centerpiece for building their nascent brands. As such, starting in 1926 they treated Route 66 as a blank canvas, with each aiming for a distinctive look. Shell favored a New England seaside motif; early Phillips 66 stations looked like a Tudor garden cottage, then they switched to a high-concept mid-century gull-wing look; while Texaco went for the dependable feel of the home of a judge or doctor. (p140)

funds their restoration. At night, Albuquerque's Central Ave (p176) is a cavalcade of vintage neon signage.

Small-Town USA

Like a good landscape photo, there's also the bigger picture. The route is dotted with scores of appealing small towns. Some so tiny yet alluring that you'll decide to make an unplanned stop, and others with such great appeal, that you'll stop for the night.

Unlike the interstate, where trying to explore a town requires you to quit cruise control, exit the highway and penetrate a shield of chains before undertaking a potentially longish drive in search of civilization, on Route 66, towns simply appear dead ahead in your windshield. Each is enticingly different, some cruising along prosperously in the 21st century, like Claremore, Oklahoma (p94), or barely one big blow away from vanishing, like Glenrio, Texas (p138), or using every possible trick to hang onto their survival on Route 66 like Seligman, Arizona (p196).

On the Open Road

Away from towns, the natural beauty you encounter is also core to the drive. The open spaces are legendary. But a sweeping view as you round a bend offers its own flash of loveliness.

Route 66 Podcast
So sincere it hurts, this ongoing series interviews Mother Road luminaries. Learn secrets of the Blue Whale or the Munger Moss Motel.

The Grapes of Wrath
John Steinbeck's 1939 book is an indictment of class struggles as the Joad family journeys to California on, yes, the Mother Road. The 1940 film made Henry Fonda a star.

Whose Names Are Unknown
Sanora Babb's 1930s novel covers the Dust Bowl and was an uncredited source for Steinbeck. It wasn't published until 2004.

A rock formation in the west or the geometric crop rows in the east can offer equal fascination.

Businesses and attractions come in a million flavors, all with the same diversity of concept, execution, offering and ownership you've now come to expect. You will be able to see, experience and buy things impossible to find elsewhere: some are wonderfully weird (p22), others – like the superb Oklahoma Route 66 Museum in Clinton (p116) – core to your Mother Road experience.

With the Mother Road's centennial in 2026, celebrations are underway along all 2400-plus of its miles and this journey of discovery – of the good, the bad and the ugly, but also the goofy and the fabulous – will get even more acclaim. There's no reason to delay, so hit the road today.

Display in Route 66 Museum, Clinton (p116)

HIGHLIGHTS

❶ Atlanta, Illinois (p52)
One of Route 66's prettiest small towns. The main square is surrounded by museums, giant advertising figures (including the 'Bunyon Giant') and a great nearby cafe known for its pie.

❷ Meramec Caverns (p70)
The original Route 66 roadside attraction and still going strong. Starting in the 1930s, the owners of the ever-expanding caves perfected the art of viral promotion on barns and bumpers.

❸ Clanton's Cafe, Vinita (p93)
Since 1927 this small-town eatery has eschewed touristy gimmicks, delivering superb chow priced for the masses. The chicken fried steak is the best anywhere.

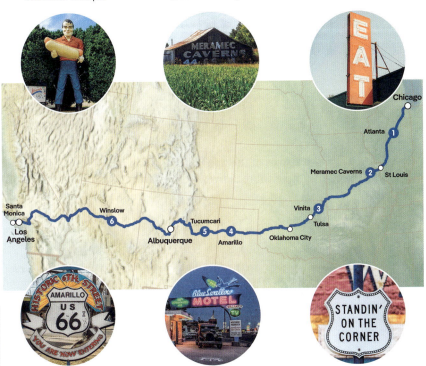

❹ SW 6th Avenue, Amarillo (p134)
A segment of Route 66 in the city, SW 6th Ave is lined with a brilliant collection of shops – many selling 1930s antiques and Mother Road merch – plus bars and restaurants, some dating to the 1940s.

❺ Tucumcari (p152)
At dusk, prepare to be dazzled by the best lineup of neon signs found along the route. Star among this notable group is the legendary Blue Swallow Motel and its '100% Refrigerated Air' slogan.

❻ Winslow (p188)
This Mother Road town hits several pitch-perfect notes: the landmark La Posada Hotel (1930) is one of the finest hotels on the road, while the Eagles song 'Take it Easy' is immortalized downtown.

Magical Open Spaces

Reveling in the wide spaces of the open road is a top reason to drive Route 66, and the route delivers from start to finish.

YOU SEE IT while you're still in Illinois: that endless horizon that sweeps around your windshield and crosses every other window of your vehicle. There's a big sky above – cornflower blue on good days and moody silver-gray on others. It starts on the oldest stretches of Route 66 south of Springfield, as you drive across table-flat farmlands little-changed since the birth of the Mother Road in 1926.

Blue Sky Farmlands

This endless vista is what Alfred Hitchcock wanted for the legendary crop-duster scene in *North by Northwest* (p90). And while people expect vast open spaces in Texas and the Southwest, they are surprised and delighted to encounter them here, barely 200 miles into their journey. One of the great promises of Route 66 is the opportunity to cast off the congestion of the interstate, the cacophony of a crowded, urbanized world and the ceaseless, franchised glare of the strip mall for something simpler that's hard to find in much of the country.

Road-trippers yearn to scale back their senses, to revel in the grandeur of little, to be freed from the tyranny of commercial stuff in the windshield. Happily, nearly every state along the route offers a chance to do just this. Illinois presents minimalist vistas of corn in summer and rich, fallow earth or even the visual purity of snow in winter. All this on the already enjoyable stair-stepping 1926 segments of Route 66 (p57) on the way to St Louis.

Rainbow Landscapes

Missouri adds texture to the empty vistas, with gently rolling hills of lush green nothingness

Route 66, Amboy (p210)
FILM STRIP: MARIQUITA ST/SHUTTERSTOCK, CHRIS HACKETT/ GETTY IMAGES, RIGHT: SOCALDREAMGIRL/SHUTTERSTOCK

in the middle of the state. Kansas never has a chance to show its amber waves of grain, as the Mother Road barely cuts off the southeast corner, but Oklahoma more than makes up for it.

The state of rich red earth is peppered with appealing small towns through its namesake city in the center, but then the promise of the west takes over and the skies and the horizons open up to wide-open spaces as far as the eye can see. This minimalist visual joy segues into the Panhandle Plains of Texas where even a doggie (cow) grazing on a clump of sod makes a dramatic visual statement. The wind blows because there's nothing to stop it. It's poetry in tans, yellows and browns set off by the blue skies and puffy white clouds. And, you might just see a soaring thunderhead, in all its menacing glory, making even this vast landscape look small.

New Mexico expands the color palette with rich browns, deep reds and hints of purple. Nothingness takes on new meaning as mesas, with their dot and dash irregularity, add drama to the horizon. These classic Southwest scenes continue into Arizona, which includes the bonus of national parks (p188). Then in the West, color and texture are stripped out of the sun-blasted deserts that become the fabled Mojave in California. From the comfort of your modern vehicle think about those who came before and survived blinding white light and searing heat.

Nearing LA, open vistas become a memory until you hit the Pacific, where the blue waters stretch to a once-again endless horizon.

PICTURING ROUTE 66

Much of the classic imagery we associate with Route 66 involves the magnificent nothingness of the American West. Central to that is the mesa, the flat-topped escarpments stretching across horizons. Think of the Road Runner and Wile E Coyote careening through a mesa-filled countryside on a two-lane asphalt highway (which was modeled on Route 66 in New Mexico and Arizona).

DRAMATIC SCENES TO CAPTURE

Winter Magic
A stark, white expanse sparkling in the sun can follow a blizzard in Illinois from November to April. Roads get plowed quickly.

Witness Weather Drama
March through October can bring lightning, thunderstorms and clouds from the Great Plains through Arizona. Watch your weather app and the sky.

Selfies in the Desert
Sunrise or sunset gives you that magical glow; bring a cloth to shade your phone or camera to avoid heat shut-downs.

HIGHLIGHTS

① South of Springfield (p57)
The small towns and charms of central Illinois are forgotten on nearly 100-year-old stretches of road that bend past farmhouses set on land so flat there's hardly a ripple.

② Near Clinton (p116)
Western Oklahoma is Dust Bowl country and you can still feel the non-stop winds blowing across the horizon. The horrors of the 1930s may be in the past, but memories – like the views – are long.

③ Best-preserved stretch of old Route 66 in Texas (p127)
Most of the Texas Panhandle is one vast open space straight outta the dreams of the open road fantasist, but this segment encapsulates it all.

MAGICAL OPEN SPACES

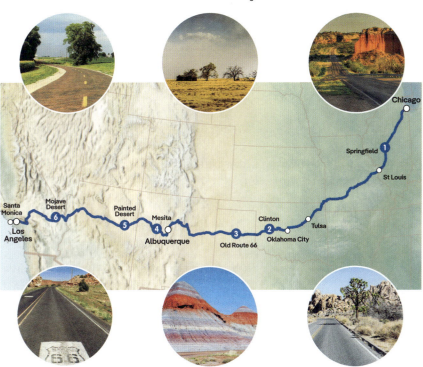

④ Mesita & Old Route 66 (p172)
Here in this tiny town begins 70 miles of pure driving pleasure through mostly wild and natural New Mexican countryside, with just enough vestiges of humanity to put all those open spaces in wonderful perspective.

⑤ Painted Desert (p188)
It's like an absurdly indulgent all-you-can-eat buffet of color that stretches as far as you can possibly see. If you haven't said 'wow' on the trip yet, you will now.

⑥ Mojave Desert (p210)
The ultimate nothingness, and one that can kill you were it not for all the modern conveniences at hand. This bare land bakes under the glare of the sun and radiates an otherworldly beauty.

Fabulous Road Food

Cutting its diagonal swath across two-thirds of the US, Route 66 passes through regions renowned for some of the nation's most iconic cuisines.

Diner Delights

Chicago has some fabulous diners (p48) and that's a great way to start your trip on Route 66. Fluffy omelets, eggs any way you like, a stack of pancakes, waffles, sausage, bacon, hash browns, the list goes on and that's just for breakfast. Lunch and dinner bring burgers, dogs, fries, soup, salads, pies, shakes and myriad more choices.

As you head west, diners are the one constant you can count on never being far from (although as you near the coast in California, they tend to be called coffee shops and you'll likely be offered a nice, fresh fruit cup). What won't be constant are the menus as regional variations crowd in: biscuits with sausage gravy start somewhere in Missouri, followed by chili in Oklahoma (p97) and, most delightfully, red and green chile and tortillas in New Mexico (p153).

Local Flavors

If diners in all their cliched, chromium glory are a staple of the Mother Road, then it's the regional cuisines that – at times literally – spice up the drive and make food one of the unmissable joys of the journey. That's why avoiding chains and their homogenized menus is a cardinal rule of any trip.

Take St Louis, a crossroads of America in transportation and food, putting its spin on everything from pizza (paper thin and made with oddball cheeses unknown in Italy) to pasta (toasted ravioli!) to its unmissable frozen custard dessert (p66).

You won't have much time in Kansas, but as you angle through, have some of the locally famous fried chicken. Then there's Oklahoma.

Toasted ravioli
ABOVE: MIKE BRAKE/SHUTTERSTOCK.
RIGHT: SEAN LOCKE PHOTOGRAPHY/SHUTTERSTOCK

First, it does chicken fried steak like no other state; you can get it at any meal and at almost any restaurant (p93). It's one of the dishes vying for official 'Mother Road Dish' status. But forget that in Oklahoma City and order a steak (p112). The beef here will spoil you when you go back to 'regular' steak.

Texas might argue the steak crown but there's no arguing its barbecue bona fides. Competition is so fierce that just being good is not good enough. Residents lay claim to their favorite pitmaster the way others cling to their plumber. Note: at the best places, go early as when the day's 'cue is gone, it's gone (p130).

In New Mexico, you might want to flatten all the tires on your vehicle, so you have an excuse to stay longer to revel in the local foods. The sophisticated flavors have their roots in techniques and ingredients that go back centuries. Arizona brings in Mexican influence, which only adds to the spice and the sophistication.

And then we reach California. Los Angeles has long been one of the world's best cities for dining, with nearly every nation represented by a community in Southern California. Cuisines are mixed and mingled and given added zest by the wealth of fresh ingredients. Just one example: that beloved Route 66 road food, the doughnut? Any Angelino will tell you the best ones are found at the scores of shops run by the region's Cambodian community.

You're gonna want to turn around and eat your way east.

BIRTH OF A CLICHÉ

Time was, Route 66 diners looked like diners anywhere: bright lights, stools at the counter and booths along the walls. As Mother Road lore took off, the diners were festooned with Route 66 signs, then merch, then red vinyl for the seating and chrome for the detailing. And, if they could find 'em (or there was a local acting school), smart-aleck waitresses. Today, you'll find 'Route 66 diners' from New York to Paris to Tokyo.

ROUTE 66 STAPLES

Chicken Fried Steak
Usually beef (can be pork or chicken), pounded thin, breaded and fried crispy/crunchy and served under a blanket of rich pan gravy with mashed potatoes.

Burgers
A menu stalwart going back to the 1930s when they were cheap and thin but often delicious (like an El Reno onion burger).

Pie
Not simple to make well. Crust needs to be flaky; fillings can be creamy (fresh banana, chocolate, coconut etc) or fruity (fresh is always best!).

HIGHLIGHTS

❶ Chicago (p36)
One of America's great food cities, from diners to soul food to creative, fresh flavors. It's a city of neighborhood restaurants where talented chefs follow their culinary dreams that you can enjoy.

❷ St Louis (p66)
This town likes its food its way. Take the pizza, which could not be any thinner or crispier – like a cracker. Then there's Ted Drewes and frozen custard, a mandatory Mother Road stop since 1929.

❸ Oklahoma City (p112)
In the 19th century, cattle drives stopped in OKC. Since 1926, it's been the stop for folks on Route 66 who've been dreaming of the city's superb steaks for the previous several hundred miles.

❹ Amarillo (p130)
Don't cross the Texas Panhandle without feasting on barbecue. Yes, there are other styles in America that have their acolytes, but this is the mother lode. Brisket, ribs and pulled pork are just the start.

❺ Albuquerque (p174)
Don't try choosing between the state's delectable red and green chile – make it Christmas, which in local parlance means you get both. Add in any of many other dishes and fresh corn tortillas, yum!

❻ Los Angeles (p232)
The surprises never stop in the world's most inventive region for food and restaurants. And amid it all are beloved classics that date back to when Route 66 was the latest thing in road trips.

Weird & Wonderful

Back when businesses lived or died by their own moxie, Route 66 was a breeding ground for wild ideas to lure in the passing public.

GOT A GARAGE? Got some tools? Want to make some dough repairing cars passing by on Route 66? What to do? You can put out a big sign, but there are a lot of big signs planted from Illinois to California. You could advertise, but what traveler reads ads, particularly one who's desperate for a mechanic?

For many budding roadside entrepreneurs in the grease monkey set, the solution to their promotional needs was a giant, 22ft-tall (sometimes more) fiberglass man holding – of all things – a muffler. It surely grabbed attention and after the first few appeared, hundreds more followed along the Mother Road and then other roadways across America.

The Muffler Men giants have always been linked to Route 66 and there's an entire subculture of Mother Road aficionados who scour the road looking for surviving examples. In fact, the original Muffler Man ended up being modified in myriad ways to promote and sell myriad goods and services, and dozens of examples can be found today.

Among the many: there's the Gemini Giant (p50) in Wilmington, Illinois; three variations of Muffler Man in Tulsa's Route 66-centric Meadow Gold District (p95); another Muffler Man tirelessly hawking used cars in Gallup, New Mexico (p179); and the beloved Chicken Boy in LA (p229).

Go Big or Go Home

Hugeness is a theme in many other Route 66 come-ons. There are motel rooms in enormous individual concrete tepees at the Wigwam Motels in Holbrook, Arizona (p188) and San Bernardino, California (p229). And perhaps the ultimate in huge, the Big Texan Steak Ranch in Amarillo, Texas, which shamelessly promotes its 72-oz steak (p130).

Eccentric Route 66

Hucksterism in any size aside, Route 66 also features plenty of spectacles that exist just to be

BEST PLACES FOR WEIRD

American Giants Museum, Atlanta, Illinois (p52)
Led by the 'Bunyon Giant,' a Paul Bunyanesque, offshoot of the Muffler Man, this unmissable museum explains all about the giant phenomena.

Poozeum, Williams, Arizona (p192)
A logical offshoot of the Uranus Fudge Factory some five states later, this museum right on Route 66 boasts of having historic turd fossils.

Elmer's Bottle Tree Ranch, Oro Grande, California (p224)
Classic road 'art' with scores of drink bottles arrayed on metal frames that jingle in the breeze.

Left: Giant cowboy, Gallup (p180); Right: Elmer's Bottle Tree Ranch, Oro Grande (p224)

weird. Easily the most photographed is Cadillac Ranch, outside of Amarillo (p136). It's a strange creation open to wild interpretation and is the ideal roadside attraction. Or as you near Tulsa, there's a life-size concrete replica of the world's largest mammal, the blue whale perched in its own little pond (p94).

Sometimes weird is in the DNA of a business. Take Uranus – the fudge place in Missouri (p74) that excretes every pun it can from its name. T-shirts in poor taste, lots of candy and a vast array of Route 66 merch make it a timeless stop that delights the road-weary.

Near the Texas border, Harley Russell (p114) provides the best reason to stop in worn-out Erick, Oklahoma. He'll have your head spinning, from the thousands of vintage signs found along the Mother Road to his bawdy musical musings. Over in Arizona, the Hackberry General Store (p198) provides relief from the desert and is the very model of what an eccentric – and unmissable – Route 66 roadhouse should be.

And the places above are just a start. One of the very best reasons to drive Route 66 is that it takes you away from plasticized America, where one freeway interchange looks like another, and instead puts you in a place where individualism and creativity reign.

SNIFFING OUT STRANGE

Almost every old town on Route 66 will have at least one business that channels the weird and wonderful spirits. You can't miss them: look for the goofy name, the strange signs, the misuse of the 66 logo, the over-hyped promises, the oddly drawn cartoon mascot, the pun-filled name etc. And then stop! You'll likely find an owner as idiosyncratic as the shop or business, ready to enliven and even enlighten your day.

UNUSUAL ROUTE 66 IN MEDIA

American Giants
An ongoing YouTube series on Muffler Men, including episodes on all 16 found along Route 66.

Wild Travels: Route 66 (2024)
An episode of the PBS series focusing on weird travel explores the stranger aspects of Route 66, including the art of Bob Waldmire.

Secret Route 66 (2017)
Authors Jim Ross and Shellee Graham recount dozens of oddball tales about the Mother Road.

Harley Russell's Sandhills Curiosity Shop, Erick (p117)

A History of Route 66

Route 66 has lived many lives during its 100 years. First, it was the roadway to opportunity, then the path to adventure, and, finally, a nostalgic road trip into America's past. Connecting the main streets of rural and urban communities along its course, it developed into a cultural phenomenon like no other highway.

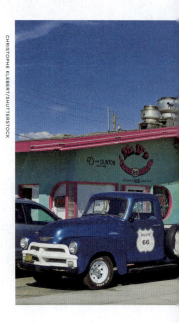

CHRISTOPHE KLEBERT/SHUTTERSTOCK

ROUTE 66 HIT the map in 1926, one of the first roads in the USA's new highway system established that year. Cyrus Avery, an Oklahoma oilman and entrepreneur, was the man with the plan: he knew that rural towns in the Midwest and Plains states were not linked to a major thoroughfare, and this made it hard for them to get their goods to market and prosper. So Avery – aka the Father of Route 66 – lobbied hard for a Chicago to Los Angeles route, cobbled together from preexisting state and local roads, that would dip southwest, connecting these neglected communities to the coast.

After an early fight over the highway's number, Avery and his colleagues began promoting Route 66 with great fanfare. The marketing campaign touted the road as the 'Main Street of America,' a clever bit of branding that continues to resonate today. The new road also hosted a cross-country foot race, generating heaps of publicity. Andy Payne won this 'Bunion Derby'

1926
Route 66 commissioned as one of the USA's first highways

1927
US 66 Highway Association forms; promotes 'Main Street of America'

1930s
Dust Bowl migrants crowd the road as they flee west

1938
Route 66 becomes the first US highway to be completely paved

with a time of 573 hours run over 84 days. That he was from Foyil, Oklahoma (p94) – one of the small towns now connected to Route 66 – made his victory particularly sweet.

Within a few years the road had become a favorite with truck drivers, thanks to the flat prairie lands it rolled through and a milder climate than the more northerly major highways, making it an easier drive year-round.

Road to Opportunity

During the 1930s, dust storms resulting from extended drought drove many families in the Plains states off their farms, especially those in Texas and Oklahoma. Roughly a quarter million of them packed what they could into their cars or trucks and headed west to California to find work in the fields. Route 66 was the road they took.

John Steinbeck wrote about the highway's newfound prominence in *The Grapes of Wrath* (1939). It was he who described Route 66 as 'the mother road, the road of flight' for its role as a refuge, protecting migrants as they escaped the Dust Bowl.

As the nation struggled through the Great Depression, Route 66 featured in the federal government's programs to provide jobs. Laborers were hired to pave the ever-busier road, and in 1938 it became the first fully paved

Mr D'z Route 66 Diner, Andy Devine Ave, Kingman (p200)

NAME GAME

Route 66 goes by many names. Initially it was known as US 60, a multiple-of-10 designation given to major east-west roads. This brief moniker lasted until eastern states complained '60' should belong to a highway starting in Virginia. So the Chicago to LA route was renamed US 62, until Cyrus Avery argued for 66, saying the double number was catchier. 'Main Street of America' was another Avery legacy that is still in use today. John Steinbeck famously dubbed it the 'Mother Road' in *The Grapes of Wrath*, as it provided new life to families heading west. It's also known as the Will Rogers Highway, honoring the beloved humorist.

1939
Steinbeck's *The Grapes of Wrath* introduces 'Mother Road' nickname

1941–45
Route 66 serves as the main route for troops and supplies during WWII

1946
Popular song '(Get Your Kicks on) Route 66' hits the airwaves

1947
Red's Giant Hamburg opens, the world's first drive-through restaurant

highway in the nation. Good thing, because three years later, the USA entered WWII, and Route 66 became a main path for moving soldiers and military supplies across the country. Mass migration to California also continued, bringing workers to the many new factories fueling the war effort. Route 66 was their road to opportunity.

Heading for Adventure

In the post-WWII economic boom, more Americans bought cars and worked in jobs that gave them increased leisure time. Road trips soon became popular as fun-seekers hopped in their cars and set out on journeys to see the sights and scenery en route to the west coast.

Already celebrated as a prime route for travelers, Route 66's allure gained traction after Bobby Troup wrote the song '(Get Your Kicks on) Route 66' and Nat King Cole sang it to the top of the charts in 1946. The idea of a carefree drive on the open road heading for adventure was hard to resist.

Motels, gas stations and diners popped up along the way to serve the new travelers. Drive-ins proliferated for those who wanted car-friendly, quick-service dining. Roadside attractions such as the whopping Blue Whale

Boots Court Motel, Carthage (p78)

1956
President Eisenhower signs Federal-Aid Highway Act of 1956

1960
Route 66 TV series premieres, romanticizing the road

1970s
Four-lane highways predominate; Route 66 falls into disuse

1985
Route 66 is officially decommissioned, removed from maps

STEP BACK IN TIME ON ROUTE 66

Pony Bridge, Bridgeport, Oklahoma (p116)
This 38-segment span was an engineering marvel when it opened in 1933; it stars in the 1940 film *The Grapes of Wrath*.

Red's Giant Hamburg, Springfield, Missouri (p76)
Considered the first drive-through restaurant, Red's catered to the booming post-WWII travel crowd and their desire for fast food.

Williams, Arizona (p192)
In 1984 this was the last bit of Route 66 wiped off the map by the interstate, but the town has hung on.

of Catoosa (p94) competed for motorists' attention – the bigger and stranger the better. Businesses installed bright, glowing neon signs beckoning drivers to pull over and buy souvenirs.

All of these features helped turn Route 66 into a cultural touchstone for American travel in the mid-20th century. But the freedom of this open road wasn't enjoyed by everyone: Black travelers weren't welcome in many towns along the highway and had to rely on the *Green Book* (p100) and other directories to guide them to safe places to eat and sleep.

Decline & Reinvention

Route 66 took a pounding from WWII truck traffic and an increase in cars hitting the road after the war. Despite upgrades to make it wider, smoother and straighter – such as the famous realignment that replaced the dangerous mountain road through Oatman, Arizona – Route 66 couldn't keep pace with the bigger, faster multi-lane highways that were being built. The Federal-Aid Highway Act of 1956 paved the way for the construction of interstate highways and by 1985 Route 66 was out of commission, thanks to five shiny new interstate highways (I-55, I-44, I-40, I-15 and I-10) that had incrementally bypassed it. Traffic decreased to a trickle, and many small towns along the original route were abandoned. Route 66 became a ghost road, flickering to life only in bits and pieces on the map.

But fans of the old highway remained, and they continued to seek its evocative, history-laden path across the belly of America. In 1999, enthusiasts worked with Congress to create the Route 66 Corridor Preservation Program to protect the road's landmarks and safeguard its role as a symbol of American hope, adventure and resilience. Today, 'Historic Route 66' is back on maps, a portal to a bygone, slower-paced era of travel.

1995	1999	2008	2026
Preservationists found National Historic Route 66 Federation	Congress passes Route 66 preservation bill to protect historic sites	World Monuments Watch List draws attention to Route 66	Route 66 marks its centennial

SIX WAYS

Ways to do Route 66

A big difference between Route 66 travelers today and those back in the day is time. Mother Road denizens once made the trip to get somewhere quickly, but now the trip itself is the destination and there are many ways to do it.

1 Long & Languid
Time *14 days*
Best for *People who want it all*

Driving Route 66 at your leisure is the dream of every Mother Road adventurer. Taking two weeks to cover the 2400 miles means you can find a seat and have an extra piece of pie in an iconic diner, spend time reveling in the view when you grab a selfie, and stay an extra night at any place that touches your soul. You need only cover about 170 miles a day – not even four hours of driving.

2 In a Hurry
Time *6 days*
Best for *People with less than a week*

The time-challenged can still have a meaningful drive. In six days, you'll need to cover 450 miles a day, which will keep you in the car a lot (fortunately, the scenery is good!), but still allows for targeted stops and experiences. In winter, though, you'll be driving at night. Any fewer days and you might as well hop on the interstate and hit the gas.
Possible overnights St Louis, Missouri; Tulsa, Oklahoma; Amarillo, Texas; Gallup, New Mexico; Kingman, Arizona

See p32 for the full route map

3 Mix & Match
Time *7 days*
Best for *Targeted enjoyment*

There's usually an interstate not far from Route 66. If pressed for time, you can hop on the interstate, hit the speed limit and make tracks – at least until you hit an aluminum wall of 18-wheelers... Keep to all stretches of the original road that stray far from the interstate, including Springfield to Joplin, all of Kansas, and Seligman to Topock.

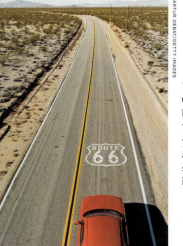

Route 66, California

ARTUR DEBAT/GETTY IMAGES

Motorcycle on Route 66, Arizona

Go to p241 for essential tip trips

4 The Core Journey
Time 6 days
Best for The uncompromising time-pressed

Get to the figurative and literal heart of Route 66 on an itinerary from St Louis to Flagstaff, Arizona, which takes in much of what defines the road. You may lose Illinois, the Mojave Desert and that first glimpse of the Pacific, but you'll get to enjoy the heart of the Mother Road: the roadside attractions of Missouri, the innumerable experiences in Oklahoma, and the beauty and wide-open vistas of Texas, New Mexico and Arizona. Plus, unmissable Albuquerque.
Possible overnights Joplin, Missouri; Amarillo, Texas

5 Go East
Time 10 days
Best for People who want to finish in the Midwest

Going west is traditionally most popular, both historically and because of the Pacific's allure. However, you can follow the lead of old-time truckers bringing loads from the Port of Los Angeles east, with the bright lights of Chicago as your goal. It's simple: just do this book in reverse. Outside of summer, dress more warmly as you go.

6 Weekends Away
Time 2½ days
Best for Short Route 66–themed escapes

Enjoy Route 66 over a weekend! Cut out of work early on Friday and drive straight on Route 66 to a nearby destination where you'll stay for two nights, maybe stopping once or twice on the way. On Saturday you explore nearby Mother Road sights and on Sunday you drive back, taking your time to do the road properly. Here are four ideas: Chicago to Springfield, Illinois; Oklahoma City to Tulsa, Oklahoma; Albuquerque to Winslow, Arizona; Los Angeles to Kingman, Arizona.

WHEN TO GO

Mar–May
Spring is a lovely time to go. Beginning in April, most everything is open, temperatures are mild and the wildflowers are in bloom.

Jun–Aug
Like anywhere, summer is peak season. Book nights at coveted motels in advance and prepare for crowds at popular sights. Balmy nights mean sitting outside under the stars. Daytime temps in the deserts are dangerous.

Sep–Nov
Autumn colors in the Midwest and the hills and mountains further west glow in the sun. Much is open through October; don't worry about booking ahead except on weekends.

Dec–Feb
Winter days are short and snow can happen nearly anywhere but California.

The Drive

A stage-by-stage, mile-by-mile account of the route. Your journey begins here.

CALIFORNIA
Needles to Barstow, p206
Barstow to Santa Monica, p220

THE SOUTHWEST
Glenrio to Albuquerque, p148
Albuquerque to Lupton, p168
Lupton to Topock, p184

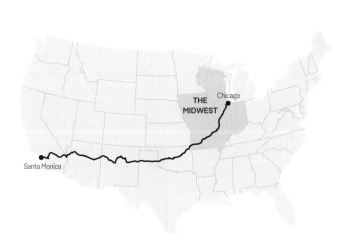

THE MIDWEST

It may not be the mesas of the Southwest or the shores of California, but the Midwest embodies Route 66's roots. Starting in lakeside Chicago, the road's course in Illinois wasn't shaped by the landscape – it's as flat as the bed of a pickup – but by the bounty of the land. The first iteration of Route 66 bent around the property lines of myriad corn and soybean farms. Crossing the Mississippi, Missouri's rivers and hills take precedence, giving the highway a gently winding, bucolic path southwest through small towns and rolling farms.

Historic Route 66 sign, Missouri
STOCKPHOTOASTUR/GETTY IMAGES

CITY GUIDE:
Chicago

Whether you start or end your Route 66 journey here, spend some time getting to know the Windy City. It'll wow you with its cloud-scraping architecture and art-filled parks. Delve into world-class museums, chow down on inventive eats and join local sports fanatics at a baseball game.

WORDS BY
KARLA ZIMMERMAN
Karla writes about travel and culture from her home base in Chicago.

Arriving

Plane Most flights arrive at O'Hare International Airport. Car rentals abound, but are cheaper downtown. To get there, take the Blue Line L train ($5, 40 minutes) or a taxi or ride-share (around $50, 30 to 60 minutes). Midway airport is on Chicago's southwest side, near where Route 66 exits the city. To reach downtown, take the Orange Line L train ($2.50, 30 minutes) or a taxi or ride-share (around $40, 20 to 40 minutes).
Train Amtrak trains arrive at Union Station at downtown's western edge. Taxis queue outside. The Blue Line Clinton stop is a few blocks south (but not a great option at night).
Driving You'll likely arrive via I-90, I-94, I-55, I-290 or I-294. The roads are multi-lane behemoths with heavy traffic and gridlock. Note that I-294 and parts of I-90 have tolls.

HOW MUCH FOR A

Pint of microbrew
$8

Italian beef sandwich
$13

Architecture boat tour ticket **$54**

Getting Around

Train The L (a system of elevated and subway trains) is the best way to travel around Chicago. Its eight color-coded lines are easy to use and get you to most sights and neighborhoods. An unlimited-ride day pass costs $5. Buy it at any L station or via the Ventra app *(ventrachicago.com)*, which also is useful for showing train times.
Cycling The Divvy *(divvybikes.com)* bike-share program has a huge network of sky-blue bikes all over the city. The $18 day pass allows unlimited rides in a 24-hour period, up to three hours each.
Driving Driving in Chicago is unpleasant. Traffic snarls not only at rush hours but most times in between. Constant road construction adds to the frustration. Use public transportation, especially around downtown and its nearby neighborhoods. That said, driving to Route 66's start point off Michigan Ave downtown is fairly easy, though congested during weekdays.
Parking Parking can be tough to find downtown and in entertainment-laden neighborhoods like Lincoln Park, Wrigleyville and Wicker Park. Look for pay boxes on main streets, where costs range from $2.50 (outlying areas) to $7 (downtown) per hour; download the **ParkChicago** *(parkchicago.com)* app to mobile pay. Downtown garages cost around $45 per day. Hotel valet parking costs around $75 per day.

For schedules and trip planning, go to Chicago Transit Authority:

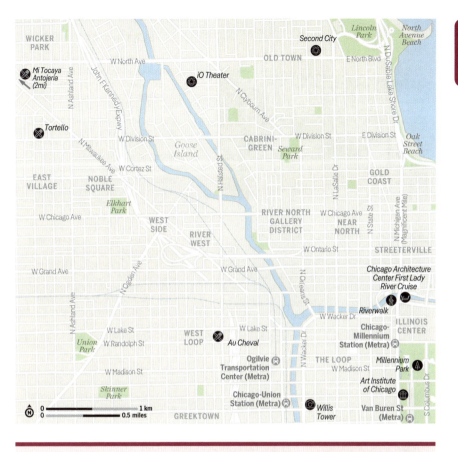

A DAY IN CHICAGO

Dive right into the main sights. Take a **Chicago Architecture Center boat tour** (p43) and ogle the most skyscraping collection of buildings the USA has to offer. Roam the **Riverwalk** (p43), then saunter over to **Millennium Park** (p41) to splash under Crown Fountain's human gargoyles and see the 'Bean' reflect the skyline.

Explore the **Art Institute of Chicago** (p39), the USA's second-largest art museum. It holds masterpieces aplenty, especially impressionist and postimpressionist paintings (and miniatures). Next, head over to **Willis Tower**, zip up to the 103rd floor and step out onto the glass-floored ledge for a knee-buckling perspective straight down.

Head to a cool neighborhood for eating and drinking: try Logan Square for **Mi Tocaya Antojeria** (p40), Wicker Park for **Tortello** (p40) or the West Loop for **Au Cheval** (p40). Then catch a late-night improv show at **iO Theater** (p38) or **The Second City** (p38).

Reckless Records

Rock the Shops: Wicker Park

Northwest of downtown, Wicker Park brims with record shops, bookstores and vintage marts perfect for an afternoon trawl. Flick through bins of post-rock and indietronica at **Reckless Records** (*reckless.com*). Pick up a fringe jacket and Bionic Woman lunchbox at **Kokorokoko** (*kokorokoko vintage.com*). Browse the used tomes filling three floors at **Myopic Books** (*myopicbookstore.com*). Loads of bars and eateries pop up in between, like **Piece** (*piecechicago.com, $*); with pizzas and house-made beers. Milwaukee Ave is the main vein, flanked by Blue Line L stations at Damen and Division.

BLAZING SKYLINE

On October 8, 1871, the Great Chicago Fire started in Patrick and Catherine O'Leary's barn southwest of downtown. Legend has it that Mrs O'Leary's cow kicked over a lantern that ignited the blaze, but other theories point to some young men who were playing cards in the barn, one of whom knocked over the lantern, or to Daniel 'Peg Leg' Sullivan, who came by the barn and accidentally dropped his pipe, which lit the fire.

However it started, the results were devastating. The conflagration burned for three days, killing 300 people and destroying more than 17,000 buildings. The 154ft-tall, Gothic-style **Water Tower** *(806 N Michigan Ave)* was one of the few structures left standing. This was due to its yellow limestone bricks, which withstood the flames, and to firefighter Frank Trautman, who soaked blankets and sails in lake water and covered the building. The tall, turreted tower soon became a symbol for a city that would rise from the ashes. And rise high, thanks to forward-thinking architects who con-verged here to help rebuild, bringing with them lofty new ideas like the invention of the skyscraper. Chicago has remained an architecture hotbed ever since.

LOL: Improv Night Out

Improv comedy began in Chicago, and the city remains a hub for the genre. Seeing a show is raucous fun, as performers create sketches based on suggestions the audience shouts out. Polished ensembles riff on politics and pop culture nightly at **The Second City** (*secondcity.com*), the most famous venue. **iO Theater** (*ioimprov.com*) is another established spot, where the Improvised Shakespeare Company ad libs wacky plays in Elizabethan verse. **Den Theatre** (*thedentheatre.com*) is a relative newcomer with fringy, offbeat shows. iO and Den typically have cheaper and easier-to-get seats. Book tickets in advance.

The Second City

Admire Endless Masterpieces

The Art Institute of Chicago houses a treasure trove of artworks. Everything from Picassos to surrealists stuff the vast galleries.

The main action happens on the 2nd floor. Stand in awe like Ferris Bueller in front of Georges Seurat's *A Sunday Afternoon on the Island of La Grande Jatte* (Gallery 240). In the adjoining rooms see canvases by Monet, Renoir and Van Gogh. It takes a while to get through the impressionist and post-impressionist paintings – there are more here than anywhere outside of France. Nearby, Edward Hopper's neon-lit diner in *Nighthawks* (Gallery 262) and Grant Wood's stern-faced couple in *American Gothic* (Gallery 263) hang in side-by-side galleries.

Make your way downstairs to enjoy an oasis of quiet in the Tadao Ando room (Gallery 109), where you'll walk through a forest of 16 pillars hiding Japanese screens. Then head to the light-drenched Modern Wing and up to the 3rd floor to gape at the blue, elongated figure of Pablo Picasso's *The Old Guitarist* (Gallery 391) and Salvador Dalí's *Inventions of the Monsters* (Gallery 395), which he painted in Austria immediately before the Nazi annexation.

From here the Nichols Bridgeway arches into Millennium Park, a fine add-on experience.

HOW TO

Nearest stop: Take the L to Adams/Wabash (Brown, Green, Orange, Pink and Purple Lines) or Monroe (Red and Blue Lines). Enter museum via Michigan Ave or Monroe St doors.

Parking: Available at Millennium Garages *(millenniumgarages.com)*

Admission: Adult $32, child under 14 free

Tip: Download the museum's free app for useful audio tours.

More info: Closed Tuesday and Wednesday; *artinstitute.edu*

Above: Lion, Art Institute of Chicago entrance; Right: *Paris Street, Rainy Day* by Gustave Caillebotte

LEFT: IAN DIKHTIAR; RIGHT: LAIOTZ/SHUTTERSTOCK

EXPERIENCE

39

Where to Sleep

Downtown has several smart architectural hotels near the sights, but limited dining options after dark. Next door, the Near North has heaps of hotels and evening action, but is pricey and a bit generic. The West Loop, Wrigleyville and Wicker Park have hip boutique hotels and abundant nightlife. They're further from the main sights but are easy enough to access via the L. Rates usually decrease the further you are from downtown. Note: hotel parking can add up to $75 per day to costs.

BEST PLACES TO SLEEP

Hampton Inn Chicago Downtown/N Loop $$ The chain's much-loved amenities in retro, vintage-car-rich environs. *hamptonchicago.com*

Publishing House Bed & Breakfast $$ Eleven mid-century modern rooms named after Chicago writers. *publishinghousebnb.com*

Robey $$ Design-savvy hotel in an art deco tower in Wicker Park. *therobey.com*

Acme Hotel $$ Industrial-chic rooms fill this energetic Near North boutique hotel. *acmehotelcompany.com*

Where to Eat

Chicago's food scene is known for being reasonably priced and pretension-free, with masterful food in come-as-you-are environs. Great neighborhoods to scope for Michelin-star and Beard Award winners include Lincoln Park, Wicker Park and Logan Square. The West Loop is where the buzziest eateries huddle. Cheap international eats abound in Pilsen (Mexican) and Uptown (Asian).

CHICAGO'S BEST-LOVED SPECIALTIES

Chicago's foremost food is deep-dish pizza, a hulking mass of crust that rises two inches above the plate and cradles a molten pile of toppings. Try it at **Lou Malnati's** (*loumalnatis.com; $$*). **Giordano's** (*giordanos.com; $$*) makes 'stuffed' pizza, a bigger, doughier version of deep dish. A third version is pan pizza: **Pequod's** (*pequodspizza.com; $$*) makes a mighty one.

Another iconic bite is the Chicago hot dog – a wiener that's been 'dragged through the garden,' ie topped with onions, tomatoes, a dill pickle and sweet relish. Try it at **Devil Dawgs** (*devildawgs.com; $*). The spicy, drippy Italian beef sandwich must also be experienced. **Mr Beef** (*666 N Orleans St; $*) assembles the gold standard, made famous in the TV show *The Bear*.

BEST PLACES TO EAT & DRINK

Au Cheval $$ Legendary cheeseburger, with a runny fried egg and melty cheddar. *auchevaldiner.com*

Tortello $$ Storefront eatery that makes fresh pasta right before your eyes. *tortellopasta.com*

Mi Tocaya Antojeria $$ Colorful Mexican spot with modern spins on regional dishes. *mitocaya.com*

Old Town Ale House $ Trendy tipplers, grizzled regulars and bawdy paintings. Cash only. *from 3pm*

Play in Millennium Park

Touch the silvery Bean, splash in Crown Fountain and pack a picnic for an evening concert in Chicago's showpiece of whimsical public art.

HOW TO

Nearest stop: Take the L to Washington/Wabash (Brown, Green, Orange, Pink and Purple Lines) or Washington (Blue Line).

Parking: Millennium Garages *(millenniumgarages.com)*.

Admission: Free

Tip: Allow extra time to get in for evening events, as all visitors must enter from either Randolph or Monroe Sts and go through a security/bag check.

More info: *millenniumpark.org*

Located downtown next to the Art Institute, **Millennium Park** bursts with free and arty sights. The mega draw is **Cloud Gate** – aka the Bean – Anish Kapoor's 110-ton, mirror-smooth sculpture. Go ahead: walk right up to it, feel it, ponder the skyline reflection and snap a picture.

Then mosey onward to Jaume Plensa's **Crown Fountain**. Its two glass-block towers have video images of Chicagoans spouting water gargoyle-style. On hot days, it's like a water park when everyone jumps in to cool down.

For a peaceful patch away from the crowd, seek out the **Lurie Garden**, abloom with prairie flowers. A little river runs through it, where folks kick off their shoes and dangle their feet.

Free concerts take place at **Pritzker Pavilion**, the swooping silver band shell designed by Frank Gehry, most nights in summer. For all concerts, but especially those by the **Grant Park Orchestra** *(grantparkmusicfestival.com)*, folks bring blankets, food, wine and beer. It's a summer ritual as the sun dips and gorgeous music fills the twilight air. To stock up, grocery store **Mariano's** *(333 E Benton Pl)* is a half-mile northeast.

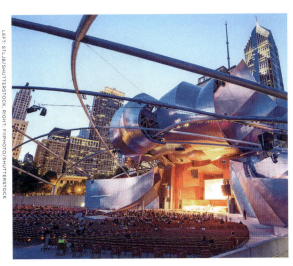

Above: Chicago skyline from Lurie Garden; Right: Pritzker Pavilion

EXPERIENCE

Catch a Game at Wrigley Field

There's nothing like spending an afternoon in the bleachers, hot dog and beer in hand, hoping for a win at the historic home of the Cubs.

HOW TO

Nearest stop: Take the Red Line L to Addison.

When to go: April through September

Cost: Varies, but roughly $40 to $110 per ticket

Tip: Buy tickets at the **Cubs website** *(cubs.com)* or online ticket broker **StubHub** *(stubhub.com)*. Upper Reserved Infield seats are usually pretty cheap. The bleachers are fun.

Five miles north of downtown, **Wrigley Field** pops up in the middle of a residential neighborhood, surrounded by houses, bars and even a fire station. The ballpark charms with its 1914 old-school features, like the hand-turned scoreboard, ivy-covered outfield walls and neon entrance sign. Seeing a game here, amid diehard Cubs fans, is a blast.

Gates open 1½ hours before the game's start time. Arrive early to check out the **Walk of Fame**, behind the bleachers in right field, to learn about Cubs greats through the ages. Watch players take batting practice, and grab a hot dog and Old Style beer.

Outside, grassy Gallagher Way hosts free movie nights and concerts on non-game days.

There are a number of great bars in the streets surrounding Wrigley Field. Try a Chicago Handshake at Wrigleyville's oldest bar, **Nisei Lounge** *(niseiloungechicago.com)*, play board games at **Guthrie's Tavern** *(guthriestavern.com)* or grab a drink just steps from the entrance to Wrigley Field's bleacher seats at **Murphy's Bleachers** *(murphysbleachers.com)*.

LEFT: KEITH HOMAN, RIGHT: JOSEPH HENDRICKSON/SHUTTERSTOCK

Above: Old Style beer; Right: Wrigley Field

Soak Up Chicago's Best Architecture

The skyline takes on a surreal majesty as you float through its shadows on a river tour, and landmark after eye-popping landmark flashes by.

Ascend to street level and browse the **Chicago Architecture Center**, where exhibits provide a primer on local buildings and designers. Excellent walking tours also depart from here. Then amble along the 1.25-mile long **Riverwalk** *(chicagoriverwalk.us)*, full of alfresco bars and restaurants from which you can admire Chicago's built environment. Give it a go swirling a rosé at **Northman Beer & Cider Garden** *(thenorthman.com)*.

Follow the crowds to the docks beneath Michigan Ave and board the **Chicago Architecture Center's First Lady** *(architecture.org)*. Yes, it's touristy, but it's also marvelous. Sit on deck and look up as you glide under stunning skyscrapers. Docents' lessons carry on the breeze, so you'll know your beaux arts from international style by journey's end.

Additional architectural delights await those keen to explore further. Step onto the ledge of Chicago's tallest skyscraper, **Willis Tower** *(theskydeck.com)*, or head to the **Rookery** *(flwright.org)* to see Frank Lloyd Wright's airy remodel. Beaux-arts beauty **Chicago Cultural Center** *(chicagoculturalcenter.org)* hosts terrific free exhibitions.

HOW TO

Nearest stop: Take the L to State/Lake (Brown, Green, Orange, Pink and Purple Lines), Washington (Blue Line) or Lake (Red Line).

Cost: Boat tours $54

Tip: Purchase tickets at the dock or online in advance.

More info: Boats run March to November; *architecture.org*

EXPERIENCE ★

Above: Willis Tower; Right: Chicago Architecture Center's *First Lady*

LEFT: RAJESH VIJAYAKUMAR, RIGHT: SERGII FIGURNYI/SHUTTERSTOCK

Chicago
ILLINOIS

The drive begins in the clamor of Chicago's Loop, not far from the lakefront. But after just a couple of hours' driving, you're in a different world. One where fields of crops provide texture and the only water you see may be a meandering stream. Following the old roads that were once Route 66, you wander from one small town to the next, becoming inured to their charms and relishing their surprises. The Illinois prairie draws you ever further, and it's further that you want to go.

Ryan Ver Berkmoes

Gemini Giant, Wilmington
ROY BOYCE/ALAMY

St Louis
MISSOURI

330 MILES · 9 HOURS' DRIVE*

* at moderate speed – it'll take longer with stops

THIS LEG:

- Chicago
- Joliet
- Wilmington
- Dwight's Texaco Station
- Pontiac
- Funks Grove Pure Maple Syrup
- Atlanta
- Springfield
- 1926 Route 66 from Chatham
- Litchfield
- Mt Olive
- Cahokia Mounds State Historic Site
- Chain of Rocks Bridge
- McKinley Bridge

Driving Notes

Following vintage Route 66 across Illinois you will mostly be on two-lane roads once you're outside of Chicago and its suburbs. Traffic is rarely an issue outside of the major cities. Every town has at least one gas station and convenience store. In winter, road conditions are only a concern if there's heavy snowfall.

Breaking Your Journey

Two days with an overnight in Springfield is the minimum for driving Route 66 in Illinois. However, if you want to do any of the experiences that follow, have time to explore the small towns and make new discoveries, you'll need more time.

Ryan's Tips

BEST MEAL The timeless menu at **Ariston Cafe**, Litchfield (p49)

FAVORITE VIEW The horizon-filling **farmlands** south of Springfield that look like Rothko paintings (p57)

ESSENTIAL STOP Strolling compact **Atlanta** with its giants, museums, shops and endless charm (p52)

ROAD-TRIP TIP Watch for those living their dream by opening a cafe serving their grandmother's pie recipes, their mom's meatloaf and other dishes made with love.

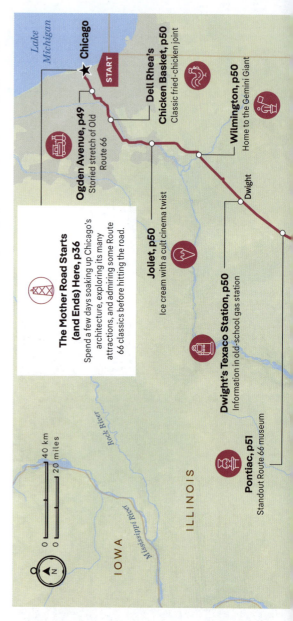

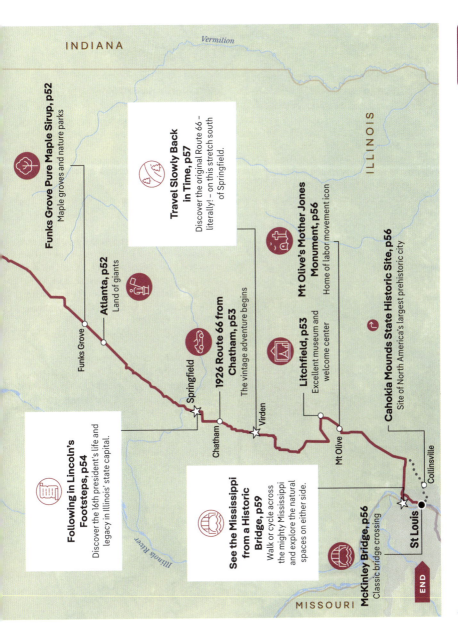

PREVIOUS STOP Route 66 begins in Chicago (p36) at iconic Michigan Ave.

Chicago

Drivers heading west would have had greater things on their mind than the cultural diversions of the Art Institute (p39), but there are two works within that relate to the open road to come: *American Gothic*, Grant Wood's much-parodied study of a stoic farm couple who might be ready to head west themselves, and *Nighthawks*, Edward Hopper's elegy for a late-night cafe with possibly road-weary patrons.

Surrounding the museum is **Grant Park**, with its spectacular centerpiece, Buckingham Fountain. It's backed by the vast expanse of **Lake Michigan**, a suitable bookend to the Pacific Ocean, some 2400 miles away.

Beginning of Historic Route Illinois US 66 sign, Chicago

Route 66's Beginning & End

From 1926 until 1955, E Jackson Blvd in Chicago's Loop, was where Route 66 started going west and ended going east. But when the street was made one-way, westbound 66 began one block north on E Adams St. Today, you'll find a much-loved selfie spot at an **official sign** reading 'Historic Route Illinois US 66 Begin' at No 77 immediately west of the Art Institute. The metal post is layered with the custom stickers that have become de rigueur for many Route 66 travelers, especially those from Europe. 'Hans & Greta Route 66 2024!!!' is typical. Look further west and you'll see the classic neon glow of the sign for the **Berghoff Restaurant**, an old Chicago classic and a harbinger of the polychromatic signage that awaits on the drive ahead.

There is a companion sign at 73 Jackson that includes 'end,' but it doesn't get the same love.

Lou Mitchell's

Exit the Loop, cross the Chicago River, jog over a block south and fuel up for your adventures ahead at **Lou Mitchell's** *(lou mitchells.com; 565 W Jackson Blvd; 6am-2pm Wed-Sun; $)*. The classic facade has proclaimed 'Serving the world's finest coffee' in red neon since this landmark opened in 1949.

Grab one of the original booths (waits are common, free doughnut holes ease the tedium) and tuck into timeless American diner fare that's a cut above the norm. Old-school waitstaff deliver big fluffy omelets, pancakes and

Chicago

Stop for 'the world's finest coffee' at Lou Mitchell's

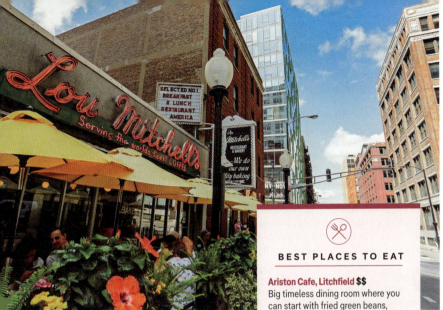

Lou Mitchell's, Chicago

BEST PLACES TO EAT

Ariston Cafe, Litchfield $$
Big timeless dining room where you can start with fried green beans, toasted ravioli or grilled chicken livers, then tuck into a steak, pork chop or pasta. *(ariston-cafe.com; 11am-8pm Tue-Sun)*

Maldaner's, Springfield $$$
Purports to be the oldest restaurant on Route 66 and it has indeed been serving upscale American fare since 1884. Try the famed beef Wellington; the lemon sherbet ice cream was inspired by Mary Lincoln's favorite dessert. *(maldaners.com; 5-9pm Tue-Sat)*

Lou Mitchell's, Chicago $$
You'll be hard-pressed to find a better breakfast along the 2400 miles of Route 66. But try anyway, huh? (See left)

thick-cut French toast with a jug of syrup. They call you 'honey' and fill your coffee cup endlessly.

Ogden Avenue

Leaving the high-rises of downtown Chicago behind and passing through the trendy West Loop, you'll hit storied Ogden Ave – **Old Route 66** – arrowing its way southwest across the city. At Cicero Ave, the vast BNSF rail yard appears on the north side: this is the endpoint for the old Santa Fe mainline, which runs alongside Route 66 much of the way to California.

The first town across the border from Chicago is workaday **Cicero**, still famous as the center of Al Capone's underworld in the 1920s.

Dell Rhea's Chicken Basket

22 miles — 20 miles

Dell Rhea's Chicken Basket

Chicago's seemingly endless collar of suburbs, with their confusing and limited lexicon of names often based on Grove, Heights, Park, Brook and more, is best (and we will say this rarely!) dealt with by hopping on the interstate – in this case I-55, the concrete ribbon that replaced Route 66 – and hitting the gas.

However, it's worth turning off at Exit 274 for an oasis of Route 66 authenticity amid the strip malls of **Willowbrook**. Dating to 1946, with roots going back a decade before, **Dell Rhea's Chicken Basket** (chickenbasket.com; $$) boasts the requisite neon sign and excellent fried chicken. The joint has a great history, and as they say: 'Get your chicks on Route 66.'

Joliet

Pop off I-55 at Hwy 53 for the old city of **Joliet**. The obvious first stop should be **Route 66 Park**, which is near the center on a bank above the wide Des Plaines River. Here you'll find a few displays about the highway, but the most notable feature is **Rich & Creamy**, which has myriad concoctions made with ice cream. You can't miss the statues of Jake and Elwood of *The Blues Brothers* cavorting on the roof. The opening scenes of the 1980 movie were shot just across the river at the **Old Joliet Prison** *(joliet prison.org)*, which is now a tourist attraction.

Wilmington's Gemini Giant

Eventually the Chicago suburbs and then the exurbs give way to the cornfields that symbolize much of Illinois for many. Follow Hwy 53 from Joliet, which traces old Route 66, and 60 miles south of Chicago you'll encounter the

Rich & Creamy ice creamery, Joliet

first of countless – and timeless – small towns found all the way to the Pacific.

Wilmington is home to the iconic and much-loved **'Gemini Giant'** – a 28ft fiberglass spaceman that stands guard in South Island Park along the Kankakee River National Trail. If he looks a little weary, it's because he's had a turbulent couple of years of ownership changes, but now he's at peace in the park and has been spiffed up. Look closely and you can see he's based on the famous 'Muffler Man' promotional statues that you can learn all about a few miles further on in Atlanta, Illinois (p52).

Dwight's Texaco Station

For 66 (!) years beginning in 1933, the **Ambler's Texaco Station** in the tiny burg of Dwight served Route 66 travelers. Built in a

---

Joliet — 19 miles — Wilmington — 23 miles — Dwight — 20 miles — Pontiac

Behold the Gemini Giant

Load up on information at Ambler's Texaco Station

residential style designed to be homey rather than invasive, it's typical of hundreds of other stations that once lined the road. You'll see many restored examples as you drive along as architectural styles evolve to match former local practices. Today the station is a handy visitor center where volunteers dispense info about the region and Route 66.

Pontiac

A must stop, **Pontiac** boasts the superb **Route 66 Association of Illinois Hall of Fame and Museum** *(il66assoc.org)*. One of the best of its kind, it tells the stories of many of the personalities who have given the road such character, such as the great Bob Waldmire (p58). Artifacts abound and the shop has unusual maps and books you won't find elsewhere.

Pontiac itself is worth exploring, with a historic courthouse square and over 25 huge murals

BEST PLACES TO SLEEP

Inn at 835, Springfield $$
This historic arts-and-crafts-style luxury apartment building from 1908 offers rooms of the four-poster bed, claw-foot bathtub variety. *(connshg.com/Inn-at-835)*

Route 66 Hotel & Conference Center, Springfield $
This locally owned indie south of the center touts its history as the first Holiday Inn built on the original Route 66. Often renovated since, rooms are comfortable and affordable, plus Cozy Dog (p52) is close by! *(rt66hotel.com)*

Carpenter Street Hotel, Springfield $
Unadorned indie hotel just north of the Lincoln sites has spacious rooms. *(carpenterstreethotel.com)*

Iconic van owned by Bob Waldmire (p58) on display at Route 66 Association of Illinois Hall of Fame and Museum, Pontiac

enlivening buildings throughout downtown. The **Cellar in Pontiac** *(721 W Washington St)* is in the old train station and has a good beer selection and bar food.

Funks Grove Pure Maple Sirup

The Funk family had already been producing maple syrup for 100 years when the first Route 66 travelers rolled past in 1926. Today, **Funks Grove Pure Maple Sirup** *(funks puremaplesirup.com)* is a minor empire of maple groves, nature parks, pumpkin patches and gourd farms lining Old Route 66 just southwest of Shirley. It retains a certain 19th-century charm and manages to cater to every seasonal and holiday gift and souvenir whim.

Atlanta

Atlanta is the land of giants – fiberglass ones that is. From the time you reach the tidy downtown, you'll see huge men looming in all directions. Known variously as 'Giant Men' or 'Muffler Men,' Atlanta boasts three variations: the iconic 'Bunyan Giant' holding a huge hot dog, a rare Texaco Man and a somewhat comical Mortimer Snerd model. The latter two are outside the **American Giants Museum** *(american giantsmuseum.com)*, which tells the story of these towering creations (p56) found all along Route 66. And for some gender equality, don't miss the pie-wielding waitress, **Lumi's Giant**, outside the **Country-Aire Restaurant** *($)* near Old Route 66 (the pies are great).

Springfield

The biggest thing – other than the occasional fiberglass giant – between Chicago and St Louis is the Illinois state capitol of **Springfield**, once the home of 16th president Abraham Lincoln (p54). It's worth at least an overnight, but no matter how long your stay, don't miss the famous **Cozy Dog Drive In** *(cozydogdrivein. com; closed Mon)* south of the center on what was once Route 66.

Along the Way We Met...

BILL LINDEN On my 66th birthday I spent a month exploring Route 66 with my wife. To us it meant traveling back to a simpler, more innocent time. We looked forward to seeing what surprises each mile would bring. My wife would buy T-shirts at several gift shops that unbeknownst to me would become a fabulous Route 66 quilt that I treasure very much! Here's to the road ahead!
Bill has been a proud Chicagoan since 1947.
BILL'S TIP: *'Don't rush it! Here's to plenty of fun pit stops and new adventures on the old Mother Road!'*

48 miles **Funks Grove Pure Maple Sirup** *Just southwest of Shirley* *11 miles* **Atlanta** *44 miles*

American Giants Museum, Atlanta

Mundane from the outside, it has two claims to fame: it's owned by the family that included the wonderful Bob Waldmire (p58) and it's the birthplace of the iconic American corn dog (although they don't call it that: here it's a 'cozy dog'). And indeed, the version of a cornmeal-battered, fried hot dog on a stick does seem superior to the pedestrian versions sold at roadside stands nationwide. Cozy Dog is also notable for the oodles of Route 66 memorabilia you can peruse while your battered dog cooks up fresh.

1926 Route 66 from Chatham

Leaving Springfield and stair-stepping your way southwest across the table-flat Illinois prairies on the original 1926 version of Route 66 can be a magical part of your trip (p57). Take Hwy 4 out of town to **Chatham** and continue south, where the vintage adventure begins.

Litchfield

When you've had enough of zigzagging along the prairie, cut back east toward I-55 and the helpfully named Old Route 66, which parallels it through a string of small towns, including **Litchfield**. Here you'll find a trio of vintage attractions. The **Litchfield Museum & Route 66 Welcome Center** *(litchfieldmuseum.org)*, right on the old road, is entirely focused on the local community and is a fine place to see how Route 66 affected one town.

Continues on page 56

Springfield — 11 miles — **1926 Route 66 from Chatham** — 53 miles — **Litchfield**

While away an afternoon at the Lincoln Sites

Refuel yourself at Ariston Cafe

Follow in Lincoln's Footsteps

The state's capital has a serious obsession with Abraham Lincoln, which is understandable: his legacy as the 16th president, his tireless fight for justice and his Civil War leadership remain awe-inspiring.

HOW TO

Nearest stop: Springfield

Getting here: Follow Old Route 66 (9th St/Business Loop I-55) into Downtown Springfield. The Lincoln sites – except his tomb – are in the center, so park once and walk.

When to go: The major sites are open daily, but you'll need to get tickets in advance. For the Lincoln Home National Historic Site, pick up free same-day tickets in person as early as possible in the day at the visitor center. For the Lincoln Presidential Library & Museum, buy tickets online in advance.

More info: The **Springfield Visitors Center** *(visitspringfieldillinois.com)* is in Lincoln's old law offices.

A Home & Neighborhood

Abraham and Mary Lincoln lived at 8th and Jackson Sts, from 1844 to 1861, then moved to the White House. This house is part of the **Lincoln Home National Historic Site** *(nps.gov/liho)*, a collection of historic and authentic buildings set on streets as they would have looked in Lincoln's time. Lincoln bought the home and Mary brought it up to her refined standards, which differed from those of Abe's frontiersman's sensibilities. Today, the house appears much like it did when the Lincolns lived there and 80% is original.

Restorers have been aided by an illustrated *New York Times* article on the home life of Lincoln that ran when he was elected. The small furniture is sized for the average person at the time. At 6ft 4in, Lincoln usually ended up sitting on the floor reading rather than enduring such 'comforts.'

Memorabilia & Triumphs

The modern **Lincoln Presidential Library & Museum** *(presidentlincoln.illinois.gov)* contains the most complete Lincoln collection in the world. Real-deal artifacts such as Abe's shaving mirror and presidential seal join whiz-bang exhibits and Disneyesque holograms that keep the kids agog. It's worth checking out both live-action performances: the nine-minute 'Ghosts of the Library' and the 17-minute 'Lincoln's Eyes.'

Lincoln's immortal line, 'A house divided against itself cannot stand…' was delivered in the **Old State Capitol** *(dnrhistoric*

WHERE TO EAT

Look for local specialty 'horseshoe,' a filling, artery-clogging fried meat sandwich covered with melted cheese.

Occupying a rambling 150-year-old mansion by Lincoln's home, **Obed & Isaac's** (obedandisaacs.com; to 11pm; $$) has a maze of sunny rooms and outdoor areas in which to drink its wildly changing menu of beers brewed on-site and enjoy its elevated bar food.

Don't miss **Maldaner's** (p49), an old-school delight, and **Cozy Dog Drive In** (p52), just south of the center.

Left: Lincoln Presidential Library & Museum; Below: Lincoln family reenactors

.illinois.gov) in the days before the Civil War. Here, detailed tours outline his early political life, which included the dramatic Lincoln-Douglas debates in 1858.

Final

After his assassination, Lincoln's body was returned to Springfield, where it lies today. Lincoln's Tomb sits in **Oak Ridge Cemetery**, 2 miles north of downtown. The gleam on the nose of Lincoln's bust, created by visitors' light touches, indicates the numbers of those who pay their respects here.

If it's a summer night, consider catching a flick at the vintage **Rt 66 Skyview Drive-In**, which has been entertaining people in their cars off Route 66 for 75 years. Year-round, the **Ariston Cafe** (p49) is aglow in neon and has 100 years of history. The food remains excellent. Note the Budweiser sign, a natural consequence of the beer's source in nearby St Louis.

Mt Olive's Mother Jones Monument

On the north side of **Mt Olive** is a monument to a pillar of the American labor movement: Mary G Harris, aka Mother Jones (1837–1930), is buried under a large monument in the **Union Miners Cemetery**, surrounded by other famous names in workers' rights, such as the folk singer Anne Feeney (note her epitaph: 'rabble rouser'). Jones spent much of her life fighting for workers' rights and against child labor.

In the center of town, don't miss a Route 66 landmark, the **Soulsby Service Station** *(710 W 1st St)*. Built in 1926, this residential-style Shell gas station was open from 1926 to 1996 and has been restored to its bright corporate plumage.

DETOUR: Cahokia Mounds State Historic Site

A surprise awaits 10 miles southeast of the Chain of Rocks Bridge: **Cahokia Mounds State Historic Site** *(cahokiamounds.org)*, site of North America's largest prehistoric city (20,000 people, more than London in the same era), dates from 1200. It's a UNESCO World Heritage Site. The 68 surviving earthen mounds, including the enormous 100ft-tall **Monk's Mound** (from which you can see the Gateway Arch and the St Louis skyline on a clear day), and the fascinating interpretive center are engrossing. Look for 'Woodhenge,' a circle of poles used for highly accurate solar observations and date keeping. The site is close to the junction of I-55/70 and I-255.

Chain of Rocks Bridge

From Mt Olive, take I-55 S and I-270 W to W Chain of Rocks Rd. Opened in 1929, the soaring **Chain of Rocks Bridge** spanned the Mississippi River and was as dramatic to look at as it was dramatic to drive. Today it's part of a park and makes for a fine pause in your journey (p59).

Continues on page 58

ROADSIDE GIANTS

Once you've seen one, you can't stop seeing them: giant men (yes, they're usually men), averaging over 20ft tall and standing outside American businesses – often along Route 66 (Tulsa has three, p99).

Most date to the 1960s, when giant figures were all the rage for roadside promotions. Produced by a California company, the figures were generically called 'Muffler Men.' As time went by variations abounded: beards, cowboy hats, even space helmets customized their looks. Some did indeed hold mufflers, others grasped axes and hot dogs. They were joined by dinosaurs, dogs, Vikings and more. Learn all about these giants at Atlanta's American Giants Museum (p52).

Travel Slowly Back in Time

South of Springfield, travel nearly 100 years back in time on original stretches of Route 66 that adhere to farm property lines as they stairstep their way across the prairie's stark beauty.

Nearest stop: Springfield

Getting here: Follow Hwy 4 south to Chatham; watch for 'Historic Route 66' signs for minor detours to vintage stretches of road.

When to go: Drive early in the day when the roads are empty, the air is crisp and the sun is shining against the cornstalks.

Exiting: Take Hwy 16 10 miles east from Gillespie to Litchfield.

This part of Central Illinois is as flat as a board: fans of *North by Northwest* will get itchy watching for malevolent crop dusters. You can almost imagine the conga lines of Model Ts rattling past the farmhouses.

Although wags will snark that it's the last time the road was paved, Illinois had a developed road system in 1926 and redesignated its fully paved Hwy 4, from Chicago to St Louis, as Route 66. The rest of the route to LA wasn't fully sealed until 1938.

As you head south on Hwy 4, look for the popular strip of **brick road** that recreates the original highway on Snell Rd north of **Auburn**. North of **Thayer**, look for the original 16ft-wide concrete **Tiller Road**. At **Virden**, pause at the main square to read about the 1898 'Battle of Virden,' when mine owners tried to break a strike and mayhem ensued.

In tiny towns like **Girard** and **Nilwood**, residents sell honey from stands. Three miles west of the latter, look for **Donaldson Road**, which preserves tracks of a turkey from early in the last century. Continue on to **Gillespie**.

Brick Route 66, Auburn

Cozy Dog Drive In, Springfield

McKinley Bridge

Driving history comes full circle at this **1910 bridge** over the Mississippi. It was the original Route 66 link to St Louis, a status it only held for four years as the deluge of cars in downtown St Louis proved unsustainable. After Route 66 was rerouted over the purpose-built Chain of Rocks Bridge to the north, this workaday Erector-set creation continued carrying local traffic until 2001, when it closed due to a lack of maintenance (an all-too-common problem with American bridges).

Finally rebuilt, you can once again cross into St Louis and Missouri as the first Route 66 travelers did 100 years ago.

BOB WALDMIRE: ROUTE 66 CHAMPION

It's not just the corn dog that can be linked to Springfield's **Cozy Dog Drive In** (p52), that is also where Bob Waldmire got his start. Bob gained fame not for his contribution to American fast food – that laurel goes to his dad, Ed – but for his remarkable artistic talents and his lifelong devotion to preserving the legacy of Route 66 and promoting its future.

See the VW bus Bob used to cruise the road hundreds of times at Pontiac's Route 66 Museum (p51) and savor his idiosyncratic art at the drive-in where he started working as a boy, meeting travelers from around the world.

10 miles

Cross the McKinley Bridge into St Louis

St Louis

See the Mississippi from a Historic Bridge

The Chain of Rocks Bridge was once a vital link on Route 66. Today, it affords sweeping views of the Mississippi and the St Louis skyline.

HOW TO

Nearest stop: McKinley Bridge

Getting here: From Illinois, follow W Chain of Rocks Rd (Old Route 66) over the Chain of Rocks Canal on and onto Chouteau Island and continue until you reach the bridge parking area.

When to go: Let the weather guide you as you'll be outside. Winter will always be a challenge.

Cost: Free

The road to the historic **Chain of Rocks Bridge** is more green than urban, despite its location. You'll think you're deep in the country as you traverse **Chouteau Island**, which is bracketed by a shipping canal on one side and the mighty Mississippi on the other. It's a grassy and wooded nature preserve popular with fishers. In 2024, the Missouri side got a lovely new park, financed by the National Park Service.

The Chain of Rocks Bridge (sometimes modified with 'Old' to differentiate it from the I-270 bridge to the north) opened in 1929. The placement of the piers would have created a hazard for boats so a 30-degree bend was inserted in the middle, which bedeviled drivers for decades to come. It closed in 1968 but was restored and reopened to pedestrians and bikes in 1999. The walk end-to-end is about 1 mile, or you can ride across the bridge from Illinois and join the **Great Rivers Greenway** *(greatriversgreenway. org)*, a network of bike trails that will take you along the Mississippi right to the heart of St Louis (about 13 miles).

EXPERIENCE

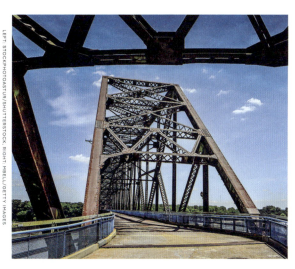

Above: Route 66 information sign; Right: Old Chain of Rocks Bridge

Seeburg 100 Wall-o-Matic music machine, Wilmington
TLF IMAGES/SHUTTERSTOCK

INSIGHT

Rhythm of the Road

Music played a key role in the highway's identity from the get-go. It was the thoroughfare by which new styles of music spread across the country, while Nat King Cole's popular '(Get Your Kicks on) Route 66' skyrocketed the route's reputation as the must-do road trip.

WORDS BY KARLA ZIMMERMAN
Karla's playlist skips from guitar-smashing rock to Senegalese mbalax. She writes about travel and culture.

ALONG WITH DUST Bowl migrants, returned WWII soldiers and postwar fun seekers, musicians were also traveling on Route 66 in its early days, bringing the electric blues, western swing and other new sounds to towns along the road.

First up in the airwaves heading east to west: the electric blues in Chicago. When Muddy Waters and friends plugged their guitars into amplifiers in the 1940s, musical grooves reached new decibel levels, and Chicago became the hub for the groundbreaking genre. The sound made its way to St Louis, where a guitarist named Chuck Berry added wild guitar riffs and lyrical melodies that morphed into rock and roll in the mid-1950s.

Onward to Springfield, Missouri, in the Ozark Mountains region, country music was hitting its stride, chock-full of fiddles, mandolins, banjos and guitars. Patsy Cline, Johnny Cash and other stars came to town for the *Ozark Jubilee* TV show that aired weekly and shared the music's twangy tunes nationally from 1955 through 1960.

Down the road in Tulsa, western swing was all the rage. The uptempo, danceable, country-meets-jazz hybrid, heavy on the fiddles, filled venues like Cain's Ballroom (still going strong today). Fiddler Bob Wills and his band the Texas Playboys shot to fame playing the style in dance halls along Route 66 from Oklahoma to California.

At the road's end in Los Angeles, West Coast blues became a dominant sound. Guitarist T-Bone Walker carried the jazzy, fast-paced spin on traditional blues from his Texas homeland to LA in the 1930s, when he traveled west on Route 66 to work in the new factories opening there. Walker also traveled east to Chicago, taking his pioneering electric blues style to the city that would soon make the sound its own.

Hit Song Jackpot

Bobby Troup had already had some songwriting success when he and his wife packed up their Buick and made their way west in 1946. During the 10-day trip along Route 66 to Los Angeles, where Troup hoped to get work in Hollywood, a tune came to him. It was pretty simple, describing the highway and rhyming several town names along the way, and he gave it a great rhyming title: '(Get Your Kicks on) Route 66.'

Within months, Nat King Cole recorded a breezy, swinging version of the song, and it was a hit. But more than that, the song inspired legions of drivers to head out on the road for fun and adventure.

New versions of 'Route 66' were recorded many times over the years. Chuck Berry played a faster, amped-up rendition, complete with crazy guitar solo, in 1961. The Rolling Stones went full rock and roll with it in 1964, while Depeche Mode recorded a trippy, propulsive, synthesizer-driven remix in 1987. It became a hit again in 2006, when John Mayer recorded a blues-rock version for the soundtrack of the animated film *Cars*. The song's staying power attests to its simple structure and enduring message about the romance of the open road.

Open Road Anthems

Route 66 ushered in a new genre of songs: those that celebrate the lure of the open road. The idea of finding freedom and excitement while spinning along in a cool car moved beyond the Mother Road to include any highway.

Steppenwolf's 1968 classic 'Born to Be Wild' shows how it's done. The opening verse commands the listener to rev their engine and then 'head out on the highway/lookin' for adventure' – the poetic start to all good road trips. Willie Nelson's 'On the Road Again' (1980) describes the joy and camaraderie of the musician's life on the road and the thrill of 'going places that I've never been.' Bruce Springsteen's 'Born to Run' (1975) offers a 'chrome-wheeled, fuel-injected' promise of escape via the open road. And there are loads more such songs. Wanderlust and the dream of freedom on four wheels remains an integral part of the American story, visceral whether you're driving Route 66 or another iconic highway.

Route 66 Playlist

Wrap your ears around these storied songs, plus a selection of our writers' road-trip favorites.

St Louis

MISSOURI

If only you could drive right through the Gateway Arch in St Louis into Missouri! The dense green rolling hills and blue waters of the Ozarks immediately make you forget the flatlands of Illinois. Route 66 runs a near-perfect diagonal southwest across the state to pick off a corner of Kansas. It's here in the Show Me state that the honky tonk roadside businesses aimed right at burgeoning Route 66 traffic first fully flowered, from auto court motels to hokey attractions.

Ryan Ver Berkmoes

Munger Moss Motel, Lebanon

TLF IMAGES/SHUTTERSTOCK

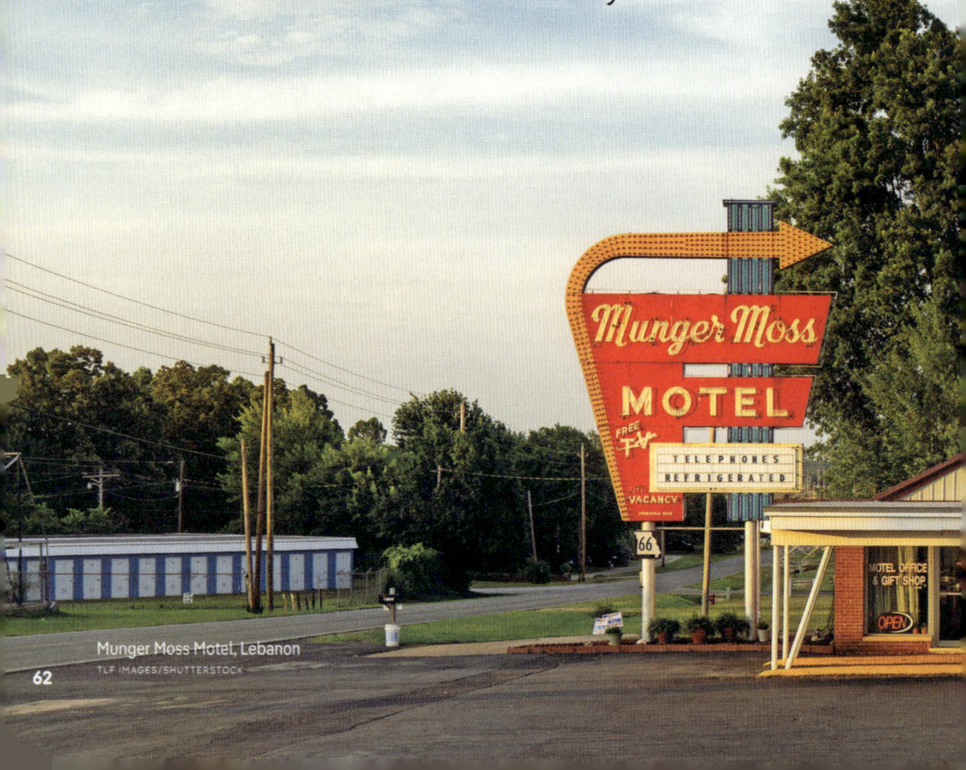

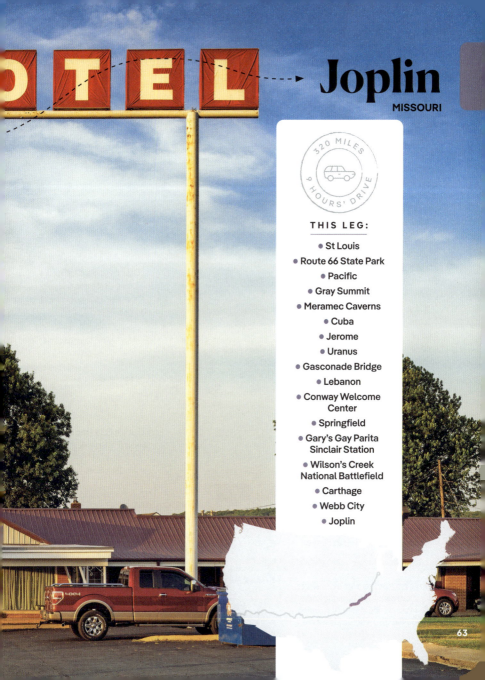

Joplin
MISSOURI

320 MILES · 9 HOURS' DRIVE

THIS LEG:

- St Louis
- Route 66 State Park
- Pacific
- Gray Summit
- Meramec Caverns
- Cuba
- Jerome
- Uranus
- Gasconade Bridge
- Lebanon
- Conway Welcome Center
- Springfield
- Gary's Gay Parita Sinclair Station
- Wilson's Creek National Battlefield
- Carthage
- Webb City
- Joplin

Driving Notes

Following Route 66 in Missouri is both easy and hard. Today's I-44 from St Louis mostly sticks to the traditional route as far as Springfield. But finding stretches of old road to escape the anonymous divided highway bubble is hit and miss. Check maps and sources carefully as your efforts will be rewarded with some of Route 66's most bucolic scenery.

Breaking Your Journey
Vintage auto courts and motels are being restored with luxuries unimagined when they were first built and small towns are spiffing up their downtowns to welcome visitors. You're never far from some characterful business along the old road ready to lure you in with a story, an ice cream or maybe a piece of pie.

Ryan's Tips

BEST MEAL A **Ted Drewes** concrete (p66)

FAVORITE VIEW From the top of **Gateway Arch** (p66)

ESSENTIAL STOP Uranus Fudge Factory (p74)

ROAD-TRIP TIP There are many visitor and information centers along Route 66 in Missouri, and staffers love being asked what their favorite places are.

Discover Springfield's Love of Route 66, p76
Break your journey in this year-round destination where Mother Road sights abound

Carthage, p78
Tree-shaded architectural gem

Gary's Gay Parita Sinclair Station, p78
Old-school Route 66 gas station

Webb City, p79
Small-town charm, 19th-century style

Joplin, p79
Site of Bonnie and Clyde shootout

Wilson's Creek National Battlefield, p78
Major Civil War battle site

PREVIOUS STOP From the McKinley Bridge, follow N Broadway to St Louis' downtown riverfront.

Gateway Arch

As a symbol for **St Louis** (p68), the **Gateway Arch** has soared above any expectations its backers could have had in 1965 when it opened. Now the centerpiece of its own **national park** *(nps.gov/jeff)*, the silvery, shimmering Arch is the Great Plains' own Eiffel Tower. It stands 630ft high and symbolizes St Louis' historical role as 'Gateway to the West.' It's the design of the legendary Finnish-American architect Eero Saarinen (1910–61).

The tram ride takes you to the tight confines at the top. Book tickets in advance online. A massive project has transformed the area around the Arch. The large **Luther Ely Smith Square** now covers the noxious I-44 and connects the Arch and its park to the rest of Downtown.

Ted Drewes

Exiting Downtown yields sweet rewards. Follow the old route of 66 southwest out of town along Gravois Ave and then Chippewa St, passing through historic neighborhoods such as Soulard.

When you see a large clapboard white building with a crowd of people standing outside, you've reached **Ted Drewes** *(teddrewes. com; 11am-10:30pm; $)*, where folks have been licking themselves silly on Route 66 since 1929. It's beloved for its super-creamy ice-cream-like frozen custard, which comes in myriad concoctions. Rich and poor rub elbows while enjoying a 'concrete,' a delectable stirred-up combination of flavors. A neighboring storefront has the inevitable gift shop and a small museum showing Route 66 travelers through the years.

DETOUR: Museum of Transportation

Huge railroad locomotives (including a Union Pacific Big Boy), historic cars and more that moves draw crowds to the vast **Museum of Transportation** *(tnmot.org)*, just 3 miles north of I-44 off I-270 west.

DiDia 150 in Museum of Transportation

Gateway Arch, St Louis

The highlight for Route 66ers is the **Coral Court exhibit**, which preserves a unit from the much-missed 1941 motor court motel that was renowned for its sleek art moderne styling. Located 1 mile west of the St Louis city limits, Coral Court's rooms had attached garages, so travelers could park their cars inside. Some thought this was for security, but most knew that the garages ensured that no one knew you were there.

 Route 66 State Park

To escape St Louis heading west, it's best to just hop on I-44 (the interstate is built

Continues on page 70

BEST PLACES TO EAT

Broadway Oyster Bar, St Louis $$
Part bar, part live-music venue, but all restaurant, this joint jumps year-round. Suck down crawfish and other Cajun treats outside with a vibe that comes upriver from America's south. *(broadwayoysterbar.com; to 1:30am)*

Ted Drewes, St Louis $
We love the banana-graham cracker Concrete combo. Don't miss seasonal flavors (see left).

Leong's Asian Diner, Springfield $
Springfield is so busy taking credit for Route 66, they forget to take credit for cashew chicken. The popular Chinese-American dish was invented here by David Leong and this restaurant is run by his family. *(leongsasiandiner.com; 11am-8:30pm)*

Route 66 State Park

26 miles · 9 miles

Explore St Louis

Slide into St Louis and revel in the unique vibe of this old city on the Mississippi River. Its culture dates back to the 18th century and it is richly endowed with sights and diversions that can easily fill a day or more. Plus, it's a sensational place for food and nightlife.

HOW TO

Getting there: All roads do indeed lead to St Louis. From Illinois, McKinley Bridge (p58) will put you close to the Riverfront. From the west, old Route 66 parallels I-44.

Getting around: Metro (metrostlouis.org) runs local buses and the MetroLink light-rail system.

Sleeping: The grand old **Missouri Athletic Club** (mac-stl.org; $$) has nice, traditional rooms in Downtown, close to the Arch. An upscale inn near Forest Park, **Cheshire** (cheshirestl.com; $$) oozes character, from its stained-glass windows to the all-encompassing British literary theme. The hodgepodge of artworks, antique furnishings and taxidermy are sure to delight.

More info: Explore St Louis (explorestlouis.com) is the official tourism information source.

Start at the Riverfront
Downtown runs west of the landmark **Gateway Arch** (p66), which rises along the Mississippi River. From here you can hop aboard a variety of boat trips. Immediately south is the 18th-century neighborhood of Soulard.

Missouri's Wildest Museum
For many, a highlight is **City Museum** (citymuseum.org), a frivolous, frilly, fun house in a vast old shoe factory. The Museum of Mirth, Mystery & Mayhem sets the tone. Run, jump and explore all manner of exhibits, including a seven-story slide. The summer-only rooftop offers all manner of weird and wonderful fun, including a flamboyant Ferris wheel and a wild slide.

Unmissable Forest Park
New York City may have Central Park, but St Louis has the bigger (by 528 acres) **Forest Park**. The superb, 1371-acre spread was the setting of the 1904 World's Fair. It's a beautiful place to escape to and is dotted with attractions, many free. Two walkable neighborhoods, the Loop and Central West End are close.

Major attractions at Forest Park include the **St Louis Art Museum** (slam.org), **Missouri History Museum** (mohistory.org), **St Louis Science Center** (slsc.org), the **Boathouse** (boathousestl.com) – both a good restaurant and a place to rent a boat – and wintertime **ice skating** (steinbergrink.com).

STLJB/SHUTTERSTOCK

EATING & DRINKING

Toasted ravioli is filled with meat, coated in breadcrumbs, then deep-fried. Practically every restaurant in the old Italian neighborhood, The Hill, serves it, most notably **Charlie Gitto's** *(charliegittos. com; 5-9pm; $$)*.

St Louis pizza is unlike any other. The crust is ultra-thin and cracker-crisp. The pizzas are square-cut and made with Provel cheese. Local chain **Imo's** *(imospizza.com; noon-10pm; $$)* is a reliable source.

And don't miss that Route 66 stalwart for superb frozen custard, Ted Drewes (p66).

EXPLORE ST LOUIS

St Louis Art Museum

Rocking Nightlife

Many music legends, including Scott Joplin, Tina Turner and Miles Davis, got their start in St Louis and jammin' live-music venues keep the flame burning. The Laclede's Landing, Soulard and the Loop neighborhoods are loaded with pubs and bars, many with live music.

St Louis native Chuck Berry rocked the small basement bar **Blueberry Hill** *(blueberryhill. com)* until the day he died in 2017. The venue hosts bands big and small, and walls covered in pop-culture memorabilia.

over most of Route 66 in Missouri) to avoid the ceaseless spread of suburbs and strip malls surrounding the city. Take Exit 265, 28 miles west, for **Route 66 State Park** *(mostateparks. com)*, with its **visitor center** and museum inside a 1935 roadhouse.

The displays are the reason to stop, but you can't help but feel like the whole place is a bit 'off.' Note that most of the park is on the other side of the Meramec River and that the historic 1932 bridge (built for Route 66) to get there has lacked a deck since 2012. (To access most of the park, which is mostly bland grasslands, you need to return to I-44 and execute a confusing array of offramps and turns.) But the real intrigue awaits: down by the river was the site of the notorious town of **Times Beach**: it was contaminated with dioxins and in the 1980s the government razed the entire area.

Meramec Caverns, Stanton

Pacific

The coming of Route 66 and the end of prohibition in 1933 gave the original owners of the **Red Cedar Inn** two good reasons to build this long-running roadhouse. Known for its stiff drinks and its following among players for the St Louis Cardinals baseball team, it had a rollicking run up until 2005 when the plug was pulled on the neon sign for the last time.

Now reborn as a **Museum and Visitor Center** *(pacificmissouri.com/324/Red-Cedar-Inn-Museum-Visitor-Center)*, the old inn has some of the state's best exhibits on Route 66. The road's history and personalities are detailed with pictures, maps and models. Sadly, the highballs are but a memory.

Gray Summit

Get out and luxuriate in the rich landscapes of the Ozarks at **Shaw Nature Reserve** *(missouribotanicalgarden.org)*, which is right off Old Route 66. Part of the Missouri Botanical Garden, the formal gem back in St Louis, this preserve covers over 2500 acres and has 17 miles of hiking trails that wind through areas devoted to tallgrass prairie, oak-hickory woodlands, floodplain forest, wetlands and more. It's an ideal place to get out of the car, stretch your legs and learn about the beautiful lands you're driving through.

Meramec Caverns

Who needs influencers? Stanton's **Meramec Caverns** *(americascave.com)* has been a model of marketing since it opened right off Route 66 in 1933. That year Lester Dill bought what looked like a mere hole in the ground, changed its name from the unpromising 'Saltpeter Cave' (saltpeter was a compound rumored to cause impotence) and started selling tickets. Soon he discovered vast geological wonderlands underground and by the 1950s he had a full-time crew painting advertisements on barns along highways across the US and teams of boys applying bumper stickers to cars in the parking lots. (You can still see a painted barn near Milepost 235 going west on I-44.)

Still run by the same family, still hugely popular and still as delightfully hokey as ever; if the stalactites aren't enough for you, there are river adventures and other diversions.

Cuba

Hollywood superstar Bette Davis passing through town on Route 66 and her husband throwing a tantrum is but one of the memorable

THE TIMES BEACH SCANDAL

In 1926, the year of Route 66's birth, a local newspaper, the *St Louis Times*, sold lots for cheap housing on a flood plain along the Meramec River in what is today's Route 66 State Park (left). Fast forward to the 1970s when the residents hired a contractor to spread used motor oil on the town's dirt roads to cut down on dust. Little did they know that the oil was contaminated with highly toxic dioxins.

By 1985, the residents had been moved out and all traces of Times Beach were erased. Today, there is little to recall about the scandal or the residents – except for a sign by the disused bridge.

Wagon Wheel Motel (p72), Cuba

Along the Way We Saw...

THE OPEN ROAD West of Springfield is when the road really begins to feel like Route 66. Prior to this, the distinct personality of Illinois overshadows the road while the encroaching trees and hills of eastern Missouri keep you in a green funnel. But with Kansas, Oklahoma and the west on the horizon, the landscape opens up. You see further, whether it's the dreams of new futures travelers once had or visions of adventure enjoyed by today's road-trippers.

TIP: *Meld your mind with the road, forget the state you're in and let Route 66 be your guide.*

Ryan Ver Berkmoes

scenes brought to life on 15 huge murals that cover walls around **Cuba**'s small downtown. Started in 2001, the **Cuba murals** *(cubamomurals.com)* each tell a story from the city's history in bold colors. QR codes give viewers the details 24/7 (the Davis backstory is a hoot).

Nearly as artful as the murals, the **Wagon Wheel Motel** is a stonemasons' work of art dating to 1934. This old-fashioned motor court has cabins crafted in Tudor Revival style from local stone and has long been a Route 66 landmark. Try to see the neon sign at night!

Jerome and the Trail of Tears

Nearly 100 years before Route 66, there was a migration through this part of the Ozarks of a different kind: the Trail of Tears, the forced relocation of thousands of Indians to lands west of the Mississippi. Several memorials recall this holocaust, including a haunting one by Larry Baggett in Jerome (right).

Continues on page 74

BEST PLACES TO SLEEP

Boots Court Motel, Carthage $
Recreates the 1940s in an architecturally significant motel with heated, hardwood floors and radios (no TVs). *(bootscourt66.com)*

Wagon Wheel Motel, Cuba $$
Since 2010 this array of 1930s stone cabins has been lovingly restored and given luxe touches; set on spacious grounds near the center. *(wagonwheel66cuba.com)*

Munger Moss Motel, Lebanon $
You'll get a good night's rest at this icon. Fab touches like fire pits in the central area for making friends make it relaxing after a day's driving. *(mungermoss.com)*

45 miles   Jerome   *10 miles*

Bear witness to history's horrors at Larry Baggett's Trail of Tears

The Trail of Tears

Thousands of Native Americans died along a web of paths across the central US collectively known as the Trail of Tears. Memorials remember this horrific chapter in US history.

HOW TO

Nearest stop: Jerome

Getting here: Larry Baggett's memorial is about 1 mile south of Jerome on the northern frontage road that's technically old Route 66 of I-44.

When to go: Weekends, although hours are erratic

Admission: Free

Info: The multi-stranded **Trail of Tears National Historic Trail** *(nps.gov/trte)* goes through nine states, including the Route 66 states of Illinois, Missouri and Oklahoma.

During the 19th century, settlers' hunger for land pushed Cherokee, Chickasaw, Choctaw, Creek and Seminole peoples off their ancestral lands. This mass displacement became the law with the Indian Removal Act of 1830. In what can at best be described as a holocaust, these five nations were force-marched along the 1838–39 Trail of Tears to today's Oklahoma. Between Rolla and Springfield, much of Route 66 follows the northern branch of the Trail of Tears.

It is estimated that thousands perished. Accounts from survivors and witnesses are horrific.

Various memorials exist, but perhaps the most moving was built by Larry Baggett. For years he was awakened by loud knocks on his door, but there would be no one there. Eventually, a Cherokee man told him that the knocking was the spirits of people walking the Trail of Tears who couldn't get across his property.

Larry modified his land to make it easier for the spirits to pass. The knocking stopped. Larry went on to learn about Indian beliefs, and built figures and symbols out of concrete and stone on his land.

Above and right: Sculptures at Larry Baggett's Trail of Tears Memorial

Uranus

What can we say: 'The best fudge comes from Uranus!' And it doesn't stop there at **Uranus Fudge Factory** (*uranusgeneralstore.com*), a shameless roadside attraction right on Old Route 66 near St Robert. No pun is left unplumbed at Uranus and it wouldn't be surprising if the employees eventually succumb to some form of PTSD as many of the worst ones are blared on a continuous loop.

The main area is, yes, a vast candy area, including brands that you may or may not remember fondly from your childhood. (Did *anyone* ever like Dots? If so, they've got Dots in Uranus.) The gift shop is sprawling (top seller: 'I [heart] Uranus' T-shirts). Diversions include circus- and magic-themed exhibits, mini-golf (guess where the ball goes...) and more.

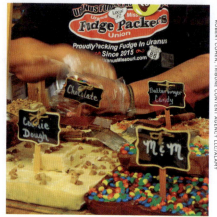

Fudge at Uranus Fudge Factory

Route 66 Gasconade Bridge

Off old Route 66, which on this stretch is also called Heartwood Rd, look for a weathered strip of old pavement heading down to an even more **weathered old bridge** over the Gasconade River. Fences keep you from walking this 1923 relic (one of the rare Missouri bridges that predates Route 66 – unlike Illinois, the state was slow on the road-building uptake), but the setting is serene and the river views calming. In summer, the roar of the cicadas can almost drown out the roar from nearby I-44.

Lebanon

One of the true icons of Route 66 awaits in the small town of **Lebanon**. Opened in 1946 and regularly updated since, the **Munger Moss Motel** (p72) is easily the most famous Route 66 motel. It's got a monster of a neon sign and Mother Road–loving owners, who have decorated the rooms with evocative photos and memorabilia. Observe the sign out front noting you've come 460 miles from the route's start and you have 645 miles to the Midpoint Cafe (p67).

Elsewhere in town, the **Route 66 Museum & Research Center** (*lebanon-laclede.lib.mo.us*) at the Lebanon-Laclede County Library has replicas of a 1930s gas station, a 1940s tourist cabin and a 1950s diner. The vintage maps and road construction blueprints will thrill any Route 66 geek.

DETOUR: Conway Welcome Center

Not just your usual freeway rest stop with a pack of 18-wheelers idling outside, the **Conway Welcome Center** has an over-the-top Route 66

Uranus	Gasconade Bridge	Lebanon	Springfield
24 miles	*15 miles*	*55 miles*	

Have fun with puns at the Fudge Factory

Load up on info at Route 66 Springfield Visitor Center

theme. Look for the signs modeled on the classic version at Lebanon's Munger Moss Motel and the huge floor mosaics showing the entirety of Route 66 from Chicago to LA.

It's on I-44 at Mile 110, near **Conway**; the features are duplicated on both sides of the road. It's between exits 107 and 113 and is only accessible from I-44.

Springfield

Springfield touts itself as the birthplace of Route 66 and while others – hello Oklahoma! – will argue with that claim, this bustling southwest Missouri city does have deep ties to the Mother Road. You can easily spend a day experiencing them (p76), which is good as Springfield is also a fine place to break your journey.

Continues on page 78

66 WHAT?

Keeping today's lexicon of terms for Route 66 straight can be a challenge, especially in Missouri, and especially west of Springfield.

Printed maps as well as digital sources like Google take divergent approaches to designating which roads correspond to the original Mother Road. Toss in variations across the decades between 1926 and 1977 and it gets more complex.

Be thankful when sources call a road 'Old Route 66' – that's usually a good sign of authenticity. Too often the situation west of Joplin is the norm: there's a state Hwy 66, which Google confusingly labels 'US Route 66.'

Munger Moss Motel, Lebanon

Enjoy Springfield's Love of Route 66

Springfield makes the most of its many ties to Route 66. The compact downtown boasts an attractive collection of historic brick buildings, while the Commercial St district has good eating and drinking options, as does the Pickwick and Cherry area. Mother Road sites abound.

HOW TO

Nearest stop: Springfield

Getting here: From the east, arrive via Business Loop I-44. From the west, it's a straight shot in on Hwy 266.

When to go: Springfield is a year-round destination. It has plenty of indoor attractions during the wintertime.

Where to stay: The much-loved **Best Western Route 66 Rail Haven** *(bestwestern.com; $)* has its roots as a 1938 Route 66 motor court. Recently renovated, the natural-stone **Rockwood Motor Court** *(rockwoodcourt.com; $)* opened in 1929.

Route 66 Legacies

Historic Route 66 arrowed across the heart of Springfield on St Louis and College Sts for most of its existence and you can still relive the feel of the road's glory days. Start at the **Route 66 Springfield Visitor Center** *(springfieldmo.org)*, which is delightfully tireless in promoting the road and the city. An excellent resource (with historic displays), staff will provide you with a refreshing drink and answer any questions.

Just west, the star of downtown is the **Gillioz Theatre** *(gillioztheatre.com)*, a lavish Spanish Colonial Revival venue where acts regularly arrived by Route 66 in its glory days.

Further west, the **Birthplace of Route 66 Park** is a work in progress along a vintage stretch of the road. It's a fine spot for a picnic and features a replica of the original **Red's Giant Hamburg sign** (the final 'er' wouldn't fit). From 1947 to 1984 Red's fried 'em up for Mother Road drivers and Springfield has long claimed that he invented the world's first drive-through window.

Celebrating Route 66

It's worth timing your trip for the nation's largest celebration of the Mother Road. Each August, the city closes off Downtown for the **Birthplace of Route 66 Festival** *(route66festivalsgf.com)*, held over a long weekend. The fun includes live entertainment, a motorcycle village, cornhole

SPRINGFIELD VS OKLAHOMA

Springfield lays claim – hard – to the title of 'The birthplace of Route 66,' but is that legit? The force behind the creation of the road and its number was Oklahoma oilman Cyrus Avery (p26). Through a series of compromises, Avery recruited Springfield promoter John Woodruff to his side. On April 20, 1926, the pair sent a telegram from Springfield to the body organizing America's highway system announcing their scheme for Route 66. So while Springfield supplied the telegram, ultimately Oklahoma supplied the juice.

Left: Birthplace of Route 66 Festival; Below: Gillioz Theatre

competitions, historic displays, beer gardens, food vendors and more.

Roadside Hype Below Ground

All manner of geologic wonders are on display at **Fantastic Caverns** *(fantasticcaverns.com)*, which wends through the eroded limestone beneath the Ozarks, northwest of Springfield. In the best of Route 66 traditions, countless billboards and other hype tout the wonders below ground. Visitors are hauled around the stalactites in trailers pulled by Jeeps and never need do any walking at all.

DETOUR: Wilson's Creek National Battlefield

The site of the first major Civil War battle fought west of the Mississippi River, **Wilson's Creek National Battlefield** (nps.gov/wicr) is a fascinating excuse for a trip off Route 66. This rolling open space looks much as it did in 1861, when a large Union force tried to surprise Confederate troops here. After a day of intense fighting that lead to 2500 casualties, the Union force retreated. Visitors can drive, walk or bike a 4.9-mile loop through the battlefield, which has explanatory signs.

Gary's Gay Parita Sinclair Station

Follow Hwy 266 west as it arrows out of Springfield on the old Route 66. It eventually joins with Hwy 96 and maintains the historic course through Carthage. This is rolling farm country, dotted with old barns and a few vintage stops.

You can't miss **Gary's Gay Parita Sinclair Station**. If the name's a mouthful, that's because it reflects several different owners over the years, including the original ones, Fred and Gay Mason. Today, the Turner family are loving stewards of this Route 66 icon, which recreates the 1930s with enough memorabilia to keep you browsing for hours.

Only 1.5 miles west, **Spencer Station** (spencerstation.myshopify.com) is another old gas station. It was custom-built for the opening of Route 66. This bit of road (now designated County Road 2062) captures the feel of 100 years ago, from the original truss bridge over the creek to the dirt road in front of the gas station, which is what much of Route 66 was like in this part of Missouri before the 1930s.

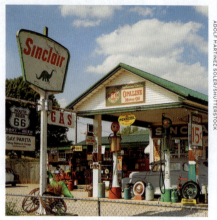

Gary's Gay Parita Sinclair Station

Carthage

Ancient Carthage was destroyed by the Romans in 146 BCE; Missouri's **Carthage** was destroyed by the Confederates in 1861. However, you'd never know it wandering its lovely, tree-shaded streets, which are lined with beautiful homes reflecting the late 1800s mineral wealth. The town's crowning glory is the 1894 **Jasper County Courthouse**, a Romanesque Revival confection of turrets and crenellations.

Learn more at the **Civil War Museum** (carthagemo.gov) and the nearby **Battle of Carthage State Historic Site** (mostateparks.com).

Spend the night near the courthouse at the **Boots Court Motel** (p72), a Streamline Moderne gem in white that's been beautifully updated. At night this Route 66 landmark is bathed in green neon.

	Gary's Gay Parita Sinclair Station		Carthage	Webb City	Joplin
23 miles		36 miles	10 miles	7 miles	
Take a detour to Wilson's Creek National Battlefield			Visit the Civil War Museum		Just 6 miles to the Kansas border

West of town, the **66 Drive-In Theatre** *(66drivein.com)* dates to 1949 and is a selfie fave with its neon signs and art deco detailing. See first-run flicks on hot summer nights on a screen that's, yes, 66ft tall.

Webb City

Just before you enter historic Webb City on US 66, you pass through tiny **Carterville**, which is worth a stop on tree-lined Main St for **Supertam on 66** *(supertamon66.com)*, an old-fashioned ice-cream shop and museum dedicated to all things Superman.

Over in **Webb City**, take time to appreciate the downtown, with its wealth of 19th-century buildings built in opulent styles reflecting the wealth brought in by the then-largest lead and zinc mines in the world. Park and start strolling at Broadway (Route 66) and Main St.

Joplin

Nearly in Kansas! At the start of the 20th century, **Joplin** was a wild city, with lawlessness fueled by mineral wealth. However, its most notorious episode occurred in 1933 when the infamous outlaws **Bonnie and Clyde** holed up here while taking a break from their crime spree. Discovered by the law, they killed two cops in a shootout and fled on Route 66, leaving behind their loot, plus a roll of film that contained now iconic photos of the duo. See these and more at the **Joplin History & Mineral Museum** *(joplin-museum.org)*.

Heading toward Kansas, turn off Hwy 66/W 7th St and take quiet Old 66 Blvd for 1 mile to the state line. Pause there for the classic roadhouse, **Hogs & Hotrods**, where, if there's not an engine revving, the only sound you'll hear is a cock crowing.

Jasper County Courthouse, Carthage

PHOTO ESSAY

The Neon Road

WITH THE EXPLOSION of car travel after WWII, came new mom-and-pop motels to serve the new travelers. Each tried to differentiate itself with kitschy themes and eye-catching neon signs, which became core to mid-century Americana.

Soon, other businesses were in on the act. Route 66 was a 2400-mile-long gallery of pop art, a fantasyland of neon-hued designs in a crazy-quilt of flashing arrows, mod trapezoidal shapes and verbiage using letters out of a font designer's acid trip. Good examples still abound in towns like Springfield, Missouri; Tulsa, Oklahoma; Albuquerque, New Mexico; and Seligman, Arizona. But Tucumcari, New Mexico, remains ground zero for flashing neon fantasies.

From left:

'100% Refrigerated Air' is the stuff of legend at the most iconic sign of them all at the Blue Swallow Motel in Tucumcari, New Mexico (p152).

How can you resist the cloying creativity of Teepee Curios, also in Tucumcari (p152)?

With a sign to match the angle of its classic mid-century roofline, Roy's Motel & Café in California's Mojave Desert is a standout (p211).

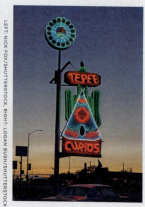

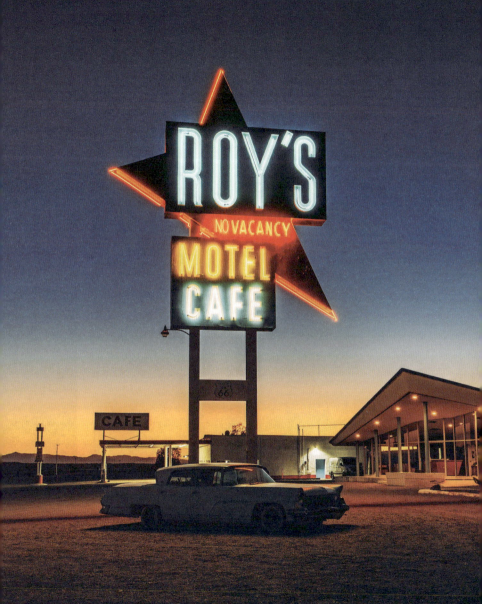

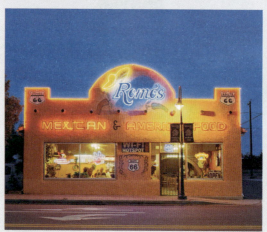

From top:
You'll spend more time decoding the sign than eating your burger at Waylan's in Miami, Oklahoma.

A warm and comforting beacon on a cold night, Romo's Diner in Holbrook, Arizona.

From left:

The second-most iconic sign on Route 66, follow the arrow into the beloved Munger Moss Motel in Lebanon, Missouri (p72).

Diners with Streamline Moderne styling, replete with chrome and glass bricks are found across the USA, and Route 66 is no exception. Here it turns the 66 Diner in Albuquerque, New Mexico into a beauty.

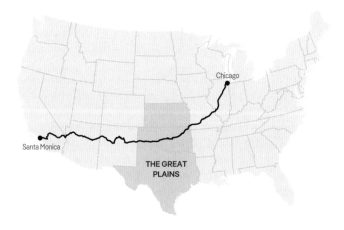

THE GREAT PLAINS

Route 66 starts flattening out during its brief foray into Kansas. In Oklahoma, the rich, red earth is striking and unforgettable. Small towns like Stroud dot the road with metronomic regularity, while Tulsa and Oklahoma City are surprisingly vibrant and urban. In the west, features drain away from the land and the wind starts to blow. You're entering the old Dust Bowl, where Route 66 became Steinbeck's 'Mother Road' and an escape west to a new life. Texas is even flatter and more featureless: its beauty is nihilistic, the horizon endless.

Old Route 66, Vega (p138)
MATTL_IMAGES/SHUTTERSTOCK

Galena
KANSAS

Oklahoma's share of Route 66 (the largest of any state) links some of the Mother Road's iconic highlights. And, indeed, the very moniker 'Mother Road' springs from Steinbeck's *The Grapes of Wrath* about Oklahomans fleeing the Dust Bowl. Listen to native son Woody Guthrie's song 'Hard Travelin' while you drive. It's about the working people on the road and includes mention of Route 66. In this segment, taste Kansas and then plunge into the sights all the way to the heartbreak and delights of Tulsa.

Ryan Ver Berkmoes

Farmland along Route 66, Oklahoma
DAVID P. SMITH/SHUTTERSTOCK

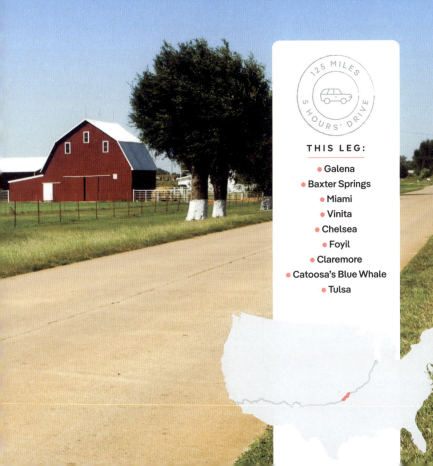

Tulsa
OKLAHOMA

125 MILES / 5 HOURS' DRIVE

THIS LEG:

- Galena
- Baxter Springs
- Miami
- Vinita
- Chelsea
- Foyil
- Claremore
- Catoosa's Blue Whale
- Tulsa

Driving Notes

Route 66 from the Missouri border to Tulsa is good to drive throughout the year. The route is well-used by the localities along it and is kept clear of any snow in winter. However, it's worth noting that some sites outside Tulsa may be seasonal and only open during warmer months. Gas stations and services are commonplace.

Breaking Your Journey

You can do the length of this portion and enjoy the sights in a day, but you won't have time for much of Tulsa. If you're starting from Springfield, Missouri, it will be a very long day. There are scattered places to stay in the towns along the way, especially Claremore. You're never far from food and drink.

Ryan's Tips

BEST MEAL The chicken-fried steak at **Clanton's Cafe**, Vinita (p93)

FAVORITE VIEW Looking down the tree-lined old road leading to Chelsea's **Pryor Creek Bridge** (p94)

ESSENTIAL STOP Tulsa's **Greenpoint** neighborhood (p98)

ROAD-TRIP TIP Park and walk Tulsa's Meadow Gold District, where new businesses catering to Route 66 travelers open all the time.

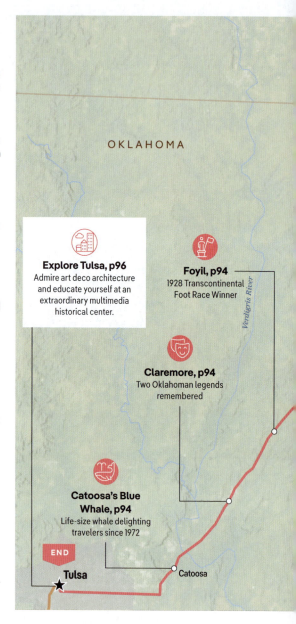

Explore Tulsa, p96 Admire art deco architecture and educate yourself at an extraordinary multimedia historical center.

Foyil, p94 1928 Transcontinental Foot Race Winner

Claremore, p94 Two Oklahoman legends remembered

Catoosa's Blue Whale, p94 Life-size whale delighting travelers since 1972

OKLAHOMA

Verdigris River

END — Tulsa

Catoosa

PREVIOUS STOP From Joplin, you're immediately in Kansas when you cross the border from Missouri.

Galena

Kansas, the sunflower state, holds a mere 13 miles of Mother Road (less than 1% of the total) but there's still a lot to see.

But first, crossing from Missouri is like entering a hellscape as you're instantly in a land still deeply scarred by years of lead mining. The 1.5-mile drive to the north end of **Galena** over old Route 66 has barely changed since 1926.

Hitting Main St, matters improve immediately thanks to, er, Mater. Yes, it's here that Pixar animators discovered a rusty tow truck that became the inspiration for the beloved character in the 2006 hit *Cars*. See the original at **Cars on the Route** *(facebook.com/CarsOnTheRoute)*, a restored gas station with lovely owners who serve lunch and tell stories about the movie. The rest of tiny Galena is a charming place for a stroll.

Baxter Springs

Four miles west of Galena, stop at the red-brick **Old Riverton Store** *(oldrivertonstore.com)* and stock up on top-notch sandwiches and Route 66 memorabilia. The 1925 property looks much like it did when it was first built – note the pressed-tin ceiling and the outhouse.

Continue on Old Route 66 to the 1923 **Brush Creek Bridge** *(nps.gov/places/brush-creek-bridge.htm),* or Rainbow Bridge, as it's popularly known. Based on the Marsh Arch design, it's an uncommonly graceful and elegant design that was once one of 70 across Kansas.

Three miles south on quiet roads brings you to **Baxter Springs**, which you'd never know was the site of a Civil War massacre and numerous bank robberies. Look for the sunflower sculpture at the north entrance to town. The multifaceted **Baxter Springs Heritage Center & Museum** *(baxterspringsmuseum.org)* has gobs of info, as does the **Route 66 Visitors Center**, which is in a restored 1930 Phillips 66 gas station.

Continues on page 93

Inspiration for Mater *(Cars)*, Galena

Galena — *Good stories at Cars on the Route* — 8 miles — **Baxter Springs** — 17 miles — *Cross the Oklahoma state border*

INSIGHT

Labor & Strife in Kansas

In 1935, in Kansas near the Missouri border, Route 66 was shut down to traffic and needed the National Guard to reopen. The legacy of the years of violence that followed can still be seen in Galena today.

A Dirty Industry

Popular images of Kansas often include flat fields of wheat rippling in the wind or tornados. Few think of Kansas and mining, yet for a good chunk of the 19th and 20th centuries it was a center of lead production in the US.

In mines surrounding Galena, thousands of workers toiled in tough conditions extracting the toxic mineral from the earth. The town reflected these harsh realities, and beginning in the 1870s it was best known for its many murders, myriad houses of prostitution and violent saloons.

Strikes & Clashes

Route 66 arrived in 1926, and followed 7th St through town. Meanwhile the miners began organizing into unions to press for better pay and conditions. The mine owners were not receptive: they responded by firing thousands of miners and replacing them with docile company shills. As elsewhere in the US, law enforcement agencies and troops were brought in at the behest of the wealthy company owners to break up the unions.

Throughout the 1930s there were violent clashes. At times striking miners blockaded Route 66 and attacked passing cars. In June 1935, strikes turned particularly violent and

ROTHSTEIN, ARTHUR, 1915-1985, PHOTOGRAPHER

Unemployed Galena miners, 1936

Route 66 was closed for much of the summer until order was restored.

Eventually the government offered legal support to the unionized workers, but by then the mines' peak production days were past. After WWII, most closed.

A Scarred Legacy

A 1937 government guidebook had this harrowing description of the landscape: 'Lying in all directions from the highway are man-made white mountains of chert, residue from the mines, topped occasionally with gaunt black mills and separated by dusty roads, railroad tracks, and patches of rock and cinder-covered wasteland.'

Today Galena – no longer notorious – depends on tourism and touts its links to the movie *Cars*, but the land remains scarred. East of the center along Route 66, you'll see ample evidence of its mining past in the desiccated landscape. Historical markers point out places where the 1930s labor riots occurred.

Drive into the Past

Route 66 in Oklahoma was like a living being. From its birth, it was continually changing and adapting. This drive takes you right back to 1926 when only 12% of the state's roads were paved.

Nearest stop: Miami, OK

Getting there: Three miles southwest of Miami, turn off US 69/Route 66 onto rural S 540 Rd.

When to go: Let the weather be your guide: skip this during wet, muddy and snowy conditions.

Tip: The National Park Service has a detailed essay on vintage Route 66 in Oklahoma *(nps.gov/places/oklahoma-road-segments.htm)*.

When Route 66 was officially born, it was an agglomeration of existing roads in a cacophony of styles. Only Illinois had a unified highway, as the state simply redesignated its existing high-quality road from Chicago to St Louis as Route 66.

Elsewhere, it was at best a patchwork, especially in Oklahoma, where it was not until 1938 that Route 66 was fully sealed.

Until then, roads were often built by local road-building societies, who invented their own individual standards. In 1926, this included all 432 miles of Route 66 that ran through the state.

Like most of Oklahoma's better roads 100 years ago, S 540 Rd is unpaved but drivable. This is a country lane and it's worth stopping just to hear the songbirds. Head south until you find some paving, where you'll find traces of the original 1921 road that became part of Route 66. It's an oddball design, even for then – a 9ft-wide single-lane layer of bricks or asphalt laid down on concrete, with gravel shoulders for when the inevitable oncoming traffic would appear. Follow this for 3.3 miles as it bends sharply west back to US 69/Route 66. A marker gives background.

Stretch of original 9ft-wide Route 66

Along the Way We Saw...

OLD ROUTE 66 The most evocative portions of Route 66 are the ones that transport you right back to 1926, such as the segments south of Springfield, Illinois, that break off Hwy 4 and meander past old farms. Then there is the drive south of Miami, Oklahoma. Only occasionally does today's rural dirt road reveal the original pavement. You're unlikely to see another car; rather, as the trees rustle overhead, you could be in the 1973 movie *Paper Moon*.
TIP: *The National Park Service details the oldest segments of Route 66 in all eight states (nps.gov/subjects/travelroute66/visit.htm).*

Ryan Ver Berkmoes

GALENA TO TULSA

Miami

Crossing the border into Oklahoma, you can see a **variation on 1930s gas station architecture** on **Miami**'s Main St, where the Marathon Oil Company erected a pint-sized Greek Revival temple to petroleum to go with its marathon-running mascot/logo.

South of town are some **beautifully preserved stretches** of original Route 66.

Vinita

One of Oklahoma's best restaurants is near the center of small-town **Vinita**. **Clanton's Cafe** (right) has been serving the model for superb chicken fried steaks since 1927. The delightfully affordable menu is laden with other top regional fare including a New York steak for under $20, pork chops and pot roast.

Most people notice – but don't order – the 'calf fries,' the local euphemism for a dish popular across cattle country that's known elsewhere as Rocky Mountain oysters, among other euphemisms. (In reality, these deep-fried nuggets are the testicles from castrated young bulls.)

BEST PLACES TO EAT

Mother Road Market, Tulsa $
Right on Route 66 at the start of the Meadow Gold District, this sprawling food hall attracts joyous groups who graze on creative offerings. Seasonal offerings dish up surprises. Nibble while quaffing local brews. *(motherroadmarket.com; 11am-9pm Tue-Sun)*

Elmer's, Tulsa $
A legendary barbecue joint where the stars include superb sausages, ham, beef, pork and more. There's also smoked salmon. *(elmersbbqtulsa.net; 11am-8pm Tue-Sat)*

Clanton's Cafe, Vinita $
Even the sides at this long-running icon are fab: don't miss the housemade French fries and onion rings. *(clantonscafe.com; 7am-8pm Mon-Fri)*

Miami — 30 miles — Vinita — 19 miles

Don't miss Clanton's Cafe

Chelsea

A town of relics, **Chelsea** is an atmospheric stop. Check out the derelict **Chelsea Motel**, part of the travel-driven building boom that saw motels explode nationwide from 1926 to the 1950s. Take a rest at the old **Pryor Creek Bridge**, which was built for Route 66 in 1926. The tree-shaded location is a bucolic idyll.

Foyil

A gracefully curving concrete road in small-town **Foyil** has stories to tell. Named Andy Payne Blvd, the western portion is original Route 66 concrete and shows the elegant engineering brought to the road's construction. At the south end, look for the **statue** of its namesake. A natural runner and Cherokee, Payne entered the first Transcontinental Foot Race in 1928. Conceived by notorious hucksters, the 'race' was an excuse to collect money from sponsors. Part of the route followed Route 66 from LA to Chicago to generate publicity for the new road.

Promoters of what was called the 'Bunion Derby' famously ignored the welfare of the runners and nearly three-quarters of the runners didn't finish. Yet Payne did, and he won with a time of 573 hours.

Claremore

Among Route 66's monikers is the 'Will Rogers Highway,' a name made official in 1952. Largely forgotten today, it's hard to understate the fame of the namesake actor and humorist in the 1920s and 1930s (opposite). **Claremore** is home to the large and engaging **Will Rogers Memorial Museum** *(willrogers.com)*, which is just 14 miles south of his birthplace in Oologah.

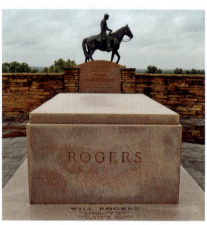

Will Rogers' tomb, Claremore

Claremore is also home to a museum where you can learn about another iconic Oklahoma talent: Lynn Riggs was a gay Cherokee playwright, whose 1930 play *Green Grow the Lilacs* was transformed into the 1943 mega-hit *Oklahoma!*, which revolutionized American musical theater. The **Claremore Museum of History** *(claremoremoh.org)* covers Riggs' fascinating life and has exhibits that include his original Smith-Corona typewriter. Route 66 through town is named Lynn Riggs Blvd.

Catoosa's Blue Whale

A beloved Route 66 icon, the **Blue Whale** of **Catoosa** has been delighting travelers since 1972. It was the obsession of Hugh Davis, who, after he retired as head of the Tulsa Zoo, kept busy on ever-larger whimsical construction projects. First, he built the swimming hole, then, a life-size concrete blue whale. The usual story is that it was a gift for his wife. However, on the Route 66 Podcast, his son suggested that the 'gift' might have been because Hugh forgot their anniversary and needed something fast and there was this huge project he'd been working on for two years...

Today you can walk through the whale's gaping mouth and out onto a pier. The entire site is rustic, dusty and a hoot.

Tulsa

Oklahoma's second-largest city, **Tulsa** (p96) is an excellent place to break your journey for a day or longer. Old Route 66 arrows straight west through town on 11th St.

The **Meadow Gold District** *(meadowgold district.com)* is well worth a few hours of your time. The enormous 1930s neon sign for the

Continues on page 99

WILL ROGERS, SUPERSTAR

Will Rogers was a hugely popular entertainer, newspaper columnist and radio star during the 1920s and 1930s. Rogers was part Cherokee and hailed from the Claremore area, a region he remained close to until his death in a plane crash in Alaska in 1935. His homespun humor was peppered with insightful quotes, such as: 'My ancestors didn't come over on the Mayflower, but they were there to meet the boat.' And his work had the common touch. 'We will never have true civilization until we have learned to recognize the rights of others.'

Blue Whale, Catoosa

Explore Tulsa

Self-billed as the 'Oil Capital of the World,' Tulsa got rich off oil drilling elsewhere, keeping its hands clean while filling its coffers – which are reflected in its high-rises and museums.

HOW TO

Getting there: From Catoosa in the east, you head south to E 11th St and then it's a straight shot in.

Getting around: MetroLink Tulsa *(tulsatransit.org)* runs the local bus network. Parking is copious.

Sleeping: The **Campbell Hotel** (p99) is a restored Route 66 gem. More opulent, the **Hotel Ambassador** (p99) is a luxury high-rise restored to its peak during the oil boom in 1929.

More info: Visit Tulsa *(visittulsa.com)*

Tip: One of the most legendary music venues along Route 66, **Cain's Ballroom** *(cainsballroom.com)* hosts rising rockers who grace the boards where Bob Wills played western swing in the '30s and the Sex Pistols caused confusion in 1978.

Downtown

Downtown Tulsa has so much art deco architecture it was once known as the 'Terra-Cotta City' for the building material typically used to create the distinctive architectural detailing. The **Philcade Building**, with its glorious T-shaped lobby, the nearby **Philtower Building** and the **Boston Avenue United Methodist Church**, rising at the end of downtown, are three exceptional examples.

Download an architectural walking guide at *visittulsa.com* (search for 'self-guided art deco walking tour'). Be sure to visit the essential **Decopolis** *(decopolis.net)* for more Tulsa architecture info. It's in the close-in Meadow Gold District, along 11th St, which is old Route 66 (p95).

Tulsa Arts District

Woody Guthrie gained fame for his 1930s folk ballads that told stories of the Dust Bowl and the Great Depression. His life and music are recalled in the impressive **Woody Guthrie Center** *(woodyguthriecenter.org)*, where you can listen to his music and explore his legacy via the works of Bob Dylan and more. There are regular concerts.

Across the street, **Guthrie Green** *(guthriegreen.com)* is an entire block of open space with an amphitheater for live music as well as regular farmers markets, festivals, classes and more.

Around Tulsa

Northwest of downtown, the superb **Gilcrease Museum** *(gilcrease.org)* sits on the manicured estate of Thomas

KIT LEONG/SHUTTERSTOCK

TOP ROAD FOOD

Great eats line Route 66. The **Mother Road Market** (p93) is a vibrant food hall with a score of vendors dishing up tasty fare, from Korean to BBQ.

Serving its namesake since 1908, **Ike's Chili** *(ikeschilius. com; $)* is served over Fritos – a local sensation called 'Frito pie.' It's located in the Meadow Gold District.

Luring you in with classic neon and chrome, **Tally's Good Food Cafe** *(tallyscafe.com; $)* is a bustling Route 66 diner. It's got Tulsa's best chicken fried steaks.

EXPLORE TULSA

Philbrook Museum of Art

Gilcrease of the Muscogee Creek Nation, who discovered oil on his allotment. Exhibits explore Native American art, textiles, pottery and more, while the surrounding free gardens make for a great stroll.

South of town, the **Philbrook Museum of Art** *(philbrook.org)* is in an oil magnate's converted Italianate villa. It houses fine Native American works and classic international art. There's also a second location, **Philbrook Downtown**, in the Brady Arts District, which shows contemporary art.

Learn How Tulsa Destroyed Itself

Learn about the Tulsa Race Massacre of 1921 on a visit to the neighborhood of Greenwood.

HOW TO

Nearest stop: Tulsa

Getting here: Greenwood is 11 blocks north of E 11th St/Route 66.

Media links: HBO's *Watchmen* revolves around the massacre and its aftermath. *Killers of the Flower Moon* (2023) features footage of the destruction.

More info: Tulsa Library *(tulsalibrary.org/tulsa-race-riot-1921)* for links and resources; Tulsa Historical Society *(tulsahistory.org/exhibit/1921-tulsa-race-massacre)* for multimedia.

On May 30, 1921, an African American teenager and a white woman were alone in an elevator in downtown Tulsa when the woman screamed. The how and why have never been answered, but the incident sparked three days of race riots in which nearly 40 blocks of Greenwood, one of America's most affluent African American neighborhoods, were destroyed by roving gangs of organized white Tulsans.

Thousands were left homeless, hundreds injured and scores killed by the riots. No one yet knows the exact toll: official estimates range from 75 to 300.

Do not miss the extraordinary **Greenwood Rising** *(greenwoodrising.org)*. Opened in 2021, this multimedia historical center near the heart of old Greenwood is unflinching in its account of what happened during the riots and it places the events in their larger contexts. The accounts of survivors, such as journalist AJ Smitherman, are searing.

Just north of Greenwood Rising, the block of N Greenwood Ave has businesses that tie into the area's culture. Check out the exhibits at **John Hope Franklin Reconciliation Park**.

Display in Greenwood Rising

John Hope Franklin Reconciliation Park

Continued from page 95

Meadow Gold brand of milk was a Route 66 landmark and a city icon. Now restored, it's surrounded by displays about the road. Anchoring the Meadow Gold District, the strip of E 11th St has much to interest Mother Road travelers, including a troika of giants! Meadow Gold Mack and **Buck Atom** are both variations on the iconic Muffler Man (p56), while **Stella Atom** brings some much-needed gender diversity.

Continuing west, at the Arkansas River Route 66 turns southwest on the eponymously named boulevard and heads out of town. Look for the **Route 66 Neon Sign Park** on the west bank of the river.

BEST PLACES TO SLEEP

Campbell Hotel, Tulsa $$

Dating to 1927, this historic hotel east of downtown has modern luxe touches including hardwood floors and plush period furniture. *(thecampbellhotel.com)*

The Ambassador, Tulsa $$$

Look in the hallway for the photos of this 10-story hotel in its glory days during the early days of Route 66. Public spaces are suitably grand; rooms have a contemporary feel. *(ambassadortulsa.com)*

Western Motel, Vinita $

Just outside town along Route 66, this motel is a no-frills special that offers clean, budget accommodations and a classic backlit sign out front. *(facebook.com/WesternMotelRoute66)*

Tulsa

16 miles

INSIGHT

A 'Green Book' Journey

Road trips have long been associated with freedom. But for Black people that freedom has often been tempered by racism. From the 1930s, the *Green Book* helped Black Americans negotiate journeys such as Route 66, and the era's legacy – from shoebox lunches to vigilant rest stops – continues to shape many journeys today.

WORDS BY **NNEKA M OKONA**
Nneka M Okona is a journalist and author based in Atlanta, Georgia.

GOOD MUSIC, SNACKS galore and the thrill of your hair blowing in the wind have anchored the quintessential 'All-American' road trip. But for some of us Americans, namely Black Americans, the freedom of being behind the wheel with somewhere to go of our own volition holds specific anxieties and traumas. Coping with these realities means most of us have enlisted ritual and process to feel safe while out in the world on the road.

The Green Book

During the 1930s, the decade right before the Civil Rights Act was passed in 1946 making Jim Crow segregation in public spaces illegal, Victor Hugo Green had an idea.

Green, a postal worker from Harlem, connected these anxieties, traumas, rituals and processes to a hypervigilance that a lot of Black people – many of whom were starting to experience upward mobility resulting in car purchases – felt around the same time that highways and byways like Route 66 were experiencing a throttled boom.

Green wanted a way to use the vast network of Black people around the United States who held spaces and homes to keep travelers safe as they drove. Prior to then, this network wasn't nearly as formalized, and it operated through word-of-mouth. Hugo wanted to offer this whisper network's information and those connections in a tangible, bound guidebook, rather than leaving Black motorists to strategize on the fly, unsure if they'd make it to their destination safely. Or even alive.

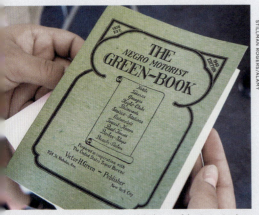

An original copy of the *Green Book*

The first edition of the *Green Book,* also called *The Negro Motorist Green Book,* was published in 1936. During its three-decade era in print, what it was known by shifted – *The Negro Travelers' Green Book* and later *The Travelers' Green Book* – just as the book evolved in its practical uses, including that of helping Black travelers navigate Route 66 with ease, comfort and their dignity intact.

Numerous *Green Book* locations are dotted along Route 66, in cities throughout Illinois, Missouri, Oklahoma, Texas, New Mexico, Arizona and California. Locations listed in the *Green Book* along the route run the full gamut: restaurants, gas stations, lodges, bars, hair salons, barbershops and, perhaps most notably, tourist homes, among the USA's earliest — if not first — iterations of the modern convention of renting a room or home within a host's space. These spaces were run by those who saw the glory and honor in being a refuge and were committed to the communal aspect of provision.

Freedom & Apprehension

Being from Atlanta, Georgia, by way of Stone Mountain, means I hold the idea of driving and that wonder of the open world in a special, albeit personal, tension, encircled in a fiery fear. My hometown of Stone Mountain, after all, is the site of the largest Confederate monument in the world. As it so happens, long road trips with a good playlist and scenes from life that zoom by in the rearview are my favorite spaces for unearthing deeper thoughts.

Without the noise and distraction of how loud our lives have naturally become, I look to driving long distances as a reprieve and a chance to reset. I yearn for them when life feels muddled. I get the freedom of driving and being the literal determiner of your fate behind the wheel. The power in that.

But for Black people like me, Black people from the South, we hold these times with both freedom and apprehension. Like I was taught at a young age: the rituals we do are a part of how we navigate travel. These rituals, these habits, these things we must always do before piling into a car to drive for hours were never simple machinations, but borne of survival.

Take me, for instance. I've driven from Atlanta all the way to Fort Worth, Texas, stopping through Louisiana for respite and fun numerous times. The last time I took this route, on the way back to Atlanta, I was stopped in a small town in Louisiana, one of those towns where the speed limit changes every 50ft. My chest burned with anxiety as I waited for the police officer to write me a speeding ticket.

This instance turned out OK, but as I drove away, my hands still rattling as they gripped the steering wheel, sweat pooled on my palms, I wondered, 'What if it hadn't?' Then those thoughts drifted to the more subtle rules of the road I've almost always employed because my parents did and their parents most likely did: always leave during daylight hours and intend to arrive during daylight, pack all your snacks in a cooler to limit stops and stay on track for an on-time arrival, and be discerning about where you stop to use the restroom when that time comes.

The granular aspect of food is of note because from the whittling-down impact of Jim Crow

> Hugo wanted to offer this whisper network's information and those connections in a tangible, bound guidebook, rather than leaving Black motorists to strategize on the fly, unsure if they'd make it to their destination safely. Or even alive.

racism that undoubtedly impacted road travel throughout the South, but really anywhere in the USA, came things like cold fried chicken. And shoebox lunches. These shoeboxes, sometimes in an actual shoebox but mostly in whatever portable small box or tin could be found, acted as a lunchbox-on-the-go for road trips. Families would put thought into what they packed in these lunches, often including proteins that were good at room temperature, such as cold fried chicken, its crunch held with the crucible of flour, baking powder, baking soda and cornstarch.

Route 66 Today

Naturally, when I think of the wonder and awe of Route 66, how energizing it must've been to travel a path that had not been taken before, my curiosity rests in the Black travelers who traveled that path. What was that experience like for them? Did their bodies shudder in fear the entire time? And what became of these essential landmarks that represented safety along the way?

Thankfully, this legacy of providing protection for Black travelers was revisited in recent years to uncover what vestiges of the past, what tangible markers of support and protection, still existed along Route 66. From 2013 until the following year, historian Frank Norris of the National Park Service led an intensive research effort[1] to both accurately and thoughtfully document *Green Book* locations along this route, taking particular care to note those structures that no longer existed. The project Norris led was known as the Route 66 Corridor Preservation Program,[2] which ended in 2019. Most of the structures were left in a state of disrepair or demolished, taking what memories were etched within their walls.

Much like those buildings that no longer stand, the *Green Book* stopped publishing right before the Civil Rights Act of 1964. Some surmise that the concept more and more was no longer relevant, as Black people could occupy public spaces more safely than in years past. The *Green Book* may be gone, but reflecting on its connection to journeys like Route 66 illuminates something vital: what has been and remains at stake for Black people traveling in this country.

Above: A family hits the road in the 1960s; Right: Jim Crow racism is evident as a man drinks from a water cooler labeled 'Colored' in 1939 Oklahoma City

> Naturally, when I think of the wonder and awe of Route 66, how energizing it must've been to travel a path that had not been taken before, my curiosity rests in the Black travelers who traveled that path. What was that experience like for them?

---

1 https://www.nps.gov/articles/000/route-66-and-the-historic-negro-motorist-green-book.htm

2 https://www.nps.gov/orgs/1453/rosi.htm

Tulsa

OKLAHOMA

The heart of Oklahoma is the heart of Route 66 country as the rolling green prairies of the Midwest segue to the dusty plains of the American West. It's here that Steinbeck based the term 'Mother Road' to describe the highway's journey across America's soul. And it's here that the road is celebrated like no place else. With the 100th anniversary celebration in 2026, festivities are breaking out and Oklahoma City has added hundreds of signs marking Route 66's paths across its neighborhoods.

Ryan Ver Berkmoes

Lake Overholser Bridge, Oklahoma City
MAGIC ALBERTO/SHUTTERSTOCK

Texola
OKLAHOMA

255 MILES
9 HOURS' DRIVE

THIS LEG:

- Sapulpa
- Stroud
- Osage County
- Chandler
- Luther
- Arcadia
- Oklahoma City
- Lake Overholser Bridge
- El Reno
- Pony Bridge
- Clinton
- Elk City
- Erick
- Texola

Driving Notes

Route 66 rarely strays far from I-40 and, short of severe weather, you can drive it year-round. Curves are broad and hills are shallow. You might time your transit of fast-growing Oklahoma City to avoid rush hours; otherwise, traffic will never be an issue and your driving will be smooth sailing. Spring has the advantage of being wildflower season.

Breaking Your Journey

Oklahoma City is the obvious place to break your journey. Stroud (with its unmissable Rock Cafe), Chandler and Clinton also make atmospheric stops, although most larger interchanges along I-40 will have bland chain hotels and fast food. In summer, be sure to book ahead.

Ryan's Tips

BEST MEAL Sirloin strip at **Cattlemen's Steakhouse** in Oklahoma City (p113)

FAVORITE VIEW Looking west across the 38 trusses from the east end of the **Pony Bridge**, with reeds waving in the Canadian River floodplain below (p116)

ESSENTIAL STOP El Reno to compare the onion burgers (p115)

ROAD-TRIP TIP Never succumb to the siren call of I-40.

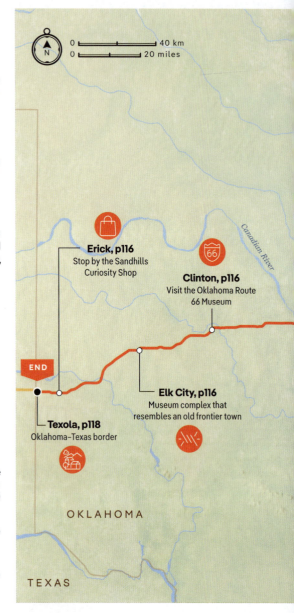

PREVIOUS STOP Tulsa looms long in the rearview mirror as you head southwest to Sapulpa.

Sapulpa

The first country town on Route 66 after Tulsa, **Sapulpa** is a good gateway to **Osage County** and its turbulent, often tragic history. The 2023 film (and 2017 book) *Killers of the Flower Moon* details some of the atrocities that have bedeviled the Osage Nation. Yet it remains a place with a rich culture and is well worth a visit to see another side of Oklahoma that's not always apparent from Route 66.

Stroud

Be sure to time your travels so that you can enjoy a meal in **Stroud** at the **Rock Cafe** *(rockcafert66.com)*, one of the best places to eat on Route 66. Opened in 1939, it's built from local stone, which has helped it survive tornadoes and a disastrous fire in 2008. The current owner, the personable Dawn Welch, bought the cafe in 1993 and was discovered by the Pixar crew in 2001: she's the basis for the Sally Carrera character in *Cars*. The food (p111) is mostly Southern, with a vague German accent.

Nearby, the modest but comfortable **Skyliner Motel** (*918-968-9556*) has the kind of soaring neon sign that sends mid-century design fanatics into paroxysms of joy.

Chandler

The impressive **Route 66 Interpretive Center** *(route66interpretivecenter.org)* in **Chandler** recreates the experience of driving the road through the decades. It's housed in a magnificent 1936 armory built from carved sandstone and designed to withstand tornadoes. The displays incorporate local art and focus on the human, rather than the mechanical experience. When you're done, be sure to pop around out back where there's a 1912 outhouse that's built like a brick, er, well, you know…

To the east on Route 66 are a couple of vintage sights: the **Lincoln Motel** *(lincolnmotelon66.com; $)* is a 1939 motor court with mustard-yellow cabin-style rooms and a big neon sign; nearly next

Continues on page 110

Skyliner Motel, Stroud

4KCLIPS/SHUTTERSTOCK

Sapulpa		Stroud		Chandler
	40 miles		14 miles	

Gateway to Osage Nation

Savor the tasty Rock Cafe

Osage County

Less than 600 full-blooded members of the Osage Nation are alive today. Their land in north-central Oklahoma is rich in beauty and culture.

HOW TO

Nearest stop: Sapulpa

Getting here: Head north on Hwy 97 or on Hwy 99 from Stroud.

When to go: Spring through fall are best to appreciate the natural beauty of the county.

Tip: Listen to the In Trust podcast about Osage headrights and mineral wealth.

More info: *visittheosage.com* and *osageculture.com*

The lush, green beauty of the Osage Nation is embodied by the **Osage Hills State Park** *(travelok.com)*, which is just northwest of Pawhuska. Sand Creek wraps around a promontory which has views of the water as it flows over rock formations.

Pawhuska was the center of the *Killers of the Flower Moon* film production. Pay a visit to the **Osage Nation Visitors Center** *(osageculture.com)*, which has art and fascinating exhibits. Nearby, the **Osage Nation Museum** *(osageculture.com)* is in an old stone chapel and is America's oldest tribal museum.

While in Pawhuska, stop for a bite to eat. The town has a star chef, Ree Drummond, aka the Pioneer Woman. Her **Pioneer Woman Mercantile** *(themercantile.com; 8am-3pm; $)* combines upscale cafe fare and a bakery. More down-home, **Trigger's BBQ** *(triggersbbq.com; noon-8pm Thu-Mon; $$)* has the expected smoky treats.

In Fairfax, the **Osage Memorial** in the **Tall Chief Theatre** *(tallchieftheater.com)* provides a history of the 'Reign of Terror.'

Get a sense of the land's majestic sweep at the **Joseph H. Williams Tallgrass Prairie Preserve**, the largest remaining protected area of its kind.

Above: Fruit tart at Pioneer Woman Mercantile; Right: Osage Hills State Park

door, the **66 Bowl** (rt66bowl.com) has modern lanes, a Mother Road theme, a glowing neon sign and a parking lot full of vintage gas station signs.

Elsewhere, the **Westfall Phillips 66 Station** downtown has been a labor of love for a series of owners who've been restoring this tiny 1934 gas station, right down to its authentic – and gaudy – colors. And, if you have a copy of the classic *EZ66 Guide for Travelers*, the author, **Jerry McClanahan** (national66.org) has his studio in town. The hours are erratic, but he welcomes visitors when he's around.

Luther

East of little **Luther** is an easily missed small building with a big story. At the corner of Route 66 and N Pottawatomi Rd, the **Threatt Filling Station** dates to 1915 when it was built by Allen Threatt to cater to African American travelers. His pick of locations was fortuitous because 11 years later the road in front became the famous highway.

Like other African American Oklahomans, Threatt hoped to pursue a better future in the state. Many had come to Oklahoma during the Trail of Tears as the enslaved people of the Five Civilized Tribes, an often-overlooked aspect of that holocaust. Threatt saw an opportunity to help Black travelers who were restricted from a wide range of services by Jim Crow and other segregationist laws. Gas stations like Threatt's – often found in the *Green Book* (p100) – were vital stops. Many stayed safe from racist gangs by parking in back and sleeping in their cars.

Today the station has been structurally restored. Look for the whimsical old carvings in the sandstone

Threatt Filling Station, Luther

Arcadia

Just before you reach **Arcadia**, look for **E Old Highway 66**. This wide, curving stretch of asphalt bordered by concrete dates to 1928. It was built when federal road money allowed for top-quality construction. Given the road is still smooth after nearly 100 years, the taxpayers got a good deal.

In town, the red-painted 1898 **Round Barn** (arcadiaroundbarn.com) was a beloved Mother Road landmark, easily spotted for its unusual design. On most days, there's a farmers market near its base.

Much less wholesome and much more gaudy, you can't miss **Pops 66** (pops66.com) just west. A 66ft LED soda bottle grabs your eye, while the hundreds of varieties of soda pop and candy from around the world grab your sweet tooth.

Luther — 10 miles — 11 miles — Arcadia — 22 miles — Oklahoma City

Stock up at the Round Barn farmers market

Spend a day or two exploring the state's capital

Oklahoma City

From east and west, Route 66 entered and exited **Oklahoma City** (OKC; p112) on the north side. Cutting across town, it never got further south than NW 23rd St, which is fine as today it's one of the city's most vibrant and interesting strips *(uptown23rd.com)*.

From the east, you hang a right onto 23rd from Lincoln Blvd at the **Oklahoma State Capitol** *(okhouse.gov)*. Built in 1917, this Greco-Roman building has large murals and a tribal flag plaza.

NW 23rd St anchors the Uptown neighborhood and is a perfect place to stroll. Cafes, shops, bars and more line the blocks, as they have for decades. At N Classen Blvd, look a block north for a Route 66 icon, the **Milk Bottle Grocery**. The now-closed shop is topped by an enormous bottle of milk that lured thirsty travelers to buy ice-cold milk from 1930 through the 1960s.

Continues on page 114

BEST PLACES TO EAT

Cattlemen's Steakhouse, Oklahoma City $$
Besides steaks, get the side salad drenched in the house garlic dressing and be sure to have some onion rings at Cattleman's Steakhouse. (p113)

Cheever's Cafe, Oklahoma City $$
Amid the Southwest flavors, the chicken fried steak is considered the best in the state. (p113)

Rock Cafe, Stroud $
The menu at Rock Cafe is Southern with a German accent. A specialty is the Jägersnitzel, a breaded pork cutlet topped with a creamy bacon and mushroom sauce served with späetzle. Top sides include onion strings, fried green tomatoes and fried pickles. Breakfast includes real hash browns. (p108)

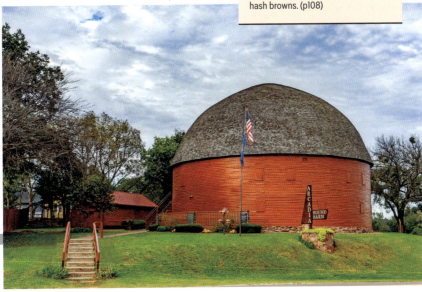

Round Barn, Arcadia

Explore Oklahoma City

Smack in the middle, Oklahoma City (OKC) is the state's booming capital and largest city. It can easily occupy a day or two of your time, with cultural diversions that reflect the local heritage (hi-yo cowboy!). Leave the touristy Brickyard area for the galleries and diversions of the Bohemian Paseo Arts District *(thepaseo.org)*.

HOW TO

Getting there: Coming from Arcadia, you enter OKC heading south on Kelly Ave and then Lincoln Blvd to NW 23rd St.

Getting around: Embark *(embarkok.com)* provides tram, bus and bike rental services. Parking is plentiful. (The parking meter was invented in OKC in 1935.)

Sleeping: Besides Route 66-oriented places (p114), good choices include the **Classen Inn Motel** *(classeninn.com; $)*, a mid-century motel near downtown, and the close by **Colcord Hotel** *(hilton.com; $$)*, a luxurious 12-story hotel in OKC's first skyscraper (1911).

More info: *visitokc.com*

Tip: Learn the stories of 39 nations at the **First Americans Museum** *(famok.org)*, a vital addition to Oklahoma's cultural scene.

OKC's Heart

Route 66 cuts its swath through attractions on the north side of OKC, especially 23rd St. The following sights are more central.

Sprawling across open land near Bricktown, the **Centennial Land Run Monument** captures the chaos and drama of the 1889 land rush that occupied a large part of the future state – and dispossessed Native Americans from their lands. Despite the enduring controversy, the land rushes remain etched in the self-identity of many Sooners.

Only the smells are missing at the **National Cowboy & Western Heritage Museum** *(nationalcowboymuseum.org)*. Here, vibrant historic displays are combined with an excellent collection of Western art.

Recounting America's worst act of domestic terrorism, the **Oklahoma City National Memorial & Museum** *(oklahomacitynationalmemorial.org)* lets the events of April 19, 1995, when a terrorist truck bomb destroyed a federal building, speak for themselves. The outdoor **Symbolic Memorial** has 168 empty chair sculptures for each of the people killed in the attack.

The **Oklahoma History Center** *(okhistory.org/historycenter)* tells the story of the Sooner State through interactive exhibits. The Native American galleries help tell a more nuanced and complete story about the state.

EATING IN OKC

Enjoy the best breakfasts in town at **Sunnyside Diner** *(eat atsunnyside.com; 6am-2pm; $)*, near Downtown. Take one bite of the fresh fare and you'll know you've found morning nirvana. Good kids menu.

OKC has a large Vietnamese community and excellent restaurants. One of the very best is **Pho Lien Hoa** *(9am-9pm; $)* on NW 23rd St.

A landmark former art deco flower shop on NW 23rd St is now the upscale **Cheever's Cafe** *(cheeverscafe.com; 11am-9pm; $$)*. It features excellent Southern- and Mexican-influenced fare.

Displays in the Oklahoma History Center

The Stockyards

You'll brush up against real cowboys in **Stockyards City** *(stockyardscity.org)*, southwest of downtown, either in the shops and restaurants or at the Oklahoma National Stockyards – the world's largest cattle market.

Buy all forms of Western gear at **Langston's** *(langstons.com)*.

Cattlemen's Steakhouse *(cattlemensrestaurant.com; $$)*, Oklahoma City's most storied restaurant, is worth a visit. This Stockyards City institution has been feeding cowpokes and city slickers slabs of prime beef since 1910. Breakfasts are an insider's secret.

Along the Way We Met...

HARLEY RUSSELL There are a lot of road signs along Route 66 which tell you the story of the road. I tell people I stole them all, but really I made deals for all of them. I have a Route 66 sign that me and Annabelle [his wife, who died in 2014] really cherished. It's the first that was on the road. *Harley is the owner of Sandhills Curiosity Shop in Erick (p117).*
HARLEY'S TIP: *People should take all the photos they want. They need to get their bumps, kicks and tricks on 66!*

Lake Overholser Bridge

In the early 1920s, Oklahoma barely had a road network. What existed were rough dirt roads that led to county seats. In 1924, the state's highway commission published a map that designated a network of highways across the state. It was a fanciful move given that the main route across the state disappeared whenever it rained, but it set a vision for the future. In 1925 work began on a landmark bridge northwest of OKC. The 748ft-long **Lake Overholser Bridge** was an engineering and aesthetic marvel and was soon part of the newly designated Route 66. Today the restored bridge is part of a lovely park. Stop for a picnic and get fresh fare at nearby **Lakeview Market** (*lakeviewmarketyukon.com*), a year-round farmers market.

El Reno

Be sure to stop for a **legendary onion burger** (opposite) in this old brick town. Before you reach **El Reno**, look for the 'Chisholm Trail Crossing' sign as you pass through **Yukon**. The storied trail was used in the 1860s and 1870s to

Continues on page 116

BEST PLACES TO SLEEP

These hotels are close to Route 66.

Bradford House, Oklahoma City $$
Built in 1912 as a luxury apartment house, it's now a boutique hotel with a wide porch and modern, comfortable rooms. *(bradfordhouseokc.com)*

District Hotel, Oklahoma City $$
The most rollicking and LGBTIQ+-friendly motel in town, this reborn mid-century motel wraps a pool that's filled with fun anytime it's warm. There's a country and western bar and a leather club. *(districthotelok.com)*

The Ellison, Oklahoma City $$
Named for famed local writer Ralph Ellison, this stylish hotel is on the far north side of town and is a high-tech marvel. *(ellisonhotel.com)*

Lake Overholser Bridge — *11 miles* — *18 miles* — El Reno — *21 miles*

 Onion burgers!

Eat an El Reno Onion Burger

What's an onion burger? It's a beef patty, layered with thinly sliced onions, which together are fried until they're caramelized, and then placed between a bun with cheese, mustard and pickles, and pressed flat.

HOW TO

Nearest stop: El Reno
Getting here: Street parking is easy.
When to go: All three burger joints are open throughout the year.
Cost: Classic onion burger $4
Tip: If there are more than two in your group, go for it and send someone to each of the three venues – you know you want to compare all three!

Although some call it a Depression burger due to the savings inherent in making a hamburger patty with 50% onions, the onion burger predates the financial collapse by several years. It was invented during a 1922 railroad strike, when beef supplies were short, and it proved a hit with customers.

Johnnie's Hamburgers & Coneys $
The first burger joint most people encounter in El Reno is Johnnie's. There's an outside option, just tables and a counter inside, but it's fairly large so the wait should be OK. The homemade pie is Johnnie's secret weapon.

Robert's Grill $
The no-nonsense option since 1926. In an unadorned stucco building with one L-shaped counter surrounding the grill. They do an especially good job of caramelizing the onions, getting them a deep mahogany color. A major option is vinegary slaw.

Sid's Diner $
The fair-weather friend: picnic tables outside and a screened dining pavilion. Order at the cash register, get a beeper, then pick up your food and grab a table under a tree. **Sid's** *(sidsdinerok.com)* has a diner breakfast menu and an ice-cream fountain.

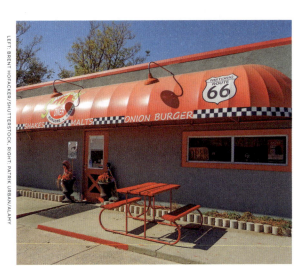

Above: Onion burger;
Right: Sid's Diner

move cattle from Texas, where they were worth $4 a head, to Kansas, where they were sent east to fetch up to $40 a head. Conflicts were legendary and inspired dozens of Westerns, the best being *Red River* (1948).

Leaving El Reno, watch for the gates for **Fort Reno** on the north side of the road. A calvary post in the 1870s, it was a prisoner-of-war camp for German and Italian soldiers in WWII. Members of the infamous Afrika Korps built the stone chapel and many are buried in the cemetery.

Route 66 is arrow-straight heading west for many miles, the 1934 result of the first major project to work out the kinks in the road.

Pony Bridge

A Mother Road highlight, the 38-truss, 4000ft-long **Pony Bridge** (aka Bridgeport Bridge) crosses the Canadian River in rhythmic style. Completed in 1932, it reopened in 2024 after a massive reconstruction. Detailed signs trace the history of the bridge and Route 66. The original made a brief appearance in the 1940 film *The Grapes of Wrath,* when the Joads stop to bury Grandpa at the west end.

Back on the 1930s Route 66, just west of **Hydro** look for the distinctive, live-over apartment at Craftsman-style **Lucille's Service Station**. Built in 1929, the station was home to the eponymous owner-operator who was known as the 'Mother of the Mother Road' until her death in 2000.

Clinton

If you take time for one museum, make it the multimedia **Oklahoma Route 66 Museum** *(okhistory.org/sites/route66; closed Sun)* in **Clinton**. Engagingly designed, in a 30-minute visit you'll get a sense of the road's sweep across eight states, how it was built in a patchwork of segments, and how it evolved across the decades. Topics include popular road eats, migration, homeless camps and racial discrimination. The gift shop has a higher order of merchandise than most, including good books.

Elk City

Several museums in one, this high-concept museum complex in **Elk City** is designed to resemble an old frontier town and includes the **National Route 66 Museum** *(visitelkcity.com/attractions/museums),* which sounds a lot grander than the reality, although displays do cover all eight states.

Erick

Continue west to **Erick**, hometown of 'King of the Road' composer Roger Miller. With the song's breezy first line floating from your

Lucille's Service Station, near Hydro

Pony Bridge — **Clinton**

38 miles — 30 miles

 Swing past Lucille's Service Station

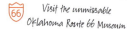 Visit the unmissable Oklahoma Route 66 Museum

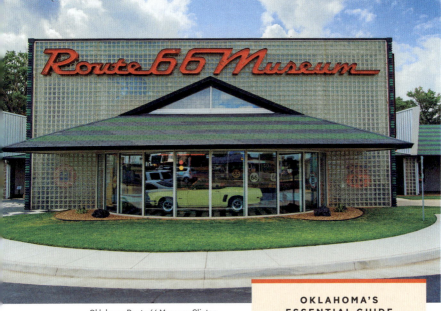

Oklahoma Route 66 Museum, Clinton

speakers ('Trailers for sale or rent...'), it's easy to put the high plains of Texas in your sights. But first stop at the **Sandhills Curiosity Shop**, an extraordinary novelty run by the profane and voluble Harley Russell (p114), who delights in telling stories and singing songs while surrounded by scads of memorabilia and thousands of vintage signs once found along Route 66 (the Pixar people did research here for *Cars*).

Along the wide streets and empty brick facades of this small town, you'll find more old stuff at the **100th Meridian Museum** (local history) and **Sams Town on 66** *(samstownon66.com)*, which also has a few campsites and cabins.

OKLAHOMA'S ESSENTIAL GUIDE

Beard tongue and oxeye sunflower join Indian blanket – the Oklahoma state wildflower – on the colorful pages of the *Oklahoma Route 66 Association Trip Guide (oklahomaroute66.com)*, an annual publishing phenomenon that's a vital and entertaining resource for Mother Road travel in the state.

At a time when publications keep shrinking, the ubiquitous trip guide keeps growing every year. Available in huge stacks at major stops until supplies run out in the fall, the guide can also be viewed online or downloaded. It has turn-by-turn maps and ads for every Route 66-related site in the state. Plus, games for the kids!

Elk City — 33 miles — **Erick**

Browse Sandhills Curiosity Shop

Abandoned gas station, Texola

Texola

A derelict four-lane vestige of Route 66 spills into Texas at **Texola**, which is just a dust devil away from being a ghost town. Right before the border, there's a large and impressive granite marker dedicating the road to Will Rogers (p95). At the border itself, no expense was spent by Texas on a minuscule sign, which is enlivened by the usual array of Mother Road tourists' stickers. (Going east, Oklahoma manages no sign at all. Over on I-40, both states make grander efforts to delineate themselves.)

OKLAHOMA & THE DUST BOWL

Like scores of others, the Joads of Oklahoma flee the Dust Bowl in John Steinbeck's *The Grapes of Wrath* for what they hope will be a better life in California and that may be one of the main reasons why people equate the Dust Bowl with Oklahoma even as other states were affected as badly or worse (p27). Between the novel and film (including Henry Fonda's memorable performance), the link to Oklahoma was cemented.

Then there's the iconic Depression-era photograph of Florence Owens Thompson in a California work camp taken by Dorothea Lange. Known as 'migrant mother,' she is from Oklahoma.

7 miles — Texola — 1 mile to the Texas border!

 INSIGHT

Cars & Route 66

In 2001, a cavalcade of Hollywood types prowled Route 66, snapping photos and taking copious notes. It turned out to be the flamboyant start to what would become the Pixar film *Cars*.

Rock Cafe (p108), Stroud

A Beloved Hit Years in the Making
Over several years, the Pixar creative team prowled Route 66 for material for *Cars,* a film about a young race car who gets stranded in a small town bypassed by the interstate and who ends up learning lessons about life. Renowned real-life Mother Road characters had their stories licensed and iconic locations were adapted for what became a hugely popular film.

To date, *Cars* is a billion-dollar franchise for Disney – which bought Pixar shortly before the film's release in 2006. There have been two sequels, a TV series, various short films and an entire section of Disneyland's California Adventure Park called Cars Land. Revenues have easily surpassed $1 billion and any business with a shred of connection to the franchise is keen to tout it along Route 66.

Real Route 66 Locations
Much of the action takes place in fictional Radiator Springs, a pastiche of small towns found in the five Route 66 states from Kansas to Arizona, where Pixar concentrated its research. (There are also locations sourced elsewhere, such as the Indianapolis Motor Speedway.)

The scenery is distinctly Southwest, of the generic mesa-rich quality that's been popular with Hollywood cartoons since Bugs Bunny took a wrong turn in Albuquerque. Real-life businesses include 'Flo's V-8 Cafe,' which was inspired by the Midpoint Cafe in Adrian, Texas (p138) as it existed in 2001 under then-owner Fran Houser. Radiator Springs Curios shop comes directly from Harley Russell and the Sandhills Curiosity Shop in Erick, Oklahoma (p117).

Sally the Porsche is drawn from Dawn Welch, owner of the historic Rock Cafe in Stroud, Oklahoma (p108). Tow Mater the tow truck was found basking in the sun in Galena, Kansas (p90). Ramone's Body Shop's heritage is the sensational Tower Station & U-Drop Inn in Shamrock, Texas (p126).

Of course, no film with a Route 66 connection would be complete without an Angel Delgadillo influence (p182). The 'Angel of Route 66' helped the Pixar team understand the existential crisis towns like Seligman, Arizona, faced when they were bypassed by the interstate and what they did to come back from the dead.

INSIGHT

Route 66 in Film & TV

An enduring saga about a family fleeing the Dust Bowl, a whimsical tale about a magical German tourist and a beloved feature-length cartoon that's a love letter to the Mother Road. These three films, Ryan Ver Berkmoes writes, have Route 66 at their core. Then there's the namesake TV series, which has nothing to do with Route 66 at all.

WORDS BY **RYAN VER BERKMOES**
Ryan is a lover of all things Route 66. As a toddler he spent Saturday mornings fascinated by the antics of the Road Runner and Wile E Coyote.

THE DISNEY/PIXAR FILM *Cars* is as much of a love letter to Route 66 as you can get on film. Many of the characters and much of the imagery in and around the fictional town of Radiator Springs are drawn from real people and places (p119).

But the film goes beyond the visual and delves into the ethos of the road. There's a key moment when Sally, a blue Porsche partly based on the persona of the real-life Dawn Welch, the proprietor of Stroud, Oklahoma's Rock Cafe (p108), gets philosophical with the film's protagonist, the race car Lightning McQueen. Looking out over a mesa-filled vista of the American Southwest with a truck-filled I-40 razoring across the landscape, Sally waxes on about the difference between travel when Route 66 was the main highway and today:

'Well, the road didn't cut through the land like that interstate. It moved with the land: it rose, it fell, it curved. Cars didn't drive on it to make great time. They drove on it to have a great time.'

In Radiator Springs, *Cars* captures the enduring loss and eternal hope of towns bypassed by the interstate in all eight Route 66 states.

Hope at the Nadir

In 1984, the twilight of Route 66 as an official highway, German filmmakers Percy and Eleonore Adlon drove the length of the Mother Road. Three years later, they made *Bagdad Cafe,* a surrealist, warm-hearted comedy-drama about a down-at-heels cafe on what's left of Route 66 in the Mojave Desert.

Still from *The Grapes of Wrath* (1940)

Under the haunting strains of the Oscar-nominated 'Calling You,' a collection of characters come to know each other and develop friendships in surprising ways, with an improbable German tourist wandering in off Route 66 as the catalyst.

Streams of trucks on I-40 and Santa Fe trains are in the background of every long shot while the Bagdad Cafe and its motel – like what's left of Route 66 – barely hang on in the time before the road itself became the star attraction. Today the actual cafe used for the film – Bagdad Cafe in Newberry Springs, California (p212) – is a major Route 66 landmark.

Parent of the Mother Road

In the novel *The Grapes of Wrath*, John Steinbeck coined the phrase 'the mother road' to describe how Route 66 was where the dirt road tributaries from across the countryside brought desperate people heading west.

The 1940 film broke with Hollywood practice and shot a fair bit of *The Grapes of Wrath* on location along Route 66 from Oklahoma to California. We see the Joads and their jalopy in small towns and wide open spaces as they journey west, culminating in their crossing the Colorado River into California on the landmark old Trails Arch Bridge (p210).

It's Not in the Name

One of the enduring myths about Route 66 is its connection to the namesake TV show. Here are the undeniable facts: *Route 66* ran for 116 episodes on CBS from 1960 to 1964. It was one of the few TV series shot entirely on location, visiting 25 states and Canada over its four seasons. And it was about two guys driving around, meeting guest stars and having adventures.

> 'Well, the road didn't cut through the land like that interstate. It moved with the land: it rose, it fell, it curved. Cars didn't drive on it to make great time. They drove on it to have a great time.'

Now for the hard truths. The theme song was not '(Get Your Kicks on) Route 66,' the enduring R&B song by Bobby Troup and Nat King Cole, but a jaunty ditty by Nelson Riddle, a Hollywood composer. The Corvette convertible driven by the lead characters was not red (as depicted in displays up and down the Mother Road), but a muted blue, green or grey. But the hardest truth of all is that *Route 66* the series had nothing to do with Route 66 the road. In fact, until late in its development, the show was known as *The Searchers*, a title that was changed lest the show be mistaken for the landmark 1956 John Ford/John Wayne Western.

As Martin Milner, who played the lead character Tod, recalled years later, series creator and producer Stirling Silliphant found the real Route 66 'boring' (the nerve, then again he was responsible for the killer bee opus *The Swarm*) and only three episodes were shot close to the road.

Location, Location, Location

A few other films – including *Easy Rider* (1969), *Natural Born Killers* (1994), *Little Miss Sunshine* (2006) and *Beneath the Dark* (2010) – have used Route 66 as a backdrop for some scenes, even though they don't center on the road itself. Among the myriad documentaries and travelogues, *Route 66: The Untold Story of Women on the Mother Road* is a moving three-part series based on the oral histories of women whose lives were closely tied to the road.

Road Runner cartoons are memorably set along Route 66 in the Southwest (keep an eye out for any Acme-brand anvils as you drive). While the running gag of a lost Bugs Bunny proclaiming 'I should have turned left in Albuquerque,' referred to the baffling course Route 66 took through the city.

Texola
TEXAS

The Mother Road arrows across Texas for 194 miles. Given the featureless landscape, one can only imagine the road ennui suffered by scores of travelers as they motored along surrounded by the beige, featureless expanses. But, as always, there were plenty of entrepreneurs ready to offer diversions for a buck or two. And, for those willing to practice some road zen, there's a minimalist peace, where fascinating details are discerned from the vastness.

Ryan Ver Berkmoes

Leaning Water Tower, Groom
MYSTIC STOCK PHOTOGRAPHY/SHUTTERSTOCK

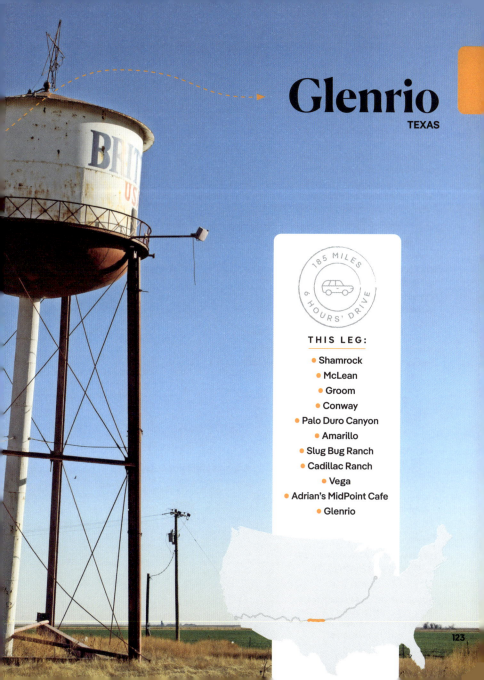

Glenrio
TEXAS

185 MILES • 6 HOURS' DRIVE

THIS LEG:

- Shamrock
- McLean
- Groom
- Conway
- Palo Duro Canyon
- Amarillo
- Slug Bug Ranch
- Cadillac Ranch
- Vega
- Adrian's MidPoint Cafe
- Glenrio

Driving Notes

Old Route 66 runs pretty true east to west. The entire route has been replaced by I-40, but through frontage and access roads plus detours through towns such as Amarillo, you can recreate most of the old route. Let the miles slip past during the 'white space' of your trip, between the green Midwest and the warm colors of the west.

Breaking Your Journey

Amarillo has been the place to break your Route 66 journey since 1926. It's got great food, nightlife and seemingly every chain hotel brand. It even has some fine indie places. If timing doesn't work, you'll find good refuge in Shamrock. Otherwise, major I-40 interchanges offer shelter and the dubious sustenance of fast food.

Ryan's Tips

BEST MEAL End-cut prime rib at the **Big Texan Steak Ranch** (p130).

FAVORITE VIEW The endless horizon at **Adrian**, midpoint on the Mother Road (p138).

ESSENTIAL STOP Walking historic **SW 6th Avenue** in Amarillo (p134).

ROAD-TRIP TIP Even frontage roads offer a serene respite from I-40. The pleasure of the drive west of Conway can't be overstated.

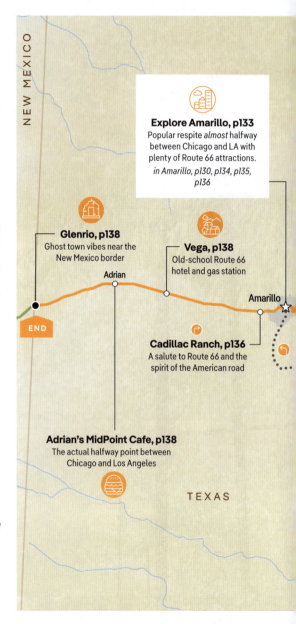

Explore Amarillo, p133
Popular respite *almost* halfway between Chicago and LA with plenty of Route 66 attractions.
in Amarillo, p130, p134, p135, p136

Glenrio, p138
Ghost town vibes near the New Mexico border

Vega, p138
Old-school Route 66 hotel and gas station

Cadillac Ranch, p136
A salute to Route 66 and the spirit of the American road

Adrian's MidPoint Cafe, p138
The actual halfway point between Chicago and Los Angeles

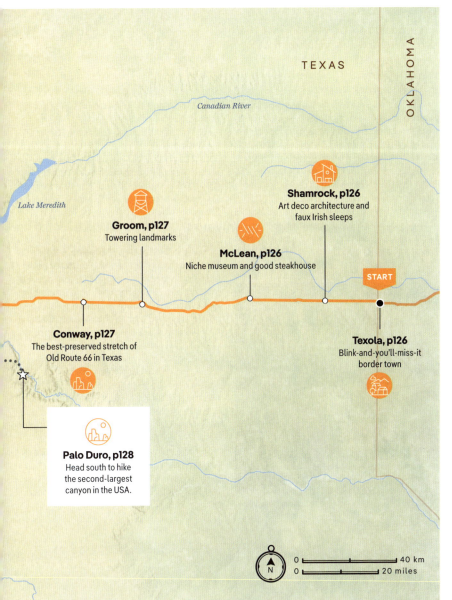

PREVIOUS STOP From Texola in Oklahoma, it's a short drive along nearly featureless landscape to the soaring surprise in Shamrock.

Shamrock

Not to be missed, the **Tower Station** in **Shamrock** is an extraordinary example of art deco design executed in light brick and green glazed tiles. The original Conoco gas station is topped by a soaring obelisk capped with a metal tulip. A shorter tower surmounts the original cafe area, the **U-Drop Inn** (a schoolboy won a naming contest with that one).

Beautifully restored with federal funds, this city-owned road palace glows with green neon at night. By day, there's a cafe serving coffee, baked goods, sandwiches and homemade pie. A large information area has a few displays devoted to Route 66 and many souvenirs. In *Cars* the building is Ramone's Body Art.

East of Tower Station are three Route 66–era indie motels. All are budget-priced and get approving reviews from guests. Two milk the faux Irish angle: the **Shamrock Country Inn** (p130) with its green tubs and the **Blarney Inn** *(blarneyinnshamrock.us; $)*, which features a Shamrock-wielding leprechaun.

McLean

The **Devil's Rope Museum & Route 66 Museum** *(barbwiremuseum.com; closed winter)* has vast barbed-wire displays (where hipsters look for new tattoo patterns) and a small but homey and idiosyncratic room devoted to Route 66. The detailed map of the road in Texas is a must. Also worth a look are the moving portraits of Dust Bowl damage and the refugees from the human-made environmental disaster.

The rest of **McLean** has a similar desolate feel. Where there was once a booming Route 66 strip of roadhouses and even a bra factory, today the wide one-way streets don't even attract tumbleweeds. Look for another restored Tudor Revival-style **Phillips Gas Station** (1929).

At McLean's west end, the **Red River Steakhouse** *(redriversteakhouse.net; $)* is an oasis in the plains, with an affordable menu of Texas classics, such as steaks, catfish, barbecue, burgers etc.

U-Drop Inn, Shamrock

Shamrock — 21 miles — McLean — 31 miles

Marvel at the Tower Station

Visit Devil's Rope Museum & Route 66 Museum

Phillips Gas Station, McLean

Groom

The next sights will appear on the horizon long before the hamlet of **Groom** appears in your windshield: the famous **Leaning Water Tower** and (one of) the **World's Tallest Cross** *(crossministries.net)*. The former was an eye-catching gimmick by Ralph Britten, owner of a long-gone gas station; the latter tops out at 190ft.

Conway

Beginning at Hwy 207, south of Exit 96 on I-44, is the **best-preserved stretch** of old Route 66 in Texas. It's not just the old 1930s concrete, which runs west like a plumb line, but

Continues on page 130

BEST PLACES TO EAT

Tyler's Barbeque, Amarillo $
Amarillo's favorite spot for barbecue is worth the love. The mesquite-grilled meats (the ribs and brisket are tops) are redolent with smoke. Get a seat so you can watch the west Texas sunset. *(tylersbarbeque.com; opens 11am Tue-Sat)*

Big Texan Steak Ranch, Amarillo $$
Steaks, more steaks, and very good prime rib; add to that excellent chicken fried steak and very good breakfasts. (p130)

Crush Wine Bar & Grill, Amarillo $$
Attracts folks in suits and skirts and cowboy boots with an inspirational wine list and creative fare. The best tables are on the upstairs patio. *(crushamarillo.com; 11am-10pm)*

Groom ○ — 17 miles — ○ Conway

Spot the Leaning Water Tower

Revel in Palo Duro Canyon

At 120 miles long and about 5 miles wide, Palo Duro Canyon is second in size in the USA only to the Grand Canyon. The cliffs striated in yellows, reds and oranges, rock towers and other geologic oddities are a refreshing delight after days on the road.

HOW TO

Nearest stop: Amarillo

Getting here: Drive south 26 miles via Hwy 217 or I-27.

When to go: Spring and fall are the best seasons, away from cold winter rain and sweltering summer daytime heat.

Admission: Palo Duro Canyon State Park $8

Tip: From June to August, check your irony at the gate and join the fun at *Texas*, an outdoor musical in the park that milks every Lone Star state cliché.

More info: tpwd.texas.gov/state-parks/palo-duro-canyon

A History of Refuge & Recreation

The multihued canyon was carved by the Prairie Dog Town Fork of the Red River. Its 26,000 acres attract hikers, horseback riders and mountain bikers, while its magnificent colors and desert light draw artists and photographers. From the visitor center (which is the best overall viewpoint), half a mile beyond the gate, the road winds down to the canyon floor, then loops on both sides of the river, passing campgrounds and trailheads.

The great gorge has sheltered and inspired people for a long time. The Clovis and Folsom peoples lived in the canyon as long as 12,000 years ago, and Coronado may have stopped by in 1541. Palo Duro was the site of an 1874 battle between Comanche and Kiowa warriors and the US Army.

Hitting the Trails

Top trails to explore the park:
Lighthouse Trail Palo Duro's most popular hiking trail leads to the Lighthouse, a hoodoo-style formation that's nearly 300ft tall. Almost all of the 5.6-mile round-trip is flat and easily traversed. The floodplain to the southwest of the trail has perhaps the park's greatest concentration of wildlife, including aoudad sheep, white-tailed mule deer and wild turkeys.
CCC Trail Cross four historic CCC bridges on your way down to the canyon floor. It's got a descent of 500ft and is 2.8 miles round-trip.

WHERE TO EAT

Food options in the park are limited to a basic cafe; bring groceries and/or a picnic from Canyon.

Feldman's Wrong Way Diner (feldmansdiner.com) has an upscale American menu with a bar and a lot of humor.

Close to the park entrance, **Sad Monkey Mercantile** (sadmonkeymercantile.com) has excellent food to go, plus top-notch deli fare for camping and picnics; and several microbrews.

Left: Lighthouse rock formation; Below: Cyclists ride the trails

Sunflower Trail The canyon's geologic wonders are on full display, including brilliant white veins of white gypsum. It is a 2.4-mile round-trip and is good for families.

Pioneer Nature This 0.4-mile looping walk to the river is good for spotting wildlife such as the horned lizard. An easy walk that's ideal for families without a lot of time.

Inside the park, **Old West Stables** (oldweststables.com) offers a variety of trips on tame horses. **Palo Duro Canyon Outfitters** (paloducanyonoutfitters.com) offers bike rental in the nearby town of Canyon.

Along the Way We Met...

KENNETH BARROW Route 66 is about living life. It's about living hope, letting your hair down and letting your cares go. You can do that by driving it, man, but you can also do it right here on SW 6th in Amarillo. All of us here, we support each other. We live the life every day. We walk outside loving life, we see each other and, I'm not kidding, the bands get going at night and there's dancing in the streets!
Kenneth works at Coffee Fixx in Amarillo (p134).
KENNETH'S TIP: *'Baby, go cruisin' on Route 66 and just enjoy the ride!'*

also the timeless Plains scenery that's table-flat, with relief provided by a grain silo or two. Get your car up to speed and enjoy the ka-thunk, ka-thunk as you race over the slabs of what's now labeled as Farm Rd 2161. After a little over 7 miles you'll be back to I-40 and frontage roads.

DETOUR: Palo Duro

Driving through the Texas Panhandle it can seem as flat as a pan. Twenty miles past Conway, head south off Route 66 to put a little Texas in your life. **Palo Duro Canyon State Park** encompasses a vast and colorful cleft in the earth that's ideal for hiking and other active pursuits (p128).

Amarillo's Big Texan

A classic Route 66 roadside attraction in **Amarillo**, **Big Texan Steak Ranch** *(bigtexan.com; 8am-10:30pm)* dispatches stretch Cadillac limos with steer-horn hood ornaments to give area hotel guests free rides. A huge Big Tex road

Continues on page 135

BEST PLACES TO SLEEP

Atrea Inn, Amarillo $
A model for modernized motels everywhere. It's bright, cheerful and great value. *(atreainnamarillo.com)*

Big Texan Inn, Amarillo $
Stay at the motel across from the Steak Ranch, or opt for the RV park, cabins, wagons (!), Airstream trailers or apartments. *(bigtexan.com)*

Shamrock Country Inn, Shamrock $
The green here stops after the neon and the bathrooms and the indoor plants and the... But the comforts keep going at this vintage motel from Route 66's heyday that remains in top form. *(shamrockcountryinn.com)*

  Take a detour to Palo Duro Canyon State Park

23 miles

Amarillo's Big Texan
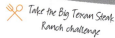 Take the Big Texan Steak Ranch challenge

1 mile

INSIGHT

The Dust Bowl

Hubris, even more than the weather, caused the economic and environmental devastation known as the Dust Bowl.

Buried farm equipment in Dallas, 1936

BEGINNING IN THE 1870s, generations of Americans were urged to 'go west'. Lacking education in good farming practices, these novice pioneers reshaped the land with disastrous consequences.

A Decade of Grief

Prior to the 1870s, the Great Plains were characterized by native grasses with tough root systems that held the thin and fragile topsoil in place. But the Homestead Act of 1862 and the government's appropriation of native lands for mostly white (and a few African American) settlers changed the landscape forever. New farmers were encouraged to till the earth, laboring under a widespread belief that 'rain follows the plow', that is, that the actual act of farming would cause rain. By 1890, over 370,000 homesteads had sprung up over 48 million acres of land.

Unscrupulous bankers encouraged farmers to take out loans to farm more land than the economy – or the environment – could support. A drought throughout the 1930s meant that seeds of grain didn't sprout; instead, the seeds of disaster were sown. The peak drought years were 1934, 1936 and 1939–40. The ever-blowing winds soon whipped up the top soil, and there were no longer any prairie grasses or crops to hold it in place. Enormous dust storms swept the countryside, burying lives, farms and towns. Farmers who had extended far beyond their means had their land, houses and belongings seized by banks.

Ultimately, an area the size of Texas was affected, with the devastation spread across the panhandle of that state, the panhandle of Oklahoma, southwest Kansas and southeast Colorado. Even northeast New Mexico suffered.

Route 66 & the Dust Bowl

Route 66 ran through the southern reaches of the misery and, as the sole developed highway, became the main means for desperate families to escape – often to the supposed greener fields of California. Most found only misery there, as the 'jobs' in the agriculture industry left them little better than indentured servants.

Many of the small towns in the heart of the Dust Bowl never recovered. In Texas, from Amarillo going west to the state line, Route 66 passes through some of the worst affected areas. Even now, the constantly blowing wind propels huge wind turbines.

Explore Amarillo

Long an unavoidable stop, roughly halfway between Chicago and LA on old Route 66, Amarillo today is still a popular respite. It also offers many attractions along old Route 66 and elsewhere in town. And, you'll want to spend time strolling and enjoying the many diversions along SW 6th Ave (p134).

HOW TO

Getting there: From the east or west, you'll arrive on I-40 or the frontage road.

Getting around: Distances are short, parking is easy.

Sleeping: Atrea Inn (p130) is an updated motel-style complex with plenty of fun touches, such as communal areas outside. **Big Texan Inn** (p130) is right across from the Steak Ranch and has comfortable faux pioneer-style motel rooms.

More info: Amarillo has great tourist resources *(visitamarillo.com)*. **Texas Route 66 Visitor Center** *(txrt66visitorcenter.com)* on SW 6th Ave has info, maps, art and gifts. On I-40, the **Texas Travel Information Center** *(txdot.gov)* has a Texas-sized amount of info about the state and Route 66.

Things to See & Do

Quarter horses, favored on the Texas range, were originally named for their prowess at galloping down early American racetracks, then a quarter-mile long. These beautiful animals are celebrated at the visually striking **American Quarter Horse Hall of Fame & Museum** *(aqha.com)*, which explores their roles in ranching as well as racing. These are often the horses you see working with cattle, owing to their sleek size.

Long before today's posh gas-guzzling RVs hit Route 66, laden with every convenience right down to the satellite dish, intrepid Americans looking for adventure had much simpler vehicles. The **Jack Sisemore RV Museum** *(rvmuseum.net)* has trailers and RVs from the 1930s to the 1970s, a time when entertainment meant watching Dad hit his head on the pint-sized door frame.

Stretch those road legs at the 600-acre **Wildcat Bluff Nature Center** *(wildcatbluff.org)*, 8 miles northwest of town, where trails wind through grasslands, cottonwoods and bluffs. Spy on a prairie dog town and try to spot a burrowing owl or porcupine while steering clear of rattlesnakes and tarantulas. There are many hiking options, including **Libb's Trail**, which is fairly short and fully accessible.

If plowing sedately along Route 66 leaves you ready for greater thrills, shake off your lethargy by careening through the double loops of the Texas Tornado roller coaster. Locally

EATING & DRINKING

The major flavors of Texas cuisines come together in Amarillo.

A top choice for Tex-Mex fare, **El Tejavan** *(eltejavan.com; 8am-8pm; $)* may look bland on the outside, but it's all piquant on the inside.

The line at Tyler's Barbeque (p127) is always long, so get there early: when it sells out, it closes. For beef, hit the **Big Texan Steak Ranch** (p127).

Crush Wine Bar & Grill (p127) has Amarillo's finest beer selection, plus a creative menu. It's in Amarillo's small downtown nightlife district.

Big Texan Steak Ranch (p130)

owned **Wonderland Amusement Park** *(wonderlandpark.com)* offers thrill rides, family rides and a water park. Check online for specific opening days and hours (and try to ignore the hideous garden-gnome mascot).

Buying Western Wear

For high-quality Western wear, consider these two sources: **Oliver Saddle Shop** *(oliver saddle.com)* has been creating leather goods for cowboys and cowgirls since 1917; **Beck Boots** *(beckboots.com)* moved to Amarillo in 1921. Their Western and work boots are legendary.

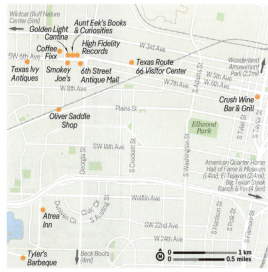

Enjoy SW 6th Ave

US Route 66-Sixth St Historic District, between Georgia St and Western St, is Amarillo's best shopping, dining and entertainment area.

HOW TO

Getting here: To follow old Route 66 from the east, take Business Loop I-40 as far as US 87, then turn south on SW 6th Ave, which going west puts you into the district. Street parking is plentiful.

When to go: There's something going on morning, noon and night year-round.

The historic **SW 6th Avenue** district is one of the most intact strips of commercial buildings linked to Route 66 in the US.

Get your morning shot at **Coffee Fixx**, which has more good cheer than seems allowed. Appropriately caffeinated, you can begin to explore the strip.

Start at the **6th Street Antique Mall** (6thstreetantiquemall.com) with over 60 vendors. Many sell Mother Road memorabilia of variable origin, from true treasures to stuff that clutters up attics and bedevils heirs who have to dispose of it.

Further west, **Texas Ivy Antiques** (facebook.com/texasivyantiques) likes to pose visitors in front of its Route 66 sign.

Look for books at **Aunt Eek's Books & Curiosities** (aunteeksonline.com), which cheerfully calls itself a 'den of uniquities.' Nearby **High Fidelity Records** (funkylittlerecordstore.com) has vinyl, CD and live performances.

Don't miss **Golden Light Cantina** (goldenlightcafe.com; $), where classic cheeseburgers, green chili stew and cold beer have sated Route 66 travelers since 1946. Across the street is **Smokey Joe's** (smokeyjoesamarillo.wixsite.com/smokey-joes; $) slings a great chicken fried steak.

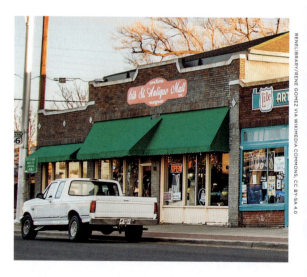

6th Street Antique Mall

Chicken fried steak with rice and beans

CHICKEN FRIED STEAK

From Chicago to LA and at virtually hundreds of points in between, you'll find chicken fried steak on menus all along Route 66.

Many an eatery claims to make the best version of the dish and two states, Oklahoma and Texas, both claim it as their own.

The origins of the dish are unknown but the recipe is as simple as the name is literal: take a cheap cut of beef, batter it up as you would to fry a chicken and then do just that: fry it. Depending on the cook (never a 'chef'), it's then swaddled in brown or white gravy.

sign welcomes travelers, who've been taunted by billboards for miles in either direction.

The legendary gimmick – the 'free 72oz steak' – is a devilish offer as you must eat this enormous portion of cow, plus a multitude of sides in under one hour, or you pay for the entire meal ($72). Contestants sit at a raised table to 'entertain' the other diners. Only about 11% pass the challenge, taking around 50 minutes. Cocky young guys seem to fare the worst; the record holder is a petite woman – a professional speed eater – who wolfed it down in four minutes, 22 seconds in 2015.

Amarillo

Wander historic SW 6th Ave

1 mile

Entry gate, Cadillac Ranch

Stunts aside, the ranch has excellent food. Adding to the fun are strolling cowboy troubadours, a beer garden with superb house-brewed beers, a buzzing bar and a gleefully honky-tonk vibe. In a word, it's a hoot.

Slug Bug Ranch

One mile west of the Big Texan, parallel to I-40, is Amarillo's latest roadside attraction. **Slug Bug Ranch** (*bugranch66.com* and *bigtexan.com/slugbugranch*) started as a cheeky come-on for a gas station in Conway in 1990. In 2023, the hucksters at the Big Texan bought it and moved it here, next to their RV park (the empire is ever-expanding).

The vintage VW Beetles still parody the Cadillac Ranch and now they've been joined by other buried beasts: retired limos from the Big Texan fleet. It's all well-organized and it's easy to spot thanks to the crowds, who gather to ogle the upended vintage VW Beetles and limos put out to pasture. Many leave their mark with spray paint.

DETOUR: Cadillac Ranch

To millions of people whizzing across the Texas Panhandle each year, the **Cadillac Ranch** (*facebook.com/1974cadillacranch*) is the ultimate symbol of the US love affair with wheels. A salute to Route 66 and the spirit of the American

Continues on page 138

Slug Bug Ranch
7 miles
Decorate a Beetle at Slug Bug Ranch

48 miles
Detour past Cadillac Ranch

INSIGHT

Route 66's Motel Evolution

Well into the 1950s, where to spend the night on the road was a constant concern. In the mid-1920s, the concept of safe, clean and convenient places where people traveling by car could sleep was unknown.

Blue Swallow Motel, Tucumcari (p152)

HOTELS IN THE 1920s could be grand, but had little parking as guests arrived by train. Flophouses for itinerant workers were not welcoming for families. Lodgings, such as they were, didn't serve a newly mobile society of people traveling on a budget. Early travelers often resorted to camping in auto camps or slept in their cars.

In the late 1920s, motor courts (collections of cottages) and motels began being built by the hundreds along Route 66. They had varying standards and varying skills behind the front desk. Usually, owners were also the operators, and skills were learned on the job.

Fit for Purpose

Standards varied widely. Boomer children have childhood stories of their suspicious mothers sniffing the air when checking into a new room and then ferociously wiping every surface with Lysol. People feared the nightmare motel mocked in a 1955 episode of *I Love Lucy*, when the gang are fleeced in a rattletrap cabin on their way to LA. (Worse, of course, happens to Janet Leigh when she checks into the wrong motel in 1961's *Psycho*.)

Motel architecture evolved to assuage traveler concerns. At first, people were as worried about their cars as they were for their families, so it was common for units to come with enclosed garages. Sprawling compounds, with nearly step-free access to each room, were near-standard.

Enter the Chains

New motels went up quickly after WWII; in Route 66 towns it's typical to see clusters of old motels built on the east ends of towns, each trying to leapfrog another in the hopes of capturing the predominantly westbound traffic (maybe with the help of a gaudy neon sign).

In the 1950s, demands for consistency drove the first formation of chains. Today's Best Western Hotels began as a loose affiliation of motels along Route 66 – each agreed to meet certain standards. Soon hundreds of Holiday Inns came along with the slogan: 'The best surprise is no surprise.'

Today, a few classic motels have been restored. Otherwise, modern hotels at freeway interchanges are as generic as the interstates.

road, it was created by burying, hood first, 10 west-facing Cadillacs.

In 1974 this 'monument to the rise and fall of the Cadillac tail fin' made its debut. The cars date from 1948 to 1959 – a period in which tail fins just kept getting bigger and bigger (the fin vanished in 1964). In 1997 the cars were relocated to a field 2 miles west of their original location due to suburban sprawl.

The cars are easily spotted off the access road on the south side of I-40. Take exit 60. The accepted practice is to draw on what's left of the disintegrating cars, which gives them an ever-changing patina. Bring spray paint in case others haven't left any around.

Vega

The original owners of the **Vega Motel** improved it continuously from the time they built it in 1947 until they sold it with the coming of I-40 in 1976. Like many motel owner-operators, they lived in a now-demolished home in the center of the complex, surrounded each night by their guests sleeping in their rooms.

While the Vega Motel is now closed, an old Route 66 Sinclair gas station (the ones with the big dinosaur) just west has been reborn as **Rooster's**, an excellent Mexican restaurant.

Adrian's MidPoint Cafe

In **Adrian**, vibrant vinyl chairs and 1950s-esque knickknacks form the backdrop for the popular **MidPoint Cafe** (closed winter; $), which is one of the highlights of these barren plains. The food is familiar (breakfast, burgers and sandwiches) and the pies are good (lots of cream varieties, they call 'em 'ugly' out of tradition).

Above: MidPoint Cafe sign, Adrian; Right: State Line Cafe, Glenrio

A minor shrine across the way declares an 1139-mile distance to each original Route 66 endpoint. Join the queue for a selfie. Note the tiny windmill, well placed as the wind never seems to stop blowing. The Midpoint opened two years after Route 66 in 1928. Fran Houser, who owned the cafe from 1990 until 2012, is the basis for Flo of 'Flo's V-8 Café' in *Cars*.

Next door, the budget **Fabulous 40s Motel** (facebook.com/Fabulous40smotel; $) gets glowing reviews for its basic accommodation sand warm welcome.

Glenrio

Just at the New Mexico border, tiny **Glenrio** makes the moniker 'ghost town' seem lively. Its heyday lasted from the 1930s until 1975, when I-40 bypassed it. Today, it could be a ready-made set for a zombie flick.

Try an ugly pie at Midpoint Cafe

📷 PHOTO ESSAY

Vintage Gas Stations

THE FIRST GAS stations in the US were little more than tin shacks. They drew the ire of neighbors and had the oil companies searching for ways to make their outlets more palatable. Because roads meandered through small towns, it was necessary to blend in with the tidy houses of these burgs.

Soon gas stations were being built in a variety of styles from Cape Cod to Tudor to Mission. This didn't change with the advent of Route 66, as it was still mostly a local road. Only as traffic took off did gas stations stop trying to blend in and instead boldly proclaim themselves.

From left:

A picnic table sits where '54 Studebakers once idled at the legendary Lucille's Service Station in Hydro, Oklahoma (p116).

As idiosyncratic today as it was back when it was a vital oasis in the desert: Hackberry General Store in Western Arizona (p198).

An early 'grand' station, the soaring Conoco Tower Station, with bus station and still-open cafe (p126) in Shamrock, Texas.

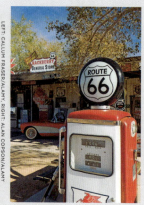

LEFT: MARK ROGER BAILEY/SHUTTERSTOCK, RIGHT: RAWF8/SHUTTERSTOCK

From above:
Prim as a springtime California poppy, the Cucamonga Service Station predates Route 66 by 11 years and represents the earliest efforts by oil companies to go beyond mere shacks (p228).

Restored Phillips 66 stations like this one in McLean, Texas (p126) blend seamlessly into their surrounding neigborhoods and are a highlight of Route 66.

From left:

The bright lights of Roy's Motel & Café (p211) in Amboy, California, helped it stand out from the crowd.

The huge Shell sign came later, but otherwise Soulsby Service Station, Illinois (p56) fits right into the homes around it.

By the 1950s, gas stations were part of roadside strips of businesses serving booming Route 66 traffic. Hokey come-ons were another way to beat the proliferating competition, as seen at the Antares Visitor Center.

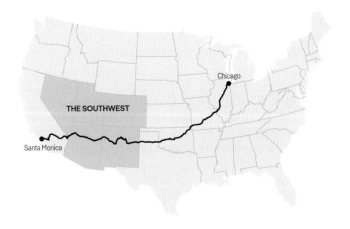

THE SOUTHWEST

This is the Route 66 of movies and cartoons. A tan, orange and brown landscape of mesas with table-tops high above sheer cliffs, lonely cacti and, yes, maybe the odd road runner. Cutting due west across New Mexico and Arizona, Route 66 traverses a harsh world with little in common with anything that has come before it. Parks capture geologic oddities that astound, while the neon glow of vintage motels colorizes the nighttime desert. Long stretches of the original road cut through Santa Fe, Albuquerque, pueblos and wilderness.

Historic Route 66 running east of Albuquerque (p163)
BRIGHT YAWNING/SHUTTERSTOCK

Glenrio

NEW MEXICO

New Mexico is yet another state where everything seems to suddenly change at the border. Beyond the fact that for decades you went from dry counties in Texas to wet ones in New Mexico, suddenly it seems the flatlands give way to the first hints of the Rockies ahead, with ripples and crags appearing in the red earth and rocks. Travelers face their first great Route 66 fork in the road: go via enticing Santa Fe or direct to Albuquerque.

Ryan Ver Berkmoes

Ruins, San Jon

Albuquerque
NEW MEXICO

**310 MILES
10 HOURS' DRIVE**

THIS LEG:

- San Jon
- Tucumcari
- Montoya
- Cuervo
- Santa Rosa
- Las Vegas, NM
- Pecos
- Glorieta Pass
- Santa Fe
- Los Alamos
- Turquoise Trail
- I-40 to Albuquerque

Driving Notes

Unlike Texas, the terrain is the journey in New Mexico. The interstate is often nearby, but there are opportunities to drive original segments of Route 66 that put you closer to the rugged, rusty-colored terrain, where the hardscrabble past is palpable. If you opt for the Santa Fe option, you'll plunge into the mountains that have challenged travelers for eons.

Breaking Your Journey

Tucumcari, with its wonderfully restored classic motels (and neon!), is an obvious choice for a night along the road. If you're doing the pre-1937 route, which takes in Santa Fe, then staying in that beguiling city is a must. Otherwise, serviceable stops dot I-40.

Ryan's Tips

BEST MEAL Chile rellenos at **Tia Sophia's** in Santa Fe (p153)

FAVORITE VIEW Any open space along **US 84** (p154)

ESSENTIAL STOP Santa Fe for its walkable vibe and history (p158)

ROAD-TRIP TIP Opt for the Santa Fe option and take the entire route *slow*. There is so much to discover and savor.

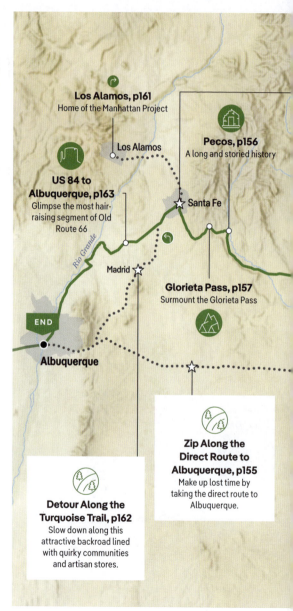

Los Alamos, p161
Home of the Manhattan Project

Pecos, p156
A long and storied history

US 84 to Albuquerque, p163
Glimpse the most hair-raising segment of Old Route 66

Glorieta Pass, p157
Surmount the Glorieta Pass

Detour Along the Turquoise Trail, p162
Slow down along this attractive backroad lined with quirky communities and artisan stores.

Zip Along the Direct Route to Albuquerque, p155
Make up lost time by taking the direct route to Albuquerque.

PREVIOUS STOP Glenrio, Texas, straddles the border with New Mexico. Just over, at I-40 Exit 256, the travel info stop has Route 66 history displays and info.

San Jon

From **Glenrio** you can go four-wheelin' on a smooth dirt and gravel road that's the old Route 66 for nearly 15 miles to the near-ghost town of **San Jon**. Don't try it if there's any hint of rain or standing water; otherwise, it's a moody, evocative and lonely ride. Look for signs of abandoned 19th-century homesteads.

The road is better continuing the 24 miles to Tucumcari. It curves amid the growing mesas and weaves around the interloping I-40. About halfway, look for the ruins of the **Cedar Hill Grocery Store**, which was once a busy stop on the highway, open 24/7.

TeePee Curios gift shop, Tucumcari

Tucumcari

The largest Route 66 town between Albuquerque and Amarillo, **Tucumcari** is situated between the mesas and the plains. It's home to a fine collection of indie motels, with at least one covering each era of lodging during the glory years of the Mother Road.

Tops by far is the beloved **Blue Swallow Motel** (p157). Listed on the National Register of Historic Places, it defines luxe 1940s lodging. There's a great lobby, friendly owners, uniquely decorated rooms and a much-photographed neon sign boasting '100% refrigerated air conditioning.'

Savor mid-century cool at the **Historic Route 66 Motel** (tucumcarimotel.com; $), with giant plate-glass doors and mesa views; look for the light plane outside. The uber-hip **Motel Safari** (p157) and the **Roadrunner Lodge** (roadrunnerlodge.com; $) both have top-rated 1960s style (the latter espouses 'Give the Interstate the bird').

Take a gander at oodles of jokey nonsense at **TeePee Curios** (facebook.com/teepeecurios; $). Among the dining choices, grab a shady table under the glowing neon outside at **Del's Restaurant** (delsrestaurant.com; $) and enjoy hearty American and Mexican fare. Afterward, walk off your feast admiring the town's **murals**.

Montoya

Beginning at Exit 321 on I-40, there is an opportunity to drive back into the 1930s on Route 66. From barely there **Palomas**, head

---

San Jon — *24 miles* — **Tucumcari**

Spot the ruins of the Cedar Hill Grocery Store

Stay at the Blue Swallow Motel

Motel Safari, Tucumcari

west for nearly 11 miles to Montoya. The road today is rough but easily drivable. You can still see evidence of the money spent by the federal government under the auspices of the New Deal in the 1930s: bridges and culverts are well-engineered and substantial. Partway along, you'll pass through a spooky tunnel under the interstate.

Montoya is just a few breaths away from ghost-town status. The collapsing remains of the sandstone **Richardson Store** are all that remain of one of Route 66's most popular stops. Until the completion of I-40, it was a traveler's oasis and people enjoyed picnics in the shade of the surrounding elm trees.

BEST PLACES TO EAT

Cafe Pasqual's, Santa Fe $$$
The menu goes beyond the standards with stars such as *huevos motuleños* at breakfast, made with sautéed bananas, feta cheese and more; later on, the meat and fish mains are superb. *(pasquals.com; to 9:30pm, closed Tue)*

La Choza, Santa Fe $
Arrive early or reserve ahead to get a table at this always popular place, which sets the standard for regional cuisine. *(lachozasf.com)*

Tia Sophia's, Santa Fe $$
Local artists and visiting celebrities outnumber tourists at this Santa Fe favorite beloved for New Mexican fare (think perfectly prepared chile rellenos). *(tiasophias.com)*

24 miles — Montoya — 20 miles

Cuervo

Leaving Montoya, stay on old Route 66 for more vintage driving, this time 20 miles to Cuervo (no relation to the tequila). The road follows the terrain through hills and mesas dotted with juniper and pinyon trees, an important source of edible nuts for Native Americans.

After about 12 miles, you'll come to **Newkirk**, which is a cautionary tale for anyone who thinks that highway rest stops are forever. A ghost town today, most of the crumbling adobe buildings were once bustling Route 66 businesses. With the Union Pacific Railroad on your right – the line runs north from El Paso, Texas – continue on to **Cuervo**, which is only slightly more lively than Newkirk. Stop often for the views across the mesas; the elevation never slips below 4000ft.

Abandoned building, Cuervo

Santa Rosa

Settled by Hispanic farmers in the mid-19th century, **Santa Rosa**'s modern claim to fame is its various lakes. Right off Route 66, the **Park Lake Historic District** protects the spring-fed lake with a surrounding park built by the WPA in the 1930s. It was popular with travelers as a place to picnic and nab a dip.

Among the family-owned places to eat along the wide swath that Route 66 cuts through town, don't miss the lovely neon glow of **Comet II Drive In & Restaurant** ($). Its menu of New Mexican fare is a delicious intro to green chilies and other local variations on Mexican cuisine.

Junction with Highway 84

At the junction of I-40 and US 84 at Exit 256, 17 miles west of Santa Rosa, you have a big decision to make: continue straight west on the post-1937 version of Route 66 to Albuquerque or take the longer pre-1937 route that goes via Santa Fe and is vastly more interesting. It's really a question of time. The older route adds nearly 100 miles to your journey and at least a day – which you may consider a real benefit!

If you stick to the more **direct route** (right), you'll be in Albuquerque in as little as two hours. Otherwise, head north for 41 miles on US 84 and enjoy the rural scenery of the New Mexico high plains. After the traffic of the I-40 corridor, it's a relief to be surrounded by nothing but nature.

After about 15 miles, watch on the east side for a **historical marker for Mela Leger**. She grew up in this thinly populated region and became a force in New Mexico for bilingual education. Her daughter, Teresa Leger Fernandez, represents this vast region in the US Congress.

Continues on page 156

Cuervo — 20 miles — Santa Rosa — 19 miles — Junction with Hwy 84 — 80 miles on US 84

Turn right on US 84 for Santa Fe or take I-40 direct to Albuquerque

Direct to Albuquerque

Drivers make good time on the direct route to Albuquerque. And that was the idea in 1937 when the route replaced the longer and more scenic route via Santa Fe.

HOW TO

Getting here: Stay on I-40 heading west after Exit 256 where US 84 heads north on the pre-1937 Route 66 alignment via Santa Fe.

When to go: I-40 is driveable year-round.

Tip: Use this option to make up for time lost on unanticipated stops earlier on the trip.

The prospect of Albuquerque fills the windshield as you head west. The promise of a much shorter trip must have been cause for joy for the road-weary masses in the late 1930s through the 1950s. Given that Route 66 journeys involved constant interruptions as another town hoved into view with its stop signs, stop lights and irresistible appeals to pause for a meal, a souvenir or a sweet, the relatively barren 90 miles to Albuquerque must have felt like a speedway.

Today, the route still feels like a speedway, albeit a crowded one. There is no option other than I-40 as it has overlaid the post-1937 version of the Mother Road.

At Exit 218, enjoy a vestige of old Route 66 culture at the **Clines Corners Travel Center** *(1 Yacht Club Dr)*, which peddles fresh fudge and screwy souvenirs.

At **Moriarty** (named for the town's first settler, not Sherlock's nemesis) stop by the **Lewis Antique Auto and Toy Museum**. Although the charming owner has passed on, his collection of vehicles that would have driven Route 66 survives and volunteers may have it open.

EXPERIENCE ★

Above: Rusty car at Lewis Antique Auto and Toy Museum; Right: Clines Corners Travel Center

DETOUR: Las Vegas, NM

The saloons and bordellos of America's original sin city, **Las Vegas, NM**, were dishing out wild times when that other Vegas was still a dry spot in the desert. Las Vegas in the 1800s was a boomtown where the Santa Fe Trail and the Santa Fe Railroad passed through, Doc Holliday gambled and Billy the Kid held court.

Starting in 1926, legions of Route 66 travelers made the 6-mile diversion north from where the road turned sharply south (where US 84 ends today) for gas, a meal and maybe a little more. Today, scores of historic buildings grace its sleepy, strollable downtown, which has repeatedly served Hollywood as a backdrop; *Wyatt Earp* and *No Country for Old Men* are just a couple of the movies filmed here. Get a doughnut or huevos rancheros at **Charlie's Spic & Span Bakery & Cafe** *($)*, also good for local gossip and New Mexican breakfasts and lunches.

Pecos

Heading toward Santa Fe from the end of Hwy 84 along pre-1937 Route 66, you are hemmed in by mountains. The **Pecos Valley** has been used by people for millennia to get from the high plains to the southwest.

Leave I-25 (or the frontage road) at Hwy 63 for **Pecos National Historical Park** *(nps.gov/peco)*, a site with a long history. It was the thriving **Pecos Pueblo** prior to European contact. Later the Spanish built a large mission (the remains of which you see today). However in one of the few times there was a successful revolt, the Pueblos expelled the Spanish in the late 1600s. The Spanish later returned and expanded the mission.

Beginning in 1821, the famous **Santa Fe Trail** passed right through here, used by thousands of settlers to colonize the Southwest. In the 1920s Route 66 arrived and with travelers came businesses, including one of the first dude ranches aimed at well-heeled tourists.

Along the Way We Saw...

SOMEONE FAMOUS My first visit to Santa Fe was memorable in many ways. I insisted on arriving in this timeless city on timeless old Route 66. 'Way better than I-25!' I [correctly] crowed. Next, I went to a recommended red chile place where the sacred stuff was transcendent. But a familiar voice behind me at the next table broke into my joy. A man was asking questions of a movie location scout. Sneaking a tourist glance, yep: Robert Redford.

RYAN'S TIP: *'If that voice at the next table sounds familiar, that's because it probably is.'*

Ryan Ver Berkmoes

Pecos

Glorieta Pass

Take a detour to visit the original Las Vegas

7 miles

19 miles

Glorieta Pass

After passing through the barely there town of Pecos on Highways 63 and 50, you have no choice but to join I-25 to surmount **Glorieta Pass** (7500ft). Today it's a bland curve, but in the pre-1937 Route 66 days, it was a more dramatic summit befitting its status as the then-highest point on the entire route from Chicago to LA.

You'll glimpse the **old Santa Fe Railroad**, which once was plied by famous trains, including the *Super Chief*. Today it gets only two a day: Amtrak's *Southwest Chief* once in each direction.

Santa Fe

Santa Fe (p158) was only a stop on Route 66 for 11 years, but it dazzled travelers during this time, much as it still does today. The road-weary can take a stroll around the Plaza and let the culture wash over them. Today, it remains a treasured destination.

Continues on page 161

BEST PLACES TO SLEEP

Blue Swallow Motel, Tucumcari $
The model for how to maintain a thriving vintage Route 66 motel. From the tiniest, guest-friendly details to the thoughtful restorations, it's a winner. *(blueswallowmotel.com)*

Motel Safari, Tucumcari $
Another thoughtfully reenergized old Route 66 motel that could have gone the way of so many others and faded away. Instead, it's been made trendy, relevant and fun. *(themotelsafari.com)*

La Fonda, Santa Fe $$$
The storied hotel that's been a dream destination for generations and never seems to change, in the best possible way. *(lafondasantafe.com)*

Catholic Mission Church, Pecos Pueblo

Explore Santa Fe

Missions, museums and art. All are players in the story of 'the city different,' a place that makes its own rules without forgetting its long and storied past. There are more quality museums, galleries and activities here than you could experience in just one visit, but give it a start.

HOW TO

Getting there: Santa Fe, the top highlight of pre-1937 Route 66 to Albuquerque, is right off I-25.

Getting around: The heart of the city is compact and walkable (p160). Park in lots within a 10-minute walk of the Plaza.

Sleeping: There are unforgettable historic options within a block of the Plaza and every kind of lodging everywhere else. Long renowned as the 'Inn at the end of the Santa Fe Trail,' **La Fonda** (p157) is Santa Fe's loveliest historic hotel. It sprawls through an old adobe just off the Plaza. Just south, **Hotel St Francis** (hotelstfrancis.com; $$) retains enough whitewashed walls and hand-crafted furniture to evoke the city's mission-era heritage.

More info: santafe.org

Tip: Don't miss the **Santa Fe Farmers Market** (santafefarmersmarket.com) every Saturday and many Tuesdays.

Where to Begin

Most people begin by walking Santa Fe's center (p160), starting at the timeless Plaza. A short distance away, don't miss one of the city's most popular venues, the **Georgia O'Keeffe Museum** (okeeffemuseum.org), which boasts the world's largest collection of her luminous works.

Several of Santa Fe's finest museums are on Museum Hill. The two unmissable ones are the **Museum of International Folk Art** (internationalfolkart.org), with its whimsical objects from more than 100 different countries, and the **Museum of Indian Arts & Culture** (indianartsandculture.org), which traces the history and culture of the Pueblo, Navajo (Diné) and Apache peoples of the Southwest.

Gallery-Hopping on Canyon Road

Santa Fe's most famous art avenue emerged in the 1920s and is a top attraction, with more than 100 of Santa Fe's 300-plus galleries. You'll find everything from rare Native American antiquities to Santa Fe School masterpieces and challenging modern work.

On Friday nights from May through October, the **galleries** (santafegalleryassociation.org) put on glittering openings early in the evening.

A few favorites include **Adobe Gallery** (adobegallery.com) for ceramics; **GF Contemporary** (gfcontemporary.com) for eclectic modern works; and **Morning Star Gallery** (morningstargallery.com) for historic Plains Indian ephemera.

EATING IN SANTA FE

When in Santa Fe, you must have the local take on New Mexico fare. You must. **Horseman's Haven** *($)* is renowned for its green chiles, which come in various strengths. Food is served quick and leans simple. Get a burrito.

Blue-corn burritos, a festive interior and an extensive margarita list make **La Choza** (p153) a favorite. Near the O'Keeffe Museum, **Tia Sophia's** (p153) is a long-standing and always packed favorite. Breakfast is the meal of choice, but lunch brings perfectly prepared chile rellenos.

Canyon Rd

Go for a Hike

There are a ton of trails around Santa Fe. Two good, easy-to-moderate hikes within an hour's drive of the Plaza are:

Aspen Vista The premier path for immersing yourself in magical fall foliage, this trail starts at about 10,000ft along the road to the ski basin; it's marked 'Trail No 150.' Mountain bikers love this one too. The first mile is very easy.

La Cieneguilla Petroglyph Site In only an hour's hike, you reach a rocky bluff that's covered with ancient Keresan petroglyphs, including images of the flute player Kokopelli.

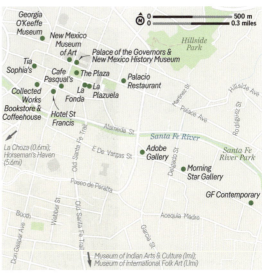

Take a City Stroll

Walking the adobe neighborhoods and the busy Plaza at its core, you feel Santa Fe's artful, earthy soul. Do as generations have done and get to know this timeless city on foot.

HOW TO

Getting here: Parking lots dot central Santa Fe.

When to go: Santa Fe is open throughout the year and winter is a popular season for visitors.

Tip: The heart of Santa Fe is compact – just wander and discover.

More info: *santafe.org*

For more than 400 years, the Plaza has stood at the heart of Santa Fe. Today, this grassy square is peopled by tourists, food vendors, skateboarding kids and street musicians.

The oldest public building in the US, the low-slung adobe **Palace of the Governors** *(palaceofthegovernors.org)* began as home to New Mexico's first Spanish governor in 1610. Here, you'll find Santa Fe's best shopping beneath the *portales* (overhanging arcades), to which Pueblo Indians travel from as far as 200 miles away to sell gorgeous handmade jewelry. Artisans, representing almost every New Mexican tribe, draw lots for the 76 prime spaces each morning.

Works by regional artists are displayed next door at the **New Mexico Museum of Art** *(nmartmuseum.org)*.

There are plenty of eating options around the Plaza. Try **La Plazuela** *(lafondasantafe.com; to 9pm; $$$)* for memorable dining; **Cafe Pasqual's** (p153) for superb New Mexican fare; **Palacio Restaurant** *(palacio restaurant.com; to 8pm Thu-Mon; $$)*, a family-run gem; and **Collected Works Bookstore & Coffeehouse** *(collectedworks bookstore.com; 9am-5pm; $)*.

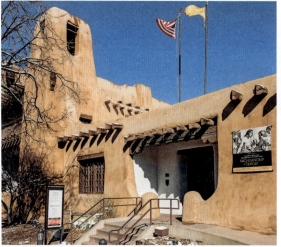

New Mexico Museum of Art

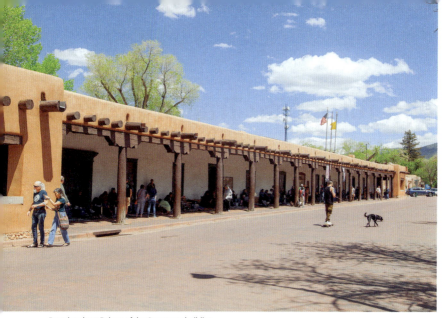

Portales along Palace of the Governors building

The I-25 corridor to Albuquerque from Santa Fe mostly matches the original 1926 to 1937 route of Route 66 and it does have a few worthy stops. However, you can also divert to the historic **Turquoise Trail** (p162) to reach Albuquerque. It's one of New Mexico's most scenic roads.

DETOUR: Los Alamos

When the top-secret **Manhattan Project** sprang to life in 1943, it turned the sleepy village of **Los Alamos** into a busy laboratory of secluded scientists, as seen in 2023's *Oppenheimer*. A 23-mile jaunt northwest from Santa Fe, Los Alamos remains a place unto itself, where the Los Alamos National Laboratory dominates

Continues on page 163

NEW MEXICAN CUISINE

New Mexico's distinctly rich, rural cuisine is a reflection of the crops the region's Pueblo Indians and Hispanic homesteaders have long grown: corn, beans, squash and chiles. Red or green chile sauce is used to smother many dishes, or it can be eaten plain with a tortilla on the side. To be clear: it does not resemble Tex-Mex chili. Other specialties include *posole* (corn stew) and *carne adovada* (red-chile marinated pork).

New Mexico is the only state with an official question: 'red or green?' You'll hear it every time you order local food. Ask for 'Christmas' to get both.

Santa Fe

Admire the Plaza's distinctive architecture

Take a detour to Los Alamos

The Turquoise Trail

The Turquoise Trail (aka Hwy 14), a National Scenic Byway, is lined with quirky communities and other diversions, which makes an attractive back road between Albuquerque and Santa Fe.

HOW TO

Nearest stop: Santa Fe

Getting here: Follow Cerrillos Rd/Hwy 14 south from Santa Fe

When to go: Many of the attractions and businesses along the Turquoise Trail close during winter.

Tip: The trail is only about 50 miles long, but given the many stops, expect to spend at least a half day along it.

More info: turquoisetrail.org

Amid scrubby desert hills pockmarked with historic mining sites, **Cerrillos Hills State Park** (emnrd.nm.gov) has 5 miles of well-marked hiking trails. Cerrillos' **Casa Grande Trading Post** (casagrandetradingpost.com) includes a turquoise mining museum packed with pioneer-era tools and mining gear.

Madrid is a boho center for artists. Stop by **Trading Bird Gallery & Gypsy Gem** (tradingbird-gypsygem.com) for creations made with locally mined turquoise. A gleeful celebration of local life, **Madrid Old Coal Town Museum** (themineshafttavern.com) has an impressive array of old tunneling equipment housed in a tavern.

You're spoiled for choice in Madrid when it's time for something sweet. **Jezebel Gallery & Soda Fountain** (jezebelgallery.com; to 5pm; $) has old-fashioned ice-cream treats. Enjoy fresh and casual fare at **Refinery 14** (refinery14.com; to 4pm Thu-Mon; $). **Shugarman's Little Shop** (shugarmanschocolate.com; to 4:30pm Thu-Sun; $) has wildly creative chocolates.

A folk-art classic, the **Tinkertown Museum** (tinkertown.com) has hand-carved dioramas of towns and other scenes.

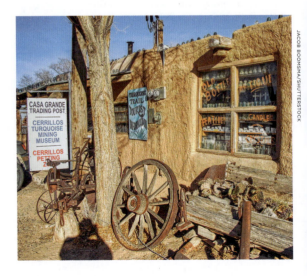

Casa Grande Trading Post, Cerrillos

Madrid, Turquoise Trail

everything – and is still developing nuclear weapons, along with more prosaic projects. Visitors will be most interested in the sights of the **Manhattan Project National Historical Park** *(nps.gov/mapr)*, which highlights things to see across the mesa dating to 1943. Since the namesake film, most people include **Oppenheimer House** on a walking tour.

To Albuquerque

Leaving Santa Fe join I-25 at Exit 267. Exit again at Exit 264 for a glimpse of the most hair-raising segment of early Route 66. Go northwest for 3.5 miles on desolate Hwy 16 until you see a **historical marker**. Look east to **La Bajada Mesa**, a lava escarpment that long was a barrier to travel. Prisoners were forced to cut a road with 23 switchbacks for Route 66, which vehicles crawled up and down from 1926 to 1932.

To everyone's relief, the treacherous route was replaced by the one now used for I-25 in 1933, before the direct route bypassed it all in 1937.

Not far south, the **Kewa Pueblo** (aka Santo Domingo Pueblo; *santodomingotribe.org*) was a popular Route 66 stop for its craft shops. Several galleries and studios abut the plaza in front of the pretty 1886 **Santo Domingo Church**, with murals by local artists.

Further along, **Silva's Saloon** *($)* in **Bernalillo** is a famous Route 66 roadhouse with hats of long-departed patrons hanging from the ceiling.

To Albuquerque

77 miles

 Follow Cerrillos Rd south from Santa Fe to take the Turquoise Trail to Albuquerque

Richardson's Trading Post, Gallup
LEE RENTZ/ALAMY

INSIGHT

'That Ain't Us': A Navajo Perspective

George R Joe grew up in Dilkon, on the southwest edge of the Navajo reservation in northeastern Arizona.

WORDS BY GEORGE R JOE
George is fluent in Navajo. His travel site, navajoguide.com, covers travel in the Navajo Nation.

WHEN I WAS in the third or fourth grade, my parents used to put me on a Greyhound bus from Winslow, Arizona, to Gallup, New Mexico. Later, all the way to Albuquerque on old Route 66, before I-40 was constructed.

As I sat on the bus in the late 1970s, I would see countless roadside signs – many of them are still there today. These signs depicted images of tepees, Plains Indians in buckskin and feathered headdresses, all urging travelers to stop and buy Native American arts and crafts. Even as a young kid, I remember thinking: That ain't us.

That's not how we look.

Some of the signs would scream, 'Turn here for Indian Village!' It always struck me as odd because Navajos don't have villages. We live in homes spread across the land, not concentrated in tight-knit clusters. As a fourth grader, I felt like an object, something to be looked at and sold, like a relic in a museum. I didn't know how to articulate this feeling, either. When I tried to explain to my late parents, they brushed it off: 'That's just how *biligaanas* (white people) do things.' So, I kept it to myself.

The bus would stop at Fort Courage near Sanders, Arizona, and passengers would get off to eat at a diner at the (now closed) replica fort. While they ate, I would wander through the gift shop, eyeing the tourist trinkets on sale. After the stop, it was back on the road, passing more billboards and stores lining the highway into Gallup.

The Jewels of Route 66

During the 1970s, the Native American arts and crafts market was booming. It was the golden era of 'Indian Jewelry,' and I lived right through it. My oldest brother was among the first Navajos in Winslow to own a storefront jewelry store. He called it 'Little Squash,' and it sat across from what is now the famous 'Standing on the Corner' Park (p189). My uncles, my father, my other brothers, cousins and just about everyone I knew was involved in making jewelry. For us, it was a prosperous time because, for the first time, many families had money. I have vivid memories of sweeping the floors and cleaning up at Little Squash at least once a week. When I think back on that time, an image sticks with me: a money-counting machine like the one you see in gangster movies. But then, just like that, it all began to fade.

A few years later, in 1984, when I was in high school, I-40 was completed, and Winslow was bypassed. I'll never forget the sadness I felt driving through downtown Winslow. It was like a ghost town. The same could be said for Holbrook and other towns along Route 66. It was like watching tumbleweeds drift across abandoned streets.

I sometimes wonder if the construction of I-40 marked the end of the Indian jewelry boom. Maybe the highway changed the flow of traffic and the tourism dried up. Whatever the cause, something shifted, and the lively, bustling streets grew quiet.

As I got older and traveled more, I realized the kind of aggressive advertising I'd grown up with that pushed Native American imagery and products like a commodity was unique to the Southwest. A few years back, I drove across the country, and nowhere else had such bold, relentless billboards and tourist traps dedicated to selling the 'Indian' image.

Changing Times

Thankfully, things are changing. In recent years, tribes have begun pushing back against these old stereotypes and narratives. In 2016, the American Indian Alaska Native Tourism Association *(aianta.org)* released a 65-page guidebook that tells the real stories of Indigenous people along the 2400-mile stretch of Route 66. More than half of the road – about 1370 miles – runs through or near Native American lands.

Today, some tribes along the route between Flagstaff and Albuquerque have tourism centers, while others maintain more limited access. The original Route 66, and now I-40, borders the southern edge of the Navajo Nation from Flagstaff to Grants, New Mexico.

> As a fourth grader, I felt like an object, something to be looked at and sold, like a relic in a museum. I didn't know how to articulate this feeling, either. When I tried to explain to my late parents, they brushed it off: 'That's just how *biligaanas* (white people) do things.'

To engage with Native culture along the Navajo stretch, contact the **Navajo Tourism Office** *(discovernavajo.com)* or visit *navajoguide.com* for more details. Around 30 miles outside Gallup, the Navajo tribal capital in **Window Rock**, Arizona, has a **museum and tribal zoo**, as well as the **Navajo Council Chambers**.

There are other tribes along this section as well: the Hopi (50 miles north of Winslow), the Acoma (near Grants) and the Zuni (30 miles south of Gallup), as well as several pueblos near Albuquerque. Further afield, Eastern Oklahoma is dense with tribes, including the Choctaw and Cherokee. Each tribe has its own unique customs and regulations. For example, on Hopi lands, photography is strictly prohibited, and visitors are not allowed into villages.

Despite the changes, there's still a chance to buy directly from Native artisans. In **Gallup**, **Earl's Restaurant** *(1400 E Historic Hwy 66)* is a great place to meet local craftspeople. Tribally owned businesses are scattered along the route, offering authentic goods. In Gallup, every Saturday you can buy authentic homemade crafts directly from craftspeople at the **Flea Market** *(visitgallup.com/blog/gallup-flea-market)*, including medicinal herbs direct from Native herbalists.

In recent years, as I've worked on developing my own travel app and have gotten involved in the film industry, I've started digging deeper into the history of these border towns along Route 66. I've become especially interested in what happened to Navajos who returned to the Winslow area after their four-year imprisonment at Bosque Redondo from 1862 to 1868. They came back and established relationships with Indian traders like the Hubbells, who ran trading posts in the area. Over time, these Navajos settled in towns like Winslow, Holbrook and Gallup, attending public schools and working alongside local populations. Today, these towns have significant Native American communities, including people from Navajo, Hopi, Apache, Sioux and Laguna tribes.

Above: Earl's Family Restaurant, Gallup; Right: Navajo Nation Council building, Window Rock

> This long, complicated history has shaped these towns and their relationships with the Native communities.

This long, complicated history has shaped these towns and their relationships with the Native communities. The conversation concerning Native Americans has evolved far beyond the presentations of the quaint but antiquated billboards of Route 66. Even more recently, people like Deb Haaland, the former US Secretary of the Interior, who grew up in Winslow, are redefining what it means to be Native in modern America. Native American directors, actors and stories are increasingly visible in films such as *Rez Ball* and *Frybread Face and Me,* and series including *Dark Winds* and *Reservation Dogs.*

The conversation about representation has evolved far beyond those old billboards on Route 66. Today, we are telling our own stories, and I hope that trend continues for future generations.

Albuquerque
NEW MEXICO

They call this the Land of Enchantment for a reason. Sure, the grittier side of Central Ave – old Route 66 – in Albuquerque may seem less than magical, but explore all 18 miles and you'll be beguiled by what's arguably the most Route 66iest of all the Route 66 cities. And from there, the road passes through old towns great and small, plateaus and pueblos, and vast desert plains spread beneath an even vaster sky, accented by amber, maroon and umber.

Ryan Ver Berkmoes

San José de la Laguna
DUKAS PRESSEAGENTUR GMBH/ALAMY

Lupton

ARIZONA

165 MILES
5 HOURS' DRIVE

THIS LEG:

- Albuquerque
- Rio Puerco Bridge
- Mesita
- Laguna Pueblo
- McCartys
- El Malpais National Monument
- Grants
- Continental Divide
- Gallup
- Manuelito
- Lupton

Driving Notes

The drive west is easy throughout the year unless the weather turns difficult. A highlight is a 70-mile stretch on the original road that passes through small towns and goes by original businesses. You can detour to see some extraordinary lava beds at El Malpais National Monument south of Grants and plan to stop longer than usual in Gallup, with its many diversions.

Breaking Your Journey

It's a bit odd to consider it, but the best place to break your journey is at the start: Albuquerque. The city has enough to keep you interested for a few days. Otherwise, Gallup is the best place in Western New Mexico for a break.

Ryan's Tips

BEST MEAL Green chile at **Frontier** in Albuquerque (p176)

FAVORITE VIEW The view from **San José de la Laguna Mission Church** in Laguna Pueblo (p172)

ESSENTIAL STOP Nob Hill on Central Ave in Albuquerque (p176)

ROAD-TRIP TIP Do all 70 miles of the original road between Exits 117 and 47 on I-47 and stop for every historical marker!

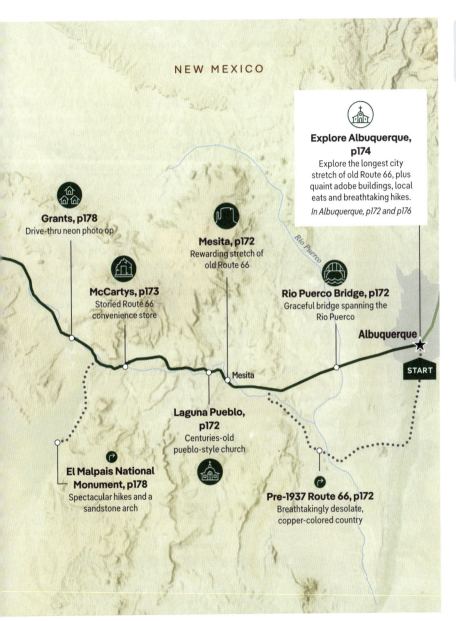

PREVIOUS STOP After the short drive from Santa Fe, you'll be ready to enjoy all that Albuquerque has to offer.

Albuquerque

Albuquerque (p174) is one of the most intriguing cities along Route 66. It's a bustling desert crossroads, with the right mix of urban and wild: the pink hues of the Sandia Mountains at sunset, swirling nightlife, a daytime culture that embraces the outdoors and the longest urban stretch of Route 66 in the nation (p176).

DETOUR: Pre-1937 Route 66

Though not as compelling as the pre-1937 Route 66 routing that ran via Santa Fe east of Albuquerque, there is an additional **pre-1937 routing** west of the city that runs south via Los Lunas and today's Hwy 6. It takes roughly 50 miles versus the later route's 30 miles.

Start on 4th St, driving south through the Barelas neighborhood (p176) from the iconic Route 66 artery Central Ave. Continue on Hwy 314 and segue over to Hwy 47 at **Isleta**. The route follows the Rio Grande and passes a mix of small farms and old homes.

Head west on Hwy 6 at **Los Lunas**. The 33-mile drive back to Route 66 and I-40 runs through desolate, beautiful, copper-colored country.

Rio Puerco Bridge

Leave Albuquerque going west on I-40 and enjoy the arid Southwest expanses until Exit 140, where you'll exit for a steely Route 66 survivor. This long (for its time) **bridge** over the deep gorge of the Rio Puerco allowed the roundabout earlier routing south of Albuquerque to be replaced in 1937. Funded by the federal government, the bridge had to be long enough not to require a central pier, which would be prone to washouts during flash floods.

The result is this graceful 250ft-long truss span that's one of the longest in the state. No longer open to vehicles, it's preserved as an important Route 66 artifact, and you can walk across it. It's close to Exit 140 on I-40.

Mesita & Old Route 66

Forsake I-40 at Exit 117 (**Mesita**) for the longest – and one of the most rewarding – **stretches of old Route 66** in New Mexico. Across 70 miles, you'll be transported back to the 1930s. Along the way, there are old trading posts, old towns and a lot of dramatic scenery, some of it hiding uranium mines deep underground.

A near-constant companion will be the mainline of the **BNSF Railway**, which runs from Chicago to LA. Back in the day, this was the Santa Fe and it was plied by speeding passenger trains such as the *Super Chief*. Today it is one of the busiest freight railroads in the world.

Laguna Pueblo

Just south of Route 66, the centuries-old **Laguna Pueblo** has a remarkable church atop its central hill. The 1699 **San José de la Laguna Mission Church** (*lagunapueblo-nsn.gov*) features exquisite murals that decorate the earthen

---

Albuquerque
★
Tour a stretch of old Route 66 right in the city

18 miles

Rio Puerco Bridge
●
Walk the bridge

24 miles

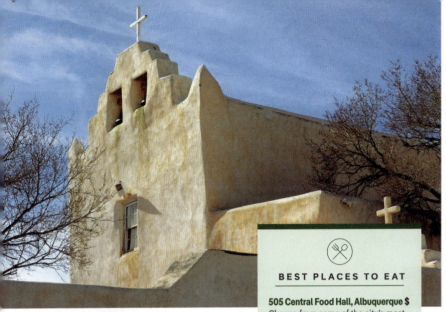

San José de la Laguna Mission Church, Laguna Pueblo

and whitewashed plaster walls. Look up at the ceiling for traditional Laguna symbols, such as a rainbow, sun, moon and stars. The grounds have a simple charm and the views from the hill take in much of the surrounding territory.

McCartys

The old road, designated Hwy 124 on this stretch, winds between hills and passes relics from the early Route 66 days, like the **Budville Trading Post**, which hung on into the 1970s.

A bit further, however, is a real survivor: the **Villa de Cubero Trading Post**. Dating to 1936, it still sells a full range of convenience store

Continues on page 178

BEST PLACES TO EAT

505 Central Food Hall, Albuquerque $
Choose from some of the city's most creative vendors at this food hall right by the KiMo Theatre Downtown. *(505central.com; 11am-9pm)*

Loyola's Family Restaurant, Albuquerque $
Pure Mother Road style, near Nob Hill. It serves no-frills New Mexican staples, including some fine chile, since before there was even a song about Route 66. *(loyolasfamilyrestaurant.com; to 1:30pm)*

Duran's Pharmacy, Albuquerque $
Yep, like the old days, it's a diner inside a pharmacy. But this one is spectacular, delivering superb local cuisine. A Route 66 classic since 1942. *(duransrx.com; to 6pm, closed Sun)*

Mesita — 6 miles — **Laguna Pueblo** — 19 miles — **McCartys**

Look out for old trading posts *Visit historic San José de la Laguna Mission Church* *Don't fall for the Hemingway story!*

Explore Albuquerque

Albuquerque's top sights are largely concentrated in and around Old Town and beside the river, while additional interesting attractions lie further afield. It's easy to spend time both inside and out – this is a city that values its active time. And don't miss Albuquerque's hoopla around 100 years of Route 66.

HOW TO

Getting there: Albuquerque is bisected by Route 66. Take Exit 167 off I-40 in the east.

Getting around: Parking in busy neighborhoods can be competitive. **ABQ Ride** (cabq.gov/transit) provides public transit.

Sleeping: A wave of updates is getting Route 66 motels ready for the next 100 years. At the 1946 **Monterey Motel** (themontereymotel.com; $$), you check in at the swank lounge and choose from a hostel room (called a StayAt) or a luxe motel room. The 1937 **El Vado Motel** (elvadoabq.com; $$$) offers characterful, luxury stays in a traditional motor court–style complex.

More info: visitalbuquerque.org

Tip: Don't miss time on Central Ave (p176), Route 66's long path through town, which is historic, gritty and vibrant.

Old Town

A great place to wander as a visitor, some of the quaint adobe buildings that line the alleyways of **Old Town** began life as private residences in 1706, when the first 15 Spanish families called the newly named 'Alburquerque' their home.

Dating from 1793, the facade of the adobe **San Felipe de Neri Church** (sanfelipedeneri.org) now provides Old Town's most famous photo op. Showpiece **Albuquerque Museum** (cabq.gov/artsculture/albuquerque-museum) has an unmissable local history gallery and a New Mexico art collection.

Anyone charmed by snakes will find the **American International Rattlesnake Museum** (rattlesnakes.com) fascinating.

Elsewhere

Collectively run by New Mexico's 19 Pueblos, the **Indian Pueblo Cultural Center** (indianpueblo.org) is an essential stop. It shares compelling stories of the Pueblos' history and artistic traditions.

The family-run **Turquoise Museum** (turquoisemuseum.com) spotlights New Mexico's signature rock. And yes, there's a gift shop. The opulent building is a minor local celebrity.

New Mexico's ongoing role in America's nuclear weapons industry is detailed at the **National Museum of Nuclear Science & History** (nuclearmuseum.org), which explores the fascinating – if sobering – history of atomic science in war and peace.

EATING OUT

New Mexican cuisine is the way to go. Near the Old Town Plaza, **Church Street Cafe** (churchstreetcafe.com; 11am-9pm, closed Sun; $$) is in an 18th-century adobe complex with a well-shaded patio. At the Indian Pueblo Cultural Center, the **Indian Pueblo Kitchen** (9am-5pm, closed Sun; $$) serves Native American–inspired fare and less common New Mexico dishes. Simple on the outside, **Mary & Tito's Cafe** (lunch Mon-Sat; $) has been serving acclaimed New Mexican cuisine, including signature red chile, since 1963.

Dried chilies hung from a *portales* ceiling

Outdoor Albuquerque

Sandia Peak Tramway (sandiapeak.com) climbs 2.7 miles from the desert floor in Albuquerque's northeast corner to the summit of 10,378ft Sandia Crest. Views are spectacular. Hiking trails lead through the woods and you can hike down.

The **Rio Grande Nature Center State Park** (emnrd.nm.gov) celebrates the famous river that courses through Albuquerque. It's laced with hiking trails along the river and *bosque* (forests on floodplains; from the Spanish word for forest), and there are interpretive gardens.

Tour Route 66 in Albuquerque

Central Ave runs across Albuquerque from east to west for nearly 18 miles and after 1937 was Route 66 for its entire length. Today, it's a fascinating stretch of urban life that mixes every hope, challenge, success and delight. Prior to 1937, Route 66 turned south along 4th St SW.

HOW TO

Getting here: From the east, enter the city from old Route 66, which is Hwy 333, or from the parallel I-40 and use Exit 167 for Central Ave SE. From the west, use I-40 Exit 149 and join Central Ave SW.

When to go: Albuquerque is enjoyable year-round with the usual seasonal caveats. **Balloon Fiesta** *(balloonfiesta.com)*, the world's largest gathering of hot-air balloons, takes place in October and all rooms are booked.

Tip: Cruise Central Ave at night for a neon spectacle.

Notable Historic Buildings & Neon

Coming in from the east, Central Ave does not get off to an edifying start. There are plenty of old motels that embody the same sketchy vibe you've seen previously in Route 66 towns bypassed by the interstate. In 1955, 98 motels lined Central, but today less than 40 remain. The 1949 **Luna Lodge**, with its commanding yellow arrow, hangs on while the tattered 1946 **Tewa Lodge** still has some of the city's best neon. Only the sign really remains of the **De Anza Motor Lodge**, but it's a great sign.

Nob Hill

Literally, the elevated portion of Central, Albuquerque's most interesting shops are in **Nob Hill**. It's worth strolling the strip and making your own discoveries. Sprawling **Frontier** *(frontierrestaurant.com; $)* has been dishing up unbeatable trad green chile across from the university since 1971.

Downtown

Flowing into Old Town just to the northwest, the city's Downtown is in the midst of a revival. The star is always the richly ornamented (1927) **KiMo Theatre** *(cabq.gov/artsculture/kimo)*, designed in a unique fusion style called Pueblo Deco.

Barelas

Prior to 1937, Route 66 ran south through the **Barelas** neighborhood on 4th St SW from

CENTRAL AVENUE

For fans of *Breaking Bad* and *Better Call Saul*, Central Ave is one long stretch of déjà vu. From 2008 to 2022, when the series were being shot locally, gritty Route 66 locations around Central figured prominently in many episodes.

The **Dog House Drive In** *(to 9pm)* was often seen, while downtown coffee shop **Java Joe's** *(to 3:30pm)* was the gangster Tuco's mural-marked headquarters. Location tours come and go as often as skeezy characters from wherever Jesse Pinkman is crashing, but there's always something on offer.

Left: KiMo Theatre;
Below: Tewa Lodge

Downtown in a long loop west to avoid the gorge that was finally crossed by the Rio Puerco Bridge (p172). A Hispanic farming community in the early 1800s, Barelas remains a center of Hispanic life in Albuquerque.

The **National Hispanic Cultural Center** *(nhccnm.org)* celebrates visual, performing and literary arts. Stroll 4th St SW and around north of Aves Dolores Huerta and Cesar Chavez for galleries, shops and cafes. **Barelas Coffee House** *(facebook.com/thebarelascoffeehouse)* is a community fave serving New Mexican fare and rich coffee.

items, from liquor to jerky to oddball candy to something kind of like pizza. It's also the home of one of the Mother Road's more preposterous stories: that Ernest Hemingway took a room out back and wrote *The Old Man and the Sea* here. Since most Route 66 sources just copy each other, we're here to say that Hemingway scholars deem the story complete nonsense. There.

From here to **McCartys**, look north and you'll see the 11,300ft summit of Mt Taylor, which is snowcapped part of the year.

DETOUR: El Malpais National Monument

The rugged **El Malpais National Monument** (nps.gov/elma) consists of almost 200 sq miles of isolated volcanic terrain beginning just south of Grants. The fields extend through the region and influenced the routing of the railroad and Route 66. About 7 miles west of McCartys, head south on Hwy 117 for spectacular sights and strenuous hikes. On a quick visit, take a short gravel road off the highway to the **Sandstone Bluffs**, which afford sweeping views of the lava fields.

Close to the Hwy 117, **La Ventana Arch** is one of the largest sandstone arches in the state. It's 18 miles south of Route 66. Get info on hiking, the lava tubes and more at the park's **El Malpais Visitor Center** near Exit 85 off I-40.

Grants

Grants first boomed as a railroad stop. Today if you sense a glow, it may be from its years as a center of uranium mining. Learn more at the **New Mexico Mining Museum** (newmexicominingmuseum.org). Or, the glow may be coming from the **Route 66 Drive-Thru Neon Sign**, a community-run gimmick to lure

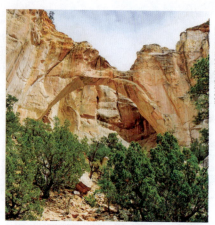

La Ventana Arch, El Malpais National Monument

Mother Road drivers off the interstate. By day it's not much, but at night the arch lights up and awaits your vehicle and selfie frenzy.

For period neon, check out the signs at the **West Theatre** and the **Sands Motel** (sandsmotel grants.us) – Elvis slept here! If all this glow leaves you thirsty, hit the aptly named **Junkyard Brewing** (facebook.com/Route66Junky ardBrewery), just east of town, which is surrounded by the hulks of vehicles that may well have once cruised Route 66.

Continental Divide

Cruising along old Route 66 after Grants, if the rolling scenery of red rocks and mesas wasn't enough to remind drivers during the first decades of Route 66 that they weren't in Illinois anymore – let alone Kansas – then the series of now-abandoned trading posts you'll pass today certainly would have made the point. Just past **Bluewater**, watch for the remains of **Bowlin's Old Crater Trading Post**, with its faded murals of cliched Native Americans and come-ons for 'Bargains' and 'Rugs.' A little way on is the similar **Rattlesnake Trading Post**.

This old road jaunt ends when you see a sign for the **Continental Divide**, although the setting is underwhelming as it's hard to imagine water flowing in any direction given the flatness. Rejoin I-40 here at Exit 47.

Gallup

Route 66 runs straight through downtown **Gallup**'s historic district, lined with renovated light-red sandstone buildings housing kitschy souvenir shops and galleries selling Navajo arts and crafts. There are over 20 noteworthy structures, built along 1st, 2nd and 3rd Sts between the 1890s and the 1940s. Included among them is the small **Rex Museum**

BEST PLACES TO SLEEP

The Imperial, Albuquerque $
This Route 66 classic motel has gone through a time warp and is now a beautifully updated boutique hotel near downtown. At the Imperial, everything gleams, even the pool. *(theimperialabq.com)*

Hotel Andaluz, Albuquerque $$
Albuquerque's finest historic hotel was built in the heart of downtown in 1939. Since then, Hotel Andaluz has been tastefully modernized while retaining its classic period details. *(hotelandaluz.com)*

Hotel El Rancho, Gallup $
Opened in 1937, Hotel El Rancho has a superb lobby resembling a rustic hunting lodge. Gallup's 'home of the movie stars' is big, bright and decorated with eclectic Old West fashions. *(elranchohotel.com)*

Sands Motel, Grants

(gallupnm.gov/341/rex-museum), displaying historical memorabilia in a former brothel.

Other noteworthy erections include a cowboy-hat-clad **'Muffler Man'** giant at John's Used Cars and the landmark 1928 Spanish Colonial **El Morro Theatre** *(elmorrotheatre.com)*.

Starting in the 1930s, the walls of Gallup's downtown buildings have been canvases for huge **murals** that trace the town's history. Download a **walking tour map** *(visitgallup.com)* and enjoy! Stop off for a meal at **Jerry's Cafe** *($)*, a Route 66 veteran that does chile – red or green – with aplomb.

Stop and stay the night at the stunning, grand and slightly preposterous **Hotel El Rancho** *(elranchohotel.com; $$)*, a Mother Road vet that had Hollywood moments when stars stayed here during Western shoots. Guests included Katharine Hepburn, Spencer Tracy, Robert Mitchum and many more. There's a John Wayne suite. Pilgrim.

Manuelito & a Film Location

Dart off I-40 at Exit 8 (**Manuelito**) to enjoy some original 1930 Route 66 concrete (now designated Hwy 118) plus some sheer sandstone called **Devil's Cliff** because it's not particularly stable, as you can tell from the steel netting.

After about 5.5 miles, film buffs will want to look to the right to the red- and yellow-streaked cliff face across the meadow. It's the **principal location** of the action in the Billy Wilder black comedy *Ace in the Hole*. Considered one of the most cynical movies ever made, it starred Kirk Douglas as a scheming reporter who connives to keep a hapless man trapped underground to further his own career. Retitled *The Big Carnival*, its grim outlook and rampant misogyny didn't

Along the Way We Met...

LAURA NITZOS Moving to Albuquerque from the East Coast in 1994, my husband and I picked up Route 66 in Oklahoma City. Somewhere in New Mexico, we stopped on the dark highway and marveled at the purple-blue wintry sky, the infinite stars, the bright full moon and the mountains beckoning in the distance. For us, as for so many others before us, the road held the promise of new beginnings and adventures, of hope and of dreams not yet conceived.

Laura is a lawyer and Albuquerque resident.

LAURA'S TIP: *'Stop often, and experience the quirky roadside attractions along the way!'*

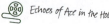
Echoes of Ace in the Hole

play with 1951 audiences and it was Wilder's first flop. Fans of the film will note that the location looks nearly the same over 70 years later.

Lupton

Old-time Route 66 attractions don't get much better than **Chief Yellowhorse**, a trading post and ancient cave that straddles the New Mexico–Arizona border at **Lupton**. You can stand in the shadow of sandstone walls bearing petroglyphs and have one foot in each state. The shop has something for everyone, from fine crafts to petrified wood to goofy souvenirs. As the sign says, '66 ♥ U.'

Note: When New Mexico is on daylight saving time from early March until early November, Arizona will be one hour earlier as it does not observe daylight saving time (except for the Navajo Nation).

NEW MEXICO'S PUEBLOS

New Mexico is home to 19 Native American pueblos. The word pueblo comes from the Spanish for 'village,' and that's what they are – small clusters of adobe houses, which often are still standing where the conquistadors found them five centuries ago. Most Pueblo people were not displaced over the centuries and have long and deep ties to their lands. For a compelling overview of these communities, visit Albuquerque's Indian Pueblo Cultural Center (p174).

Some pueblos are more welcoming of visitors than others. Besides Kewa (p163) and Laguna (p172), **Zuni Pueblo** is known for creative jewelry and wild scenery; it's 35 miles south of Gallup.

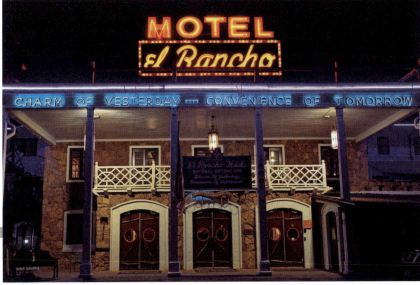

Hotel El Rancho, Gallup

The Guardian Angel of Route 66

There was a time not so long ago when Route 66 nearly disappeared from the public imagination. It took a small-town barber, Angel Delgadillo, to bring it back to life. Mark Johanson spoke to the Mother Road's savior.

WORDS BY **MARK JOHANSON**

Mark is an American journalist based in Chile whose stories regularly appear in National Geographic, Travel + Leisure and the BBC, among others.

ANGEL DELGADILLO can still visualize the glory days of his youth when he'd use the headlights of cars traveling along Route 66 to make shadow puppets on the modest storefronts of his small Arizona town. He also remembers the darker days, after I-40 opened to the public, when the headlights moved off to the horizon.

'The town of Seligman died at 2:30pm on September 22, 1978,' he recalls. 'We were the first small community in Arizona to get bypassed by I-40, and it took us years to figure out why the traveling public quit on us.'

Route 66 channeled 9000 daily cars through Seligman. Overnight, that traffic vanished. 'We knew we were going to get bypassed,' Delgadillo says, 'but we didn't know how devastating it would be.' The death of Route 66 is etched deep into the timeline of Delgadillo's life. But so, too, is its revival. That's because this humble barber, now in his 90s, was instrumental in putting Route 66 back in the spotlight.

The Rebirth of Route 66

The legendary 20th-century highway from Chicago to Los Angeles rose to prominence during the Great Depression and gained a new life as the ultimate path across America for road-tripping families from the 1950s to 1970s. Yet, the end was nigh for its themed motels, neon-lit diners and audacious roadside attractions by the mid 1980s, when five soul-crunching interstates had replaced Route 66 almost in its entirety.

Angel Delgadillo

That's where the story could have ended if it weren't for an idealistic Arizona barber who noticed folks trickling back into his town a decade after they'd abandoned it. 'They were searching for their tire marks, their history and the America of yesteryear,' he says. 'They wanted to find the highway of their childhood.'

All this nostalgia got Delgadillo thinking: what if he could convince Arizona to designate the segment of Route 66 through Seligman as a historic byway (and, in the process, save his town from economic collapse)? He called a meeting in February of 1987 and formed what was to become the first Historic Route 66 Association in the United States. The group sent letters to the Arizona Department of Transportation asking for support. When none came, they knocked on doors, demanding to be heard.

Nine months later, the state government created new Route 66 signs and put them up between Seligman and Topock, 140 miles away, preserving the longest remaining stretch of Route 66 in the country. Soon, Delgadillo was fielding calls from the seven other states along the historic road which, within three years, all had their own associations replicating his work. The highway at the heart of the American identity was officially reborn.

Attracting a New Generation

Delgadillo is now known as the 'Guardian Angel of Route 66.' Though he retired in 2022 after 75 years of barbering, his shop acts as a gift store where he handcrafts birdhouses and welcomes his frequent visitors. Often, Delgadillo is called upon to consult on local history.

If you've seen the 2006 Pixar film *Cars* you already know Seligman by its fictional name Radiator Springs. Director John Lasseter came to this teeny town to interview Delgadillo, drawing inspiration for the movie from the stories he heard.

'Prior to *Cars*, the only people who ended up in Seligman were grown-ups,' Delgadillo says. 'When they put that movie on the air, it captured the imagination of children. It inspired a new generation to become interested in Route 66 – and they're the ones who will inherit what we started.'

You can see glimpses of Radiator Springs in real-life places like the Snow Cap Drive-In, a classic greasy spoon built by Delgadillo's brother Juan in 1953 out of scrap lumber from a nearby rail yard. Its walls are now covered in mementos (business cards, money, IDs) left by travelers from as far away as Japan and Brazil. Down the road is the Supai Motel, whose soaring neon sign recalls the heyday of this route for road-trippers. A succession of kitschy gift shops leads the way out of town.

'People come here to reminisce,' says Delgadillo, glancing out his shop window at the 'Mother Road.' 'We treat everyone like we did 50 or 60 years ago, with respect and honor. You're not a number to us; you're a person. And so, you get to experience life as it was way back when.'

> The death of Route 66 is etched deep into the timeline of Delgadillo's life. But so, too, is its revival. That's because this humble barber, now in his 90s, was instrumental in putting Route 66 back in the spotlight.

Lupton
ARIZONA

History, scenery and the open road. An alluring combination that makes traveling across Arizona on Route 66 so irresistible. Yes, there are showstoppers – the Painted Desert, the Grand Canyon, – but you'll remember the long, intoxicating miles under endless skies for as long as the icons in between. And yet, there are so many reasons to stop. Old towns steeped in history and surprises appearing around a bend, whether an impossibly beautiful rock formation or a sleeping burro blocking the road.

Ryan Ver Berkmoes

Cool Springs Station

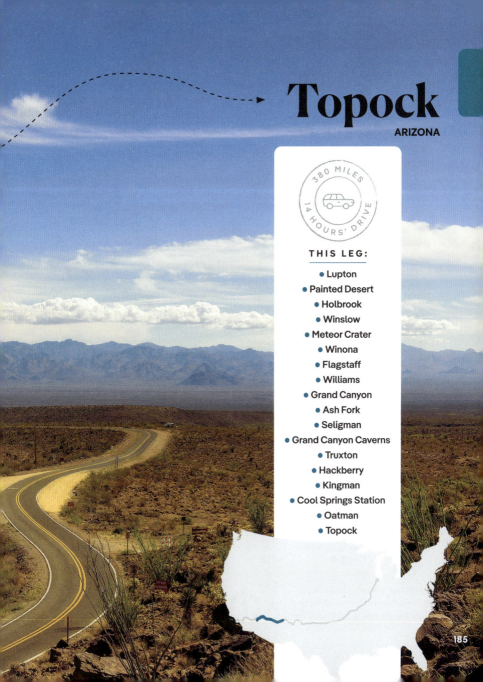

Topock
ARIZONA

380 MILES · 14 HOURS' DRIVE

THIS LEG:

- Lupton
- Painted Desert
- Holbrook
- Winslow
- Meteor Crater
- Winona
- Flagstaff
- Williams
- Grand Canyon
- Ash Fork
- Seligman
- Grand Canyon Caverns
- Truxton
- Hackberry
- Kingman
- Cool Springs Station
- Oatman
- Topock

Driving Notes

In a little under 380 miles, traversing Arizona on Route 66 offers every kind of experience. From the wide-open spaces and smooth roads of the east to the high elevations and pine forests of the center and then on to the hot and dry deserts of the west, capped by the roller coaster of a drive via Oatman. It's never dull!

Breaking Your Journey

Arizona offers many opportunities to break your journey. The cities of Flagstaff and Kingman are natural stops. Smaller, but no less appealing, are Williams and Winslow, especially the latter with its world-famous hotel. Even Seligman and Holbrook have fine options for a night. In the latter you can have the unique experience of bedding down in a concrete tepee.

Ryan's Tips

BEST MEAL Dinner at the **Turquoise Room** (p189)

FAVORITE VIEW The Painted Desert as seen from **Tawa Point** (p190)

ESSENTIAL STOP Walking the historic center of **Flagstaff**

ROAD-TRIP TIP Enjoy every minute driving old Route 66 from Exit 146 on I-40 all the way west to Topock and the California border

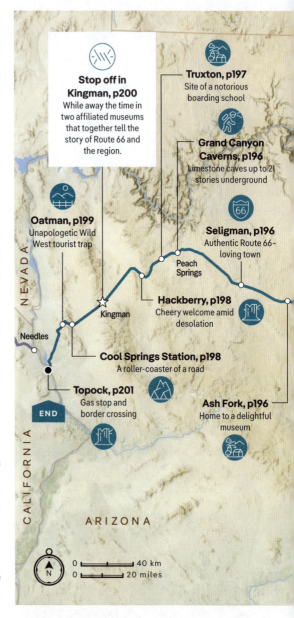

Stop off in Kingman, p200
While away the time in two affiliated museums that together tell the story of Route 66 and the region.

Truxton, p197
Site of a notorious boarding school

Grand Canyon Caverns, p196
Limestone caves up to 21 stories underground

Oatman, p199
Unapologetic Wild West tourist trap

Seligman, p196
Authentic Route 66–loving town

Hackberry, p198
Cheery welcome amid desolation

Cool Springs Station, p198
A roller-coaster of a road

Topock, p201
Gas stop and border crossing

Ash Fork, p196
Home to a delightful museum

PREVIOUS STOP Tiny Lupton spills over the New Mexico–Arizona border.

Lupton

Crossing into Arizona at **Lupton**, the transition is less dramatic than other state border crossings. The rolling, tree-dotted hills of the dry plains continue. Note that from early March until early November, Arizona (except for the Navajo Nation) is one hour earlier than New Mexico.

Once you're barreling along I-40 (there's no worthwhile old Route 66 alternative), you'll see the remains of a modern-day tourist trap at Exit 348. The much-touted **'Fort Courage'** crumbles on the north side of the highway. It was an ill-conceived effort to milk the old sitcom *F Troop*, a low-rated TV show from the mid-1960s.

Wigwam Motel, Holbrook

DETOUR: Painted Desert

Every Mother Road traveler should make time for the one national park that protects a stretch of original Route 66. Not only does the **Petrified Forest National Park** offer extraordinary beauty, it can be enjoyed by those on a tight schedule. It's easy to see all the highlights (p190) of the extraordinary **Painted Desert**, which are not easily discerned from I-40.

Holbrook

The closest town to the Petrified Forest, **Holbrook** has many motels, including the iconic **Wigwam Motel** *(sleepinawigwam.com; $)*, which was once part of a chain. Dating to 1950, each room is a self-contained concrete tepee outfitted with restored 1950s hickory log-pole furniture. The town's main drag, Navajo Blvd, is dotted with bright neon at night.

Some 17 miles west on I-40 is another Route 66 icon. The **Jack Rabbit Trading Post** *(jackrabbittradingpost.com)* is memorable for its laconic bunny logo alongside the motto 'Here it is' out front. (Once there were hundreds of billboards hawking the post from here to Missouri.) Inside you'll find tons of Route 66 merch.

Winslow

Winslow's star is the Mission Revival **La Posada Hotel** (p199), a 1930 sprawling masterpiece by Mary Jane Colter. It was the last great railroad hotel built for the Fred Harvey Company

Lupton

73 miles

 Take the Painted Desert detour

Winslow

BEST PLACES TO EAT

Turquoise Room, Winslow $$
The main restaurant in the La Posada Hotel offers a seasonal menu of creative Southwestern fare. Servers are good at recommending unfamiliar items. *(theturquoiseroom.net)*

Proper Meats + Provisions, Flagstaff $
Superb for road food and picnics near or far. Sensational sandwiches, house-made salami and pancetta are the stars of the charcuterie board, with cheese, figs and olives. *(propermeats.com; to 5pm, closed Mon)*

Sultana Bar, Williams $
In a time when too many bars are little more than venues for dozens of sports-blaring screens, this unapologetic old dive offers live music, taxidermized animals and raucous fun. *(facebook.com/theworldfamoussultanabar)*

along the Santa Fe Railroad. (It's still the Amtrak station.) Elaborate tilework, Navajo rugs and other details accent its elegance. The decor goes with the splashy canvases of Tina Mion, one of the artists who bought and restored the hotel in 1997. The **Turquoise Room** (right) offers the best meal between Flagstaff and Albuquerque.

In the old train station nearby, the **Affeldt Mion Museum** *(ammwsa.com)* shows works from the local community. Downtown, loudspeakers guarantee you an earworm at **Standin' On the Corner Park** *(standinonthecorner.com)*. A mural of that famous girl in a flatbed Ford and more celebrate the Eagles' song 'Take It Easy.'

Continues on page 192

Marvel at the Painted Desert

When you first see the Painted Desert stretching to the horizon at Petrified Forest National Park, with its panoply of colors swirling and blending like a kaleidoscope, you'll be awed. That the 'trees' embody these colors is a bonus, and the Route 66 angle – that's pure icing.

HOW TO

Nearest stop: Painted Desert

Getting here: The park is easily accessed by westbound traffic from I-40. A 28-mile scenic road ends in the south at US 180, and then it's 19 miles to Holbrook. Going east, do this in reverse.

When to go: The park can be enjoyed year-round.

Cost: Per car $25

Tip: Visitor centers and the Painted Desert Inn have snacks. The closest selection of lodging is in Holbrook.

More info: nps.gov/pefo; the Painted Desert Visitor Center is close to I-40 and the Rainbow Forest Museum is near US 180. Both have info and exhibits.

Entering the Park

The 28-mile one-way **drive** through the park can be managed in an hour, which will give the time-pressured a chance to glimpse many of the wonders, but two hours is more realistic.

At the **visitor centers**, ask for the passel of brochures beyond the basic map everyone receives. They cover how wood gets petrified, Route 66 and more, and make for fine reading out amid the beauty of the park.

North of I-40

The first stops past the entrance offer the first views of the **Painted Desert**. Of these, hold out for **Tawa Point**, as its vantage of the vast polychromatic vista is the most sweeping. The spectacle sits below the plains you've driven on until now, so the first glimpse never fails to startle.

Don't miss the **Painted Desert Inn** (right), and wander some of the north-facing walks at **Hòzhò Point**.

Old Route 66

The rusted-out **1932 Studebaker** may be one of the most photographed old cars in the US. It signifies where the Mother Road crossed the grassy plains of today's park. The lonely line of wooden telephone poles trace the alignment the highway used from 1926 to 1958, but you'll be hard-pressed to find any other trace, so thorough has nature been in erasing the pavement in the decades since.

MAKE TIME AT THE INN

Though not open as a lodge, it's worth stopping at the beautiful **Painted Desert Inn**. What you see today reflects the work of three supremely talented people. National Park Service architect Lyle Bennett created a style of architecture used throughout the West; he redesigned the inn in the late 1930s. Hopi artist Fred Kabotie crafted the exquisite murals. In the late 1940s, Mary Jane Colter, an extraordinarily talented architect, added her influence. Colter was also the genius behind Winslow's **La Posada Hotel** (p199) and several landmarks at the Grand Canyon.

Left: Painted Desert viewed from Tawa Point; Below: Painted Desert Inn

Petrified Forest

South of I-40 is where to find petrified wood. But first, walk the remains of **Puerco Pueblo**, a sophisticated 14th-century village. And be ready for more geologic wonder at **The Teepees**, where the slate and maroon banding of the mesas seems unreal in late afternoon sun.

Exit your vehicle at **Blue Mesa** and walk the trails to fully appreciate the luminous wonder of the petrified wood, which captures the colors of the Painted Desert in miniature. Go to the furthest reaches to escape the crowds and appreciate the alien beauty of this forbidding valley.

DETOUR: Meteor Crater

A mile across and 600ft deep, the second-most impressive hole in Arizona was formed by a meteor that tore into the atmosphere about 50,000 years ago, when giant sloths still lived in these parts. The privately owned **Meteor Crater** (meteorcrater.com) is a massively hyped attraction that opened to Route 66 travelers in 1953.

Lookout points surround the crater's edge. The visitor center has plenty of diversions (note: the 'Apollo 11 capsule' was used for training – it is *not* the one that went to the moon). It's 18 miles west of Winslow and 6 miles south of I-40.

Winona

Prior to 1947, Route 66 took a looping route through the ever-denser ponderosa pine forests to the north of **Winona** on the way to Flagstaff. Bid farewell to the jockeying 18-wheelers on I-40 at Exit 211 and join what's now designated County Rd 394. After a short distance, the closed 1924 **Walnut Canyon Bridge** comes into view. It's a soaring truss design that you can walk across. Surviving original segments of Route 66 at either end are still the rich red of the local gravel used for the asphalt. Continue through the rolling hills of ranch country.

Flagstaff

Flagstaff's ties to Route 66 are palpable in its walkable downtown (right). It's a good place to break your trip and delight in the mix of cultural sites and access to outdoorsy pursuits like mountain biking and skiing.

Just south of downtown, the name will make it hard to resist the allure of the **Mother Road Brewing Company** (motherroadbeer.com), which has a taproom beside Route 66.

Hiker looks out over Meteor Crater

Leaving town on I-40, if your image of Arizona is of red rocks, cacti and deserts, the drive west from Flagstaff will dispel it, as this jaunt across high elevations (over 7000ft) takes you through the world's largest ponderosa pine forest.

Williams

As a major gateway to the Grand Canyon (p194), **Williams** stays vibrant and still milks every link it can to Route 66. The center is lined with historic 1800s buildings. Attractions include the unmissable **Poozeum** (poozeum.com; free!), which combines elements of a natural history museum with a sideshow. It boasts the world's largest collection of coprolites (fossilized feces, but you knew that, right?) and the longest dinosaur turd this side of Uranus.

Continues on page 196

Walk Flagstaff

Flagstaff packs a lot of history into a compact and walkable downtown. Restored historic hotels and motels welcome guests. Strolling the streets, you'll find bakeries, cafes, bookstores and outdoor stores.

HOW TO

Nearest stop: Flagstaff

Getting here: Route 66 passes right in front of the Flagstaff Visitor Center on Santa Fe Ave.

When to go: Flagstaff has activities for every season.

Tip: Get a picnic downtown and watch the trains go by.

More info: *flagstaffarizona.org*

Every visit to Flagstaff should start at the extraordinary ❶ **Flagstaff Visitor Center** in the 1926 Santa Fe train station. It's Route 66's best – among tough competition. Learn about Flagstaff's essential role in the Apollo program, its public art and more. They also offer walking tours and audio guides. Watch a train thunder past, then set off east to San Francisco St where you'll see the city's ❷ **1889**

Historic Hotel Monte Vista

Train Station, a tidy red stone building from 1889. Cross the tracks south to Phoenix Ave and stop at the corner of Phoenix Ave, which was Route 66 until 1934, when traffic got so bad the highway was moved to Santa Fe Ave to the north. Ponder the large 2014 ❸ **Mother Myth Mural** here, which tells the story of Route 66 from right to left, because so many people traveled it from east to west.

Cross back into town to the corner of San Francisco St and Aspen Ave. The ❹ **Hotel Monte Vista** is an example of a vintage hotel that's had a fine restoration (the nearby Weatherford Hotel is another). Walk a half block west to ❺ **Heritage Square** and relax with a drink and plot your next Flagstaff experience.

Detour: Gaze into the Grand Canyon

No matter how much you read about the Grand Canyon or how many photographs you've seen, nothing really prepares you for the sight of it. One of the world's seven natural wonders, it's so startlingly familiar and iconic you can't take your eyes off it. It's a superb Route 66 detour.

HOW TO

Nearest stop: Williams

Getting here: From Williams, it is a 56-mile drive straight north on Hwy 64.

When to go: The Grand Canyon can be visited year-round, though summer can get prohibitively hot at midday.

Cost: Per car $35

Eating and sleeping: There are myriad options inside the park and at Grand Canyon Village.

A fun tip: Arrive before 10am or after 2pm to avoid the longest wait times at the entrances.

More info: *nps.gov/grca*

History

The canyon's immensity, the sheer intensity of light and shadow at sunrise or sunset, even its very age, scream for superlatives. At about two billion years old – half of Earth's total life span – the layer of Vishnu Schist at the bottom of the canyon is some of the oldest exposed rock on the planet. And how it was exposed is the Colorado River, which continues to carve its way 277 miles through the canyon as it has for the past six million years.

Viewpoints

Short, easy and spectacular (it's just a 0.5-mile round-trip), the paved trail to **Bright Angel Point** is a Grand Canyon must. Beginning from the back porch of the Grand Canyon Lodge, it goes to a narrow finger of an overlook with fabulous views.

The worn winding staircase of Mary Colter's 70ft stone **Desert View Watchtower** leads to the highest spot on the rim (7522ft). From here, unparalleled views take in not only the canyon and the Colorado River, but also the San Francisco Peaks, the Navajo Reservation and the Painted Desert.

Marvelously uncrowded **Shoshone Point** is a rocky promontory with some of the canyon's best views.

Walking the Canyon

Beginning in Grand Canyon Village, the popular **Rim Trail** follows the rim west 13 miles to

TAKE THE TRAIN

Riding the historic **Grand Canyon Railway** *(thetrain.com)* to the South Rim takes a bit longer than if you were to drive, but you avoid traffic and disembark relaxed and ready to explore the canyon. The train drops you off a few minutes from the historic El Tovar and canyon rim. The trains start in the classic Route 66 town of Williams. You can park there and ride to the canyon, spend the day touring the magnificence and then return.

Left: Grand Canyon viewed from Shoshone Point;
Below: Desert View Watchtower

Hermits Rest, dipping in and out of scrubby pines and connecting a series of scenic points and historical sights. Portions are paved, and every viewpoint is accessed by one of the three shuttle routes.

The **Trail of Time** borders the Rim Trail just west of **Yavapai Geology Museum**. Here, every meter of the trail represents one million years of geologic history, with exhibits providing the details.

Among the myriad tours, **ranger-led walks** along the rim are a great way to learn about natural history and contemporary Grand Canyon issues.

At the east end of town, stop off at the open-air **Welcome and History Park**, where you'll find preserved railroad cars and a sign with photos and the history of Route 66 and Williams.

Several places to eat have a Mother Road theme and the chromium diner look is popular. For authentic old, stop in for toot (drink) at the 'world famous' **Sultana Bar** (p189), a dive that kept early Mother Road drivers lubricated as it was a speakeasy during prohibition.

Ash Fork

The endearing, volunteer-run **Ash Fork Route 66 Museum** *(facebook.com/ashfork rt66historicmuseum)* is proud of its ties to Route 66 and was preparing for the road's centenary well in advance. Check out the large model of the town in its heydey – which was the 1950s.

Back on I-40, you can exit again in only 7 miles (Exit 139) to enjoy an extended 160-mile run on old Route 66 as it curves through the increasingly arid Arizona plains and passes through the delightful tourist town of Seligman to Kingman. Watch for recreated red-and-white **Burma Shave signs**.

Seligman

Tiny **Seligman** embraces its Route 66 heritage with verve, thanks to the Delgadillo family, the Mother Road's biggest boosters.

Angel (p182) is dancing with 100 but he still has a tale to tell. You may catch the 'Angel of Route 66' at **Angel & Vilma's Original Route 66 Gift Shop** *(route66giftshop.com)*. Poke around for souvenirs and admire license plates sent in by fans from all over the world.

One door east, **Delgadillo's Snow Cap** *($)* is an institution renowned for the ceaseless gags it plays on customers (beware of the mustard!). Schtick aside, the cheeseburgers are good and the onion rings crispy. Elsewhere, the mascot manages to avoid copyright infringement by a hair at **Route 66 Road Runner** *(route66road runner.com; $)*, which serves comfort food and cold beer in a 1936 Chevy dealership. The **Historic Route 66 Motel** *(route66seligman arizona.com; $)* features immaculate rooms, while **Aztec Motel & Creative Space** (p199) takes a vintage motel canvas and draws a new-age haven.

Grand Canyon Caverns

On the way to **Peach Springs** (old Route 66 is Arizona 66 until Kingman), the tribal capital of the Hualapai Indian Reservation, there's another roadside cave waiting to lure you underground. The **Grand Canyon Caverns** *(gccaverns.com)* were discovered in 1927

Burma Shave sign between Seligman and Kingman

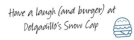

Delgadillo's Snow Cap, Seligman

by a woodcutter who literally stumbled across (or into) them. These limestone caves have fascinated visitors ever since. Up to 21 stories underground, the dry caverns can be explored on a variety of tours. Stay at the **Caverns Inn** *($)*, which features an underground suite that appealed to Mother Road travelers during the Cold War 'duck-and-cover' era.

Truxton

For 42 miles from **Truxton** to Kingman, Route 66 passes through increasingly arid, forbidding territory. Pixar took inspiration for the *Cars* town Radiator Springs from various Mother

> **DEATH & REBIRTH IN WILLIAMS**
>
> Were it not for the ongoing renaissance of Route 66, Williams (p192) would be the road's memorial, a place of mourning for a lost slice of Americana. It was here on October 13, 1984 (not a Friday!), that the last bit of old Route 66 was replaced by the interstate, with the remains of the route being officially deconsecrated the following year. Beloved crooner Bobby Troup (he'd turn 66 in five days) was brought in to perform ('Get Your Kicks on) Route 66' one more time for the occasion.

Peach Springs — 37 miles — Truxton — 15 miles

Hualapai Indian Reservation and Grand Canyon Caverns

Along the Way We Met...

BARNEY All day long tourists drive through going too fast. They act like we don't own the place. And leave your window open so I can see if you have food. I hear tourists moan, 'Phew, it smells like donkey here!' Well, we have to smell them all day every day. Talk about phew! And they all want freebies! A burro's gotta earn a living too. You want a selfie, fine, but how 'bout some oats, OK?

Barney the burro is a lifelong resident of Oatman.

BARNEY'S TIP: *'Don't make an ass of yourself.'*

Road towns. Given the likelihood of radiators blowing here back in the day, this drive would have been inspirational.

In **Valentine**, the isolated canyon was the sight of horrible abuses. From 1903 to 1937, the **Truxton Canyon Training School** was one of the notorious government boarding schools for Indian children who were forcibly removed from their homes and culture. They were subjected to brutal discipline, disease and forced labor.

Hackberry

Coming out of the narrow canyons, with the railroad still alongside, the views open up north to the desert basin of Mojave County. Dust devils and towns with unbucolic names like Chloride speak to the forbidding nature of the landscape. Amidst the odd unwelcoming roadhouse, the cheery 1934 **Hackberry General Store** lures passersby with its eccentrically decorated gas station. It was once owned by famed Route 66 artist Bob Waldmire (p58).

Kingman

Route 66 curves through **Kingman** as Andy Devine Ave, named for the hometown hero, a Hollywood star famous as the perpetually befuddled driver of the eponymous *Stagecoach* in John Ford's Oscar-winning 1939 movie. It's worth stopping here for its **walkable downtown** and excellent Route 66 museum (p200).

Cool Springs Station

Until 1953, Route 66 followed a perilous path to California that continues to bedevil drivers today. The middle portion of the 55-mile Oatman Hwy is a roller-coaster of a road that's not for the faint of heart. It's not uncommon to see people lose their nerve and attempt three-point turns on blind curves, desperate to leave this corkscrewing asphalt hell. But for most drivers, especially ones who pull over so faster drivers can pass and those who stop to enjoy the sweeping views, the drive is a highlight. With clear air, you might see three states at once.

Hackberry — Refresh at Hackberry General Store

28 miles

Kingman — Don't miss the excellent museums

20 miles

Cool Springs Station — Cool refreshments!

9 miles

Oatman

Right before the road gets hairy, stop off for a refreshment at **Cool Springs Station** *(route 66coolspringsaz.com).*

Oatman
The 7 miles after Cool Springs Station are the curviest. Try to imagine fully laden trucks navigating Sitgreaves Pass (3586ft) amid station wagons filled with sweaty families. Watch out for **burros**. They are the prolific descendants of pack animals abandoned by miners and they like to sleep in the road.

Oatman is a ramshackle hillside town that had a brief heyday after a 1915 gold strike. Since the 1940s, it has reinvented itself as an unapologetic Wild West tourist trap, complete with staged gunfights, gift shops with goofy names and genial watering holes where crusty residents will cadge a beer and cackle 'Don't worry, the burros don't bite!'

Continues on page 201

BEST PLACES TO SLEEP

La Posada Hotel, Winslow $$
If you stay in one hotel in Arizona, make it this architectural landmark that never takes itself too seriously. *(laposada.org)*

Motel DuBeau Travelers Inn, Flagstaff $
Opened as a motor court on Route 66 in 1926, it survived the rerouting of the road in the 1930s, thanks to the surviving neon sign tower. With updated rooms, it's ideally located for walking Downtown. *(modubeau.com)*

Aztec Motel & Creative Space, Seligman $
Not just renovated, but reimagined, this old motel is ready for another 100 years of Mother Road guests. *(theaztecmotel.com)*

Burros, Oatman

Stop off in Kingman

Kingman's compact downtown with its museums makes a great place to take a break in either direction on Route 66. Trains pound past as they have for over 150 years.

Nearest stop: Kingman

Getting here: Andy Devine Ave curves through Downtown Kingman. There is parking by the Powerhouse.

When to go: Enjoy stopping in Kingman year-round.

Cost: Combined adult admission to Route 66 and Mojave Museums $10

Tip: The historic downtown train station is home to the **Kingman Railroad Museum** (kingmanrailroadmuseum.com; Fri-Sun) and a large model railroad.

More info: explorekingman.com

Start at the **Powerhouse Visitor Center**, a hefty 1907 building that supplied the juice needed to build Hoover Dam, 74 miles northwest. Pick up the detailed walking tour guide, then hurry upstairs to the unmissable **Route 66 Museum** (mohavemuseum.org/route-66-museum). Covering an entire floor, there's an informative historical overview of travel along the Mother Road that hits the highs and lows, but the real strength of the displays are the stories of people whose lives were changed by traveling Route 66. There are tales of escape, desperation, immigration, transformation and simple delight.

Close by, the **Mohave Museum** (mohavemuseum.org) tells tales about diverse subjects from mining towns to Andy Devine. There's a wall of portraits of US first ladies, all by the same artist. Don't miss the petrified lightning.

Kingman has numerous motels along Andy Devine Ave, including the old **El Trovatore Motel** (eltrovatoremotel.com; $), which honors vintage celebs and has a top-notch sign. Downtown Kingman offers retro diners like **Mr D'z Route 66 Diner** ($), which serves up the Harley Dog – a real hog of a dog with spicy sauce.

El Trovatore Motel

Mr D'z Route 66 Diner, Kingman

Continued from page 199

Oatman is day trip country. Lunch places abound, but dinner and places to sleep don't. Buy some snacks and make friends with the burros.

Topock

The road to **Topock** is fairly genial. The main reason to stop is for gas, whether you're going east (there's none until Kingman) or west (in California gas may be at least $3 more per gallon). Hop onto I-40 for the quick trip over the desiccated **Colorado River**, its once mighty flow diverted by thirsty desert metropolises.

ARIZONA'S CUISINE

Native American, Hispanic and Anglo influences permeate Southwestern cuisine. Traditional crops form the foundation: corn, beans, squash, and, of course, chiles. Meat comes from all three influences. Mexican fare in Arizona is Sonoran, with specialties such as *carne seca* (dried beef). Meals are usually served with refried beans, rice, and flour or corn tortillas; chiles are mild. Huevos rancheros is the quintessential breakfast: eggs prepared to order are served on top of two fried corn tortillas, loaded with beans and potatoes, sprinkled with cheese and served swimming in chile or salsa. Breakfast burritos are similar and served everywhere.

1963 Buick Wildcat convertible
B CHRISTOPHER/ALAMY

INSIGHT

My Life & Route 66

Growing up in 1960s California, Route 66 was a constant presence in Ryan Ver Berkmoes' life. Even today, he can't stop driving it.

WORDS BY **RYAN VER BERKMOES**
Ryan Ver Berkmoes is still wondering what happened to his beach ball, which blew out of the car window somewhere along Route 66 iin 1964.

I FIRST DROVE Route 66 when I was four. Granted, I wasn't behind the wheel, but I was sitting behind my Dad, who was at the wheel of our 1963 Buick Wildcat convertible. It was a swank car that my mother cherished. Though it may have looked flashy as hell, it was a sickly kitten at heart, known for its propensity to overheat at the first sign of warm weather or a vague incline in the road.

Like legions of Route 66 travelers before them – including the Joads of *The Grapes of Wrath*, published some 25 years before – my parents had debated endlessly about when to undertake driving across the feared Mojave Desert. We sat around Barstow for hours until the temperature dropped enough that the odds of the Buick betraying us, so that we ended up as bleached bones by the roadside, were manageable.

Even at a young age, I loved road trips. My head was on a swivel taking in the action outside the windows. My enduring memories of the trip are of the interstate highway construction. At times we'd drive on new two-lane concrete next to another two-lane ribbon under construction. Four-year-old me – who cherished his Tonka trucks – couldn't get enough of the enormous machines building the road.

I can still see the images of the barriers that would regularly shunt us off the new road onto the old road and hear my Dad muttering about 'going slow.' There's a family photo from the trip showing me in front of some nonsensical gift shop in what I'm pretty sure is Seligman, Arizona – the town that got bypassed by I-40 in 1978 and which is a primary inspiration for Radiator Springs in *Cars*.

Mother Road Legacies

In our family, one Route 66 story was often told through the decades. My grandparents drove out to visit my family in 1958 (I wasn't even a gleam yet). They stopped in Needles and waited for the sun to go down so they wouldn't perish in the desert and then made the run across to Los Angeles, where they would turn north on US 101.

They survived the Mojave only to run aground in LA, with its complex and baffling freeway interchanges. Like Bugs Bunny making a wrong turn in Albuquerque, they made several in LA and were soon off the freeway in a Badlands of unfamiliarity. Panicked and confused, my grandfather called my parents and shouted: 'Help! I am in hell!' (He eventually asked directions and reached my family with his tail between his legs.)

Most families I knew had their own Mother Road stories. The parents of a very good friend were from Texas and had arrived in California in the 1930s. They were reticent to talk much of their past. Looking back now, I realize they could have been the Joads. Their part of the Texas Panhandle was devastated during the Dust Bowl years (p131).

My friend's mother worked several jobs to afford nursing school while his father got a job as a government laborer and worked his way up. Eventually, they were able to buy a simple house where they raised four kids. But the telling detail was that the house was on an acre of land on which they planted a small orchard plus fruit and vegetable gardens. My friend's father, a humble man of few words, once said to me: 'This reminds me of what I left behind.'

My Life & Route 66

During my sophomore year of high school, I got to get out of school for a few weeks for a road trip – via Route 66 – to Indiana. (School vs Indiana? No contest!) It was the first time I marveled at how the terrain around you can change dramatically just by crossing a state line. The ocher and umber mesas of New Mexico replaced by the featureless flatlands of Texas, the rich red earth of Oklahoma replaced by the rolling green hills of Missouri, which in turn are replaced by the flat cornfields of Illinois.

I had a magical experience that has shaped my life to this day. While we drove through the Mojave Desert, I was reading an excerpt from Steinbeck's road trip book *Travels with Charley: In Search of America*. In it, Steinbeck sits on the back of his camper shells and watches a coyote watching him. And where are they? The Mojave Desert. When I realized the coincidence, I got chills in my spine that resolved into a wanderlust that has never left my soul. To this day, I drive Route 66 every year or two, delighting in what awaits around every bend and over every hill.

> Even at a young age, I loved road trips. My head was on a swivel taking in the action outside the windows.

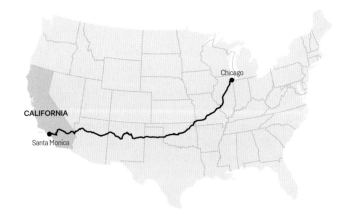

CALIFORNIA

Welcome – and *bienvenidos* – to California, the last stretch of Route 66. Pass through desertscapes dotted with remnants of the Mother Road's heyday, from the ruined remains of decommissioned gas pumps to old-timey diners. Visit small cities where the iconic Route 66 shield is emblazoned everywhere and watch the desert fade into SoCal suburbia as you drive east toward the Pacific Ocean. Savor these final miles on the road, for you'll soon be in Santa Monica, snapping one last selfie at the end-of-the-trail sign.

Motel sign at Bagdad Cafe, Newberry Springs (p212)
PICTURESQUE JAPAN/SHUTTERSTOCK

Needles

CALIFORNIA

This section of the Mother Road goes deep into the desert, through wide, empty expanses with sandy landscapes that are dwarfed by the enormity of the sky. It's one of many stretches in the vast American West where you can easily drive for miles without seeing another soul, much less a cactus. Sure, there are a few populated towns along the way – and even more roadside attractions – but in many stretches of this drive, you get the eerie sensation that ghosts outnumber the residents.

Margot Bigg

Roy's Motel & Café, Amboy
CL SHEBLEY/SHUTTERSTOCK

Barstow
CALIFORNIA

186 MILES
4 HOURS' DRIVE

THIS LEG:

- Needles
- Goffs Schoolhouse
- Amboy
- Joshua Tree National Park
- Newberry Springs
- Rock-A-Hoola Waterpark
- Yermo
- Barstow

Driving Notes

From Needles, take County Route 66 (CR 66) – which follows the trajectory of Route 66 – through vast stretches of sandy desert that are dwarfed in places by the enormity of the sky. While this part of the route is usually dry as a bone, the July to September monsoon season can bring with it flash floods and road closures.

Breaking Your Journey

A short detour off old Route 66, Yermo is a good place for a stop, with a couple of places to eat and a visitor center. That said, you'll have more options if you hold out until Barstow. You can also make a full-day drive out of it by detouring to Joshua Tree for a couple of hours and then heading back and finishing the stretch.

Margot's Tips

BEST MEAL A giant dill pickle and a bottle of sarsaparilla at **Calico Ghost Town** (p216)

FAVORITE VIEW The pre-sunset shadows at **Joshua Tree National Park** (p213)

ESSENTIAL STOP Goffs Schoolhouse (p210)

ROAD-TRIP TIP Some parts of this stretch lack convenience stores, so pack adequate water and snacks

Barstow, p215
The perfect stopover for train enthusiasts

Channel Your Inner Miner at a Historic Ghost Town, p216
Step back in time as you wander the streets of a real 1881 silver mining town.

Rock-A-Hoola Waterpark, p215
Derelict waterpark with photographic appeal

Newberry Springs, p212
Classic cult cinema photo op

See Anti-Communist Art in the Desert, p214
Larger-than-life sculptures promoting democracy and freedom on the edge of town.

Joshua Tree

PREVIOUS STOP Leave Topock, Arizona, by taking I-40 across the Colorado River and into California.

Needles

As you cross the Colorado River into California, take Exit 153 toward Park Moabi Rd/Historic Route 66 and double back toward the river to view a Route 66 icon: the **Trails Arch Bridge**. Completed in 1916, it was the longest arch bridge in the US until 1928 and the original Route 66 river crossing until 1947. This gorgeous stretch featured in *The Grapes of Wrath* (1940).

Back on I-40, it's around 10 miles to Exit 142, which will get you into **Needles**. Take a right onto J St and drive for about three blocks until you reach the T-junction with Front St. In front of you is **Rotary Park**, a small roadside stretch with a decommissioned red caboose and a couple of train cars. The park's star attraction is **Rocky the Route 66 Snake**, a community-created sculpture made of hundreds of painted rocks. Visitors are encouraged to add a painted rock to help Rocky grow.

From here, you're just a block away from **El Garces**, an early-20th-century train depot. If you want to peek inside, contact the **Needles Regional Museum**, just across the street *(needlesregionalmuseum.org; closed summer)*.

Goffs Schoolhouse

Leaving Needles, follow I-40 west to CR 66/Goffs Rd through a barren stretch of desert. You won't find any gas or convenience stores along here; what you can expect is plenty of train tracks and possible delays at crossings.

About 16 miles along Goffs Rd, you'll reach **Goffs Schoolhouse** *(themojaveroad.org; 9am-4pm Fri-Sun)*, a one-room schoolhouse dating from 1914 that has been transformed into a robust museum featuring a hodgepodge of Mojave Desert–related history exhibits and Route 66 ephemera. Explore the sandy outdoor museum surrounding the schoolhouse, which preserves the rusty remains of the tiny railway and ranching community of **Goffs**. Highlights include an old cemetery and a wooden replica of nearby Fort Piute. Loaner guides are stored inside a metal replica of the schoolhouse, a few steps from the entrance.

Amboy

Route 66 continues south from Goffs to **Fenner**, where it intersects with I-40. This stretch is sometimes closed due to road damage from floods. If you see a 'road closed' sign, take I-40 west to Exit 78 and then head south along Kelbaker Rd, which connects to the old route (just east of Amboy) after 11.5 miles. If the road *is* open, you can take it south into vast, and often eerily empty, expanses of desert, passing deteriorating remnants of the route's heyday.

One such ruin is the **Road Runner's Retreat**, 1.7 miles west of Chambless. The 30ft sign at this Googie-style restaurant and service station makes for a great photo stop; at the time of research, volunteers were working on restoring the sign to its former neon-illuminated glory.

Needles • — *30 miles* — • Goffs Schoolhouse

Coast through expansive desert landscapes   *Check for road closures*

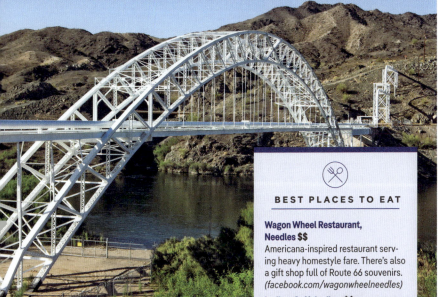

Old Trails Arch, between Topock, AZ, and Needles, CA

The next town over is **Amboy**, once a thriving Route 66 boomtown. These days, the town is mostly abandoned, but you can still stop at **Roy's Motel & Café** *(visitamboy.com)* for fuel and snacks. Area photo ops include a trifecta of murals painted by highway artist John Cerney, an old painted car and the derelict remains of **St Raymond's Church**.

A 2-mile drive west of Amboy leads to the turnoff for **Amboy Crater**, a 250ft-high cinder cone that juts out from a lava field. A moderately challenging trail leads to the center; the 4-mile hike takes most people two to three hours (round-trip) and is best avoided during the sweltering summer.

BEST PLACES TO EAT

Wagon Wheel Restaurant, Needles $$
Americana-inspired restaurant serving heavy homestyle fare. There's also a gift shop full of Route 66 souvenirs. *(facebook.com/wagonwheelneedles)*

Ludlow Café, Ludlow $$
Old-school Route 66 roadside cafe with hot breakfasts in the morning and burgers, sandwiches and salads for lunch and dinner. *(68315 National Trails Hwy)*

EddieWorld, Yermo $
Detouring off the old Route 66, a two-story cupcake beckons travelers to California's self-proclaimed largest gas station, where you'll find three fast-casual joints serving pizza, ice cream and sushi. *(eddieworld.com)*

Barstow Station, Barstow $
Unabashedly kitschy roadside stop with an assortment of fast-food favorites, including a McDonald's modeled after a fake train station. *(1611 E Main St)*

57 miles — Amboy

Hike to the rim of Amboy Crater

Along the Way We Met...

LAURA MISAJET I love our mission: to collect and preserve the history of the east Mojave Desert. We publish books about the history of the East Mojave Desert...and we take groups to see old mine sites and petroglyph sites in what is now the Mojave National Preserve. We also help maintain the old Mojave Road, which is a famous east–west route that came through what is now the preserve, and the East Mojave Heritage Trails. *Laura is the Director of Museum Operations & Public Outreach at the Mojave Desert Heritage and Cultural Association (themojaveroad.org), the nonprofit organization that maintains the Goff's Schoolhouse property.*

LAURA'S TIP: *There are sections of Route 66 where bridges have been washed out, so check road closures before you set out.*

DETOUR: Joshua Tree National Park

Known for its ethereal desert landscapes dotted with bulbous rock formations – as well as its eponymous Joshua trees – this sprawling **national park** (right) is one of the more unusual in the US. Located where the Mojave and Colorado Desert ecosystems intersect, it's a worthwhile detour 53 miles (around one hour) out of Amboy, particularly for hikers and rock climbers. It's also an International Dark Sky Park, so you can expect excellent stargazing opportunities.

Newberry Springs

From the Amboy Crater, it's a 60-mile drive along Route 66 to **Newberry Springs**, the site of a popular Mother Road photo op: the **Bagdad Cafe** (*bagdad-cafe-usa.com*). This

Continues on page 215

BEST PLACES TO SLEEP

Hampton Inn, Needles $$
Comfortable, central chain hotel with free breakfast. (*hilton.com/en/hotels/eedithx-hampton-needles*)

Calico Ghost Town Campground $
County-managed ghost town with climate-controlled cabins, plus RV camping with and without hookups. BYO bed linens. (*sbcountyparks.com*)

Route 66 Motel, Barstow $
Simple roadside motel with on-point branding and air-conditioned rooms. (*route66-motel.com*)

---

60 miles   **Newberry Springs**

 Head off-track at Joshua Tree National Park

 Stop for a photo op at the Bagdad Cafe

Explore Joshua Tree National Park

Named for the Joshua trees *(Yucca brevifolia)* that dot its boulder-strewn landscapes, otherworldly Joshua Tree National Park merits a detour for its scenery alone.

HOW TO

Nearest stop: Amboy

Getting here: Turn south on Amboy Rd and follow the signs to the city of Twentynine Palms on the northern edge of the park.

When to go: Fall and spring are the ideal times to visit, with pleasantly warm temperatures and cool nights, perfect for stargazing. Summers can be oppressively hot.

More info: *nps.gov/jotr*

Get your bearings (and fill your water bottle) at the **Visitor Center** *(6554 Park Blvd; 7:30am-5pm)* before heading into the park. If you're fond of botany, head straight to the **Cholla Cactus Garden**, 12 miles from the north entrance, where a quarter-mile boardwalk leads into a natural garden full of hedgehog and beavertail cacti, purple desert lavender and teddy bear cholla.

Then head northwest along Pinto Basin Rd until you reach the **Arch Rock Nature Trail**, a 1.4-mile lollipop trail that leads past a few curiously shaped rock formations. Drive north to Park Blvd and take a left, driving until you reach the 0.4-mile **Cap Rock Nature Trail**, which leads past stands of Joshua trees, or continue north to the **Barker Dam Trail**, a flat 1.1-mile loop that passes by an ancient rock art site. If you continue up Park Blvd instead, you'll soon reach **Hemingway Buttress**, a climber favorite featuring gorgeous rock formations fronted by Joshua trees.

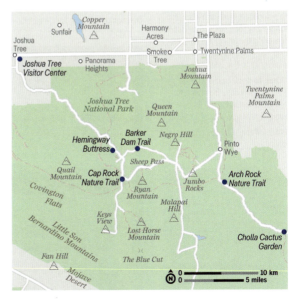

See Anti-Communist Art in the Desert

With its larger-than-life sculptures that all share a common theme – opposition to the Chinese Communist Party – Liberty Sculpture Park is perhaps the most surprising roadside attraction in the area.

Nearest stop: Yermo

Getting here: The park's entrance is at 37570 Yermo Rd, the main thoroughfare through Yermo. A long dusty road flanked by banners featuring the images of famous anti-communists leads from the main gate to the sculpture area.

When to go: Liberty Sculpture Park is open daily from 9am to 8pm, but the light is at its best around sunset.

More info: *en.libertysculpturepark.com*

If you love large-scale art installations and hate communism, Yermo's **Liberty Sculpture Park** might be for you. Stretching for nearly 40 acres, and touting itself as the 'world's largest sculpture park dedicated to the themes of fighting for democracy and freedom and opposing communist tyranny,' this sandy roadside expanse showcases over a dozen massive sculptures erected in honor of the victims of historic events (most notably the Tiananmen Square Massacre) as well as those who have been imprisoned or tortured under communist governments.

You can drive through the park or wander around. While there doesn't seem to be much order in how the sculptures are positioned, all are well signposted.

Sculptures in the park include a pyramid of skulls topped with a giant red hammer-and-sickle symbol and a massive relief depicting the 1989 events at Tiananmen Square. The nonprofit park was founded by Chinese-New Zealander sculptor Weiming Chen, who also serves as its lead artist.

MARGOT BIGG

Liberty Sculpture Park

roadside eatery served as the main shooting locale of the 1987 cult film of the same name, and draws in movie buffs from around the world who sign their names on its chestnut exterior.

DETOUR: Rock-A-Hoola Waterpark

From Newberry Springs, continue west along Route 66 to Barstow via the tiny town of Dagget, or leave old Route 66 and head north for 15 miles until you reach one of the region's quirkiest roadside attractions: the heavily graffitied remains of **Rock-A-Hoola Waterpark** (previously known as Lake Dolores Waterpark – plug 'Dolores Lake' into your GPS). The attraction first opened in the 1960s, when waterparks were still a novelty, and went through a few ownership changes and relaunches until the early noughties, when it was finally shut down and left for ruin. These days, it's primarily the domain of daring skaters and graffiti artists, whose colorful art can be seen across derelict buildings, pools and on the shallow walls of what was once a lazy river.

Vintage railroad car, Western America Railroad Museum, Barstow

Yermo

About a 10-mile drive southwest of the Rock-A-Hoola Waterpark along Yermo Rd is the town of **Yermo**, where the Mexican-inspired fast-food chain Del Taco was founded in 1964. You can stop for a photo at the **Original Del Taco** *(38434 E Yermo Rd; $)*, but be aware that it's now a burger joint.

Just down the road, **Thrift-N-More** *(457 W Yermo Rd; closed Sun)* is a good place to hunt for cheap vintage home decor. Another mile west leads to the **Liberty Sculpture Park** (left).

From Yermo, it's around a 4-mile drive north to the **Calico Ghost Town Regional Park** (p216), a 19th-century ghost town that's been transformed into an impeccably preserved county-run park.

Barstow

I-15, I-40 and CR 66 converge in **Barstow**, the first proper city in miles, driving east to west. It's also the first place you're likely to get decent deals on gas (by California standards) after miles of price gouging at the pumps. Barstow is the land of budget hotels and fast-food chains, as well as the site of the **Historic Harvey House** *(685 N 1st Ave)*, a 1911 train depot that currently houses an Amtrak station and the **Western America Railroad Museum** *(barstowrailmuseums.com; Fri-Sun)*. Until 2024, the building also housed the Route 66 Mother Road Museum, now closed after a 24-year run.

Take a detour past Rock-A-Hoola Waterpark

Channel Your Inner Miner at a Historic Ghost Town

Head to the hills above Yermo to see one of the best-preserved ghost towns in California, complete with Wild West attractions, a 19th-century mine and – for those who dare – a campground.

HOW TO

Getting here: Calico Ghost Town is about 4 miles north of I-15 in Yermo. Parking is in a dusty lot just beyond a pay booth.

When to go: Open daily throughout the year, except Christmas. The best weather is in spring and fall; summers can be hot and crowded.

Cost: Adults $8, children four to 11 $5, kids under three free

More info: parks.sbcounty.gov/park/calico-ghost-town-regional-park

Tip: While the main road through town is wheelchair-accessible, some of the older structures are not accessible.

The History

At first glance, **Calico Ghost Town** has the look and feel of an Old West theme park, but it's very much the real deal. The city was founded in 1881 as a silver-mining settlement, but its life was cut short the following decade, when the value of silver plummeted. Calico was abandoned soon after and remained as such until the 1950s, when Walter Knott, a boysenberry mogul who's best known as the mastermind behind the Knott's Berry Farm theme park near LA, bought the old town and restored many of its old buildings (and built a number of replicas), transforming Calico from a derelict ruin into a family-friendly attraction that's both educational and delightfully hokey.

A Walk Through Town

Most of Calico's attractions are housed in clapboard and stucco structures that line a half-mile-long road that runs uphill from the parking area.

Begin your journey at the visitor center, to the left of the entrance, where you can see a few photos of the town in its heyday. From here, head into the town – you'll quickly notice that a majority of the old structures have been transformed into gift shops selling everything from moccasins to Route 66 merch, many with souvenir penny presses and Wild West adaptions of

CHEEKY CHUKARS

One of the first things most visitors to Calico notice is the abundance of chukars, a type of striped pheasant that waddles about Calico in droves. These striped birds, which are native to Asia, were not around during Calico's mining heyday – rather, they were imported from India in 1928 and released into the California wild a few years later. These days, the cute and harmless critters are very much part of the Calico community; while you shouldn't feed them, chukars certainly make great photo subjects.

Left: Streetscape, Calico; Below: Calico Cemetery

animatronic Zoltar fortune tellers machines. There's also a **photo studio** where visitors can dress up in 19th-century cowpoke finery and get sepia-hued souvenir prints, as well as several restaurants and cafes.

While much of Calico feels designed to separate you from your money, it's also full of treats for history fans, including a replica schoolhouse, two museums and a subterranean mine that some say is haunted. There's a rustic **cemetery** to the left of the entrance, where the bodies of many Calico residents were interred, as well as a **campground** (p212) where daring souls can spend the night.

INSIGHT

Finding Freedom on the Open Road

What happens when an explorer can't explore? That's the existential question Andrew Bender faced when the COVID-19 pandemic struck. A few months and 7800 miles later, he found salvation on the open road.

WORDS BY **ANDREW BENDER**

Los Angeles–based Andrew Bender has spent more than two decades covering California for Lonely Planet.

FIRST, LET'S ACKNOWLEDGE that I've been lucky. Since my first assignment for Lonely Planet in 2001, covering the far corners of eastern Germany, I've been exploring the world for guidebooks: 40 days and 40 nights above the Arctic Circle in Norway, cycling (and cycling and cycling) the canals of Amsterdam, attempting to learn the Way of Zen with priests in Kyoto, stepping back in time in rural Korea, brushing elbows with the yacht set on Nantucket, plumbing the big city bustle of Taipei, and venturing up and down my home state of California. Each adventure added another shiny coin to my soul bank.

Even the COVID-19 pandemic could have been much worse. Sure, I was stuck, but I was stuck in *Santa Monica* – the Promised Land at the end of Route 66, replete with an expansive beach for social distancing, an endless ocean for contemplating and palm-lined neighborhoods for wandering beneath tangerine sunsets. I taught myself to bake scones and hem the pajamas that had needed it for years.

But coming home alone to the same four walls – day in, day out, night in, night out for months – began to take its toll.

In June 2020, I finally hit on it: if I was going to be by myself within four walls, they might as well be the walls of a car.

The Last Six Project

I set myself a mission: to visit the handful of US states that had thus far eluded me. I called

Open road, South Dakota

it the 'Last Six Project'. I rented an SUV, laid a camping mattress in the back, stocked up on masks, hand sanitizer, granola bars, a box of wine and the guitar I hoped to eventually learn, and headed north.

I rolled through the first four states, ticking them off The Last Six and finding something special in each:

State 1: Idaho. The under-visited, aptly named Craters of the Moon National Park mirrored the desolation I was feeling. Yet, rambling undeterred in its hills, vents and caves imparted hope.

State 2: Montana. Sitting on a stone in the middle of a glassy lake in Glacier National Park, I meditated upon a craggy mountain face.

State 3: Wyoming. Yellowstone. Bison traffic jams. Painted pools echoing infinity. Lightning crackling over Devil's Tower.

State 4: North Dakota. Land of Unexpected Kindnesses, where complete strangers paid for my dinners and morning coffee and swore the servers to secrecy.

Where Had I Been?

Finally, just before July 4, Independence Day, I arrived in **State 5: South Dakota**, where the reason for the entire trip finally clarified – a reason I had never anticipated. After visiting the must-dos – hiking the Badlands, eating/gawking at Wall Drug, marveling at expanses of prairie and gaping at Mt Rushmore – in a small town in the Black Hills I wandered into a gallery specializing in art by the Lakota people. There, a Lakota archaeologist held court, explaining the iconography embedded in these pieces, and the philosophy behind them: we are one with the Earth, and the Earth is one with us. There's nothing we truly own – it all belongs to nature. And no matter our background, faith, income or education, we're all trying to get to the same place.

It sounded cosmically familiar: virtually word for word the sentiment I'd heard from the Zen priest in Kyoto. That's when it hit me: I'd spent decades wandering the world, when all along the same universal truths were right here, from the original inhabitants of my own heartland.

But coming home alone to the same four walls – day in, day out, night in, night out for months – began to take its toll. In June 2020, I finally hit on it: if I was going to be by myself within four walls, they might as well be the walls of a car.

Later, driving across South Dakota's vast, open spaces, after one of those pounding, only-on-the-plains rainstorms that render windshield wipers useless, a perfect arc of a rainbow framed the road before me as if in confirmation.

Heading Home

By the time I got to **State 6: Kansas**, my homeland felt different to me – or I felt different in it. Surrounded by the simplicity of the Tallgrass Prairie National Preserve, in that moment nothing was more important than feeling the wave of the greens and yellows on the ground or imagining myself above in the boundless azure punctuated by rolling puffs of white. I was at peace.

A month after I left, I returned to my home at the end of the Mother Road, bopping my head and singing as I passed through each town: 'Flagstaff, Arizona, don't forget Winona, Kingman, Barstow, Saaaaaaan Bernardino!' The pandemic was far from over, but finding this one, essential truth was worth the whole journey. I had returned a stronger man.

Barstow

CALIFORNIA

The sparse landscapes of southeastern California quickly fade into SoCal suburbia on this final stretch of Route 66. Leave the big wide open behind you and inch closer to Santa Monica, where the route terminates. While it can be tempting to race through the final few miles of the Mother Road, this is a marathon, not a sprint. Slow down and take in the scenery – the finish line is mere miles away.

Margot Bigg

Elmer's Bottle Tree Ranch, Oro Grande
DONVICTORIO/SHUTTERSTOCK

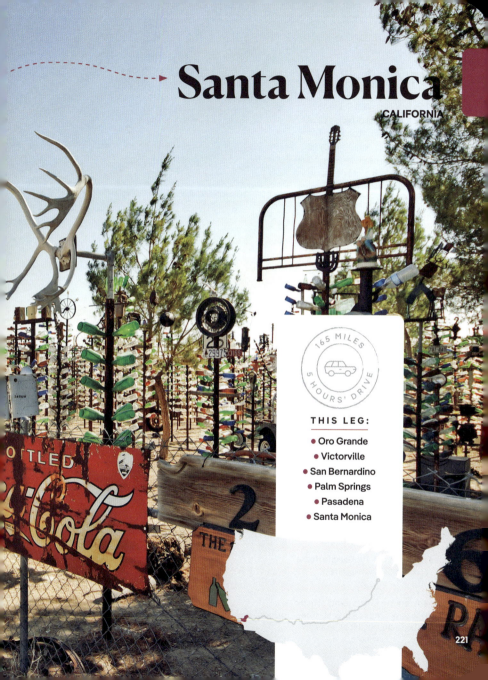

Santa Monica
CALIFORNIA

165 MILES
5 HOURS' DRIVE

THIS LEG:
- Oro Grande
- Victorville
- San Bernardino
- Palm Springs
- Pasadena
- Santa Monica

Driving Notes

This final section of Route 66 is where the last bits of barren desert give way to the urban sprawl of Los Angeles County. You may hit traffic once you head west out of San Bernardino, which might get worse as you get closer to the end of the route in Santa Monica. Try to resist the temptation to jump on the freeway.

Breaking Your Journey

Victorville is a decent place to stretch your legs and grab a bite, but it's not the prettiest place. San Bernardino and Pasadena – the two largest cities on this stretch – are better options for an overnight stay. Each has plenty of places to eat and sleep, but Pasadena is more charming (with the hotel prices to show for it).

Margot's Tips

BEST MEAL The Soul Bowl at **Native Foods** in Palm Springs (p227)

FAVORITE VIEW The technicolor sunset over the Pacific Ocean in **Santa Monica** (p230)

ESSENTIAL STOP The **Gamble House** (p228) in Pasadena

ROAD-TRIP TIP Expect plenty of traffic on the drive across LA to Santa Monica. Don't attempt this on an empty stomach.

CALIFORNIA

The Road to Santa Monica, p228
The final (or first!) stretch

Pasadena, p228
Mid-century Americana awaits

END — Santa Monica

Los Angeles

Watch the Sunset in Santa Monica, p230
Pick up your completion certificate and head to the pier to celebrate your incredible journey.

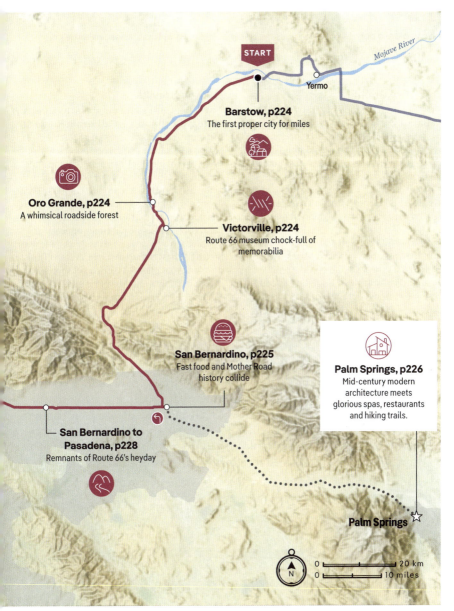

PREVIOUS STOP Main St becomes the National Trails Hwy in Barstow, leading away from suburban sprawl and into the quiet of the desert.

Oro Grande

Hop on the National Trails Hwy (CR 66) in **Barstow** and continue for roughly 25 miles, past the town of Helendale. To your right, you'll see the **Sage Brush Inn**, an old stone structure made of rugged stacked stones – it's rumored to have once been a roadside brothel.

From here, it's just under a mile to **Oro Grande** and **Elmer's Bottle Tree Ranch** (the bottletreeranch.com), a magnificent installation made up of 'bottle trees,' metal frames adorned with colorful beer and soda pop bottles that give the appearance of glass leaves. When the wind passes through, the bottles tremble ever so slightly, resulting in a jingling sound that resounds throughout the roadside 'forest.'

Victorville

Continue south for about 10 miles to **Victorville** to visit the **California Route 66 Museum** (califrt66museum.org; 16825 D St), a 45,000-sq-ft gallery that's chock-full of seemingly every type of Mother Road memorabilia under the sun, from road sign–inspired fairy lights to vintage signboards. A reproduction 1950s-style diner, old Phillips 66® gas pumps and a ramshackle wooden outhouse (not intended for guest use!) add to the old-timey appeal.

Visitors are invited to pose inside a hippie-decorated VW bus (enthusiastic volunteers will insist on taking your photo). There's a gift shop selling souvenir T-shirts and ice-cold bottles of syrupy Route 66 soda pop. If you're feeling peckish, head

Along the Way We Saw...

MILITARY TANKS While I expected to see plenty of roadside oddities during my Route 66 drive, I certainly didn't anticipate seeing an ultra-long train zooming through the sandy desert, carrying what appeared to be well over 100 military tanks, as I did one early weekday morning. It was an alarming and fascinating sight, but apparently not unusual. I would later learn that people often spot trains full of tanks traveling through Southern California. The tanks are typically destined for area training centers or coastal ports.

TIP: *You never know just what you'll see in the desert: keep your phone or camera handy.*

Margot Bigg

Barstow — 32 miles — Oro Grande — 5 miles

Wander the glass roadside forest

Emma Jean's Holland Burger Café, Victorville

north up D St for 2 miles until you reach **Emma Jean's Holland Burger Café** (right), a historic diner that's been serving up hearty breakfast favorites – and burgers – since 1947.

 ### San Bernardino

The sprawling city of **San Bernardino** was once a major stopover on Route 66 and makes a good place to take a break. Don't miss the **Historic Site of the Original McDonald's** *(1398 N E St)*, situated where Dick and Mac McDonald first went into business, back in 1937. Today it's a museum full of collectibles, from old restaurant ashtrays to vintage Happy Meal toys.

Continues on page 228

BEST PLACES TO EAT

Emma Jean's Holland Burger Café, Victorville $
Classic old-timey diner focused on breakfasts, burgers and hand-spun milkshakes. *(hollandburger.com)*

Mitla Café, San Bernardino $$
A Mother Road institution that's been serving hearty American breakfasts and massive Mexican combo plates since 1937. *(mitlacafesb.com)*

Russell's, Pasadena $$
American diner food meets French-inspired treats at this Pasadena favorite, which has been operating since 1930. *(30 N Fair Oaks Ave)*

Mel's Drive-In, Santa Monica $$
Ring the 'route-completed' bell when you arrive at this end-of-the-route institution, where the menu features everything from vegan burgers to turkey dinners. *(melsdrive-in.com)*

Victorville — *41 miles* — San Bernardino

Explore the California Route 66 Museum

Explore Palm Springs

The 1950s aesthetic is very much alive in Palm Springs, and nowhere else will you see so much mid-century modern architecture in one place. However, Palm Springs is more than just pretty buildings. Its glorious spas, restaurants and hiking trails make it an ideal place to break your journey, whether for a few hours or a few days.

HOW TO

Getting there: Take I-10 E to the CA-111 (Exit 111). Continue for around 10 miles to downtown Palm Springs.

Getting around: Parking is plentiful in Palm Springs, so it's easy to get around by car. If you'd rather explore on two wheels, bike lanes are abundant and rentals are widely available (and some hotels loan bikes).

Sleeping: The Palm Springs area has plenty of overnight options, from **The Skylark** (theskylark.com; $), a 1950s hotel that retains much of its mid-century charm, to the ultra-colorful **Saguaro** (thesaguaro.com; $$). Most of the area's swankiest digs are in neighboring Rancho Mirage, including the ultra-luxe **Ritz-Carlton, Rancho Mirage** (ritzcarlton.com; $$$).

More info: Palm Springs Visitors Center (visitpalmsprings.com; 2901 N Palm Canyon Dr)

Immerse Yourself in Art

Modern and contemporary art are the big focus at **Palm Springs Art Museum** (psmuseum.org; $20), but it also has a solid collection of Mesoamerican pieces on display. Don't miss the museum's **Faye Sarkowsky Sculpture Garden**, which showcases 14 outdoor sculptures in a 4-acre expanse. To see local artists in action, head to the **Backstreet Art District** (backstreetartdistrict.com; 2600 S Cherokee Way). Art walks with studio visits take place on the first Wednesday of the month.

Take a Hike

On the lands of the Agua Caliente Band of Cahuilla Indians, the **Tahquitz Canyon Trail** is a short but strenuous hike that covers 1.8 rocky miles with 350ft of elevation gain. For something more relaxed, head 4 miles south to the **Andreas Canyon Trail**, an easy 1.2-mile loop that leads past pretty rock formations. For a high-elevation alternative, take the **Palm Springs Aerial Tramway** (pstramway.com) up to **Mt San Jacinto State Park**, where 50 miles of hiking trails await.

Pamper Yourself

Wrap up a day of hiking – or just treat yourself to a little bit of self-care – at the much-lauded **Spa at Séc-he** (thespaatseche.com), which offers mineral springs baths along with high-end facials, body scrubs, cryotherapy and flotation tanks. For a spa experience with a touch of mid-century Hollywood flair,

EATING OUT

Palm Springs favorites include **Rooster and the Pig** (roosterandthepig.com; 356 S Indian Canyon Dr; $$), which fuses American and Vietnamese flavors, and **Farm** (farmpalmsprings.com; 6 La Plaza; $$), beloved for its French-style breakfasts. For a plant-based treat, head to the flagship location of **Native Foods** (nativefoods.com; 1775 E Palm Canyon Dr; $), which dishes up vegan sandwiches, burgers and more, or make your way to **Chef Tanya's Kitchen** (cheftanyaskitchen.com; 706 S Eugene Rd; $$).

Palm Springs Art Museum

book a package at **L'Horizon Resort and Spa** (lhorizonpalmsprings.com).

Party on Arenas Road

Palm Springs has a huge LGBTIQ+ community, and has long been a popular vacation destination for gay men. All are welcome at the city's gay bars and clubs, the bulk of which are on downtown's Arenas Rd. Must-visits include casual **Streetbar** (psstreetbar.com), the oldest gay bar in town, and **Toucans Tiki Lounge** (toucanstikilounge.com), known for its solid lineup of drag shows.

From here, it's about a 2-mile drive to the hearty Mexican meals at **Mitla Café** (p225), a classic Route 66 stop since 1937, and a 5.5-mile drive to the local **Wigwam Motel** (right), which sits right on the Mother Road.

DETOUR: Palm Springs

While Route 66 has its share of great buildings, nowhere does mid-century modern architecture better than **Palm Springs**, 54 miles southwest of San Bernardino. The sunny city – an old favorite among Hollywood stars, artists and members of the LGBTIQ+ community – is equally loved for its arts and culinary scenes and its easy access to swanky golf courses and desert hiking trails. While many motorists combine a visit to Palm Springs with a trip to **Joshua Tree National Park** (p213), it's also an easy 50-minute drive to get to the city on a detour from San Bernardino via I-10.

San Bernardino to Pasadena

From San Bernardino, head east along W Foothill Blvd for 18 miles until you reach the **Cucamonga Service Station** (cucamongaservicestation.net; 9670 Foothill Blvd; closed Mon-Wed). It was built in 1915, making it one of the few remaining structures on the route that predates the Mother Road. The service station was restored and converted into a museum a century later and now showcases a small collection of Route 66 and fuel-related objects.

An 8-mile drive west leads to the **California Botanical Garden** (calbg.org; 1500 N College Ave, Claremont), an 86-acre estate devoted to the native plants of California. From here, it's a 20-mile drive to the **Aztec Hotel** (301 W Foothill Blvd, Monrovia), a Mayan (not Aztec) Revival National Historic Landmark dating to 1924. Although there are a few storefronts on the front of the building, the hotel itself has been closed to the public since 2012. However, you can still catch a glimpse of the lobby if you peek through the windows on the main door.

Pasadena

Continue west for another 10 miles and you'll be in historic **Pasadena**. Don't miss the **Gamble House** (gamblehouse.org; 4 Westmoreland Pl; tours Tue, Thu-Sun), a gorgeous mansion built in the American arts-and-crafts style. The historic home is known for both its stained-glass interiors and for its role as Doc Brown's house in the 1985 film *Back to the Future*.

From here, it's a 3-mile drive south to the **Fair Oaks Pharmacy and Soda Fountain** (fairoakspharmacy.net; 1526 Mission St), which has been in business since 1915. Stop in for an ice-cream sundae or a Coke float, or try a 'phosphate' – a traditional soda fountain drink made of carbonated water, syrup and a tangy splash of phosphoric acid. The pharmacy also has a large gift shop full of candies and toys that were popular in the 1950s and '60s along with plenty of Americana-inspired gifts.

The Road to Santa Monica

While parts of Route 66 in **Los Angeles** (p232) are no longer intact, you can still follow much of the route through the city. But first, head west for about 3 miles to **Galco's Old Town Grocery** (sodapopstop.com; 5702 York Blvd), a century-old grocery store selling seemingly every type of soda pop ever made. A 'soda creation station' at the back of the store allows you to DIY your own fizzy drinks by mixing syrups with carbonated water. There's even a hand-operated bottle-cap sealer.

Then drive a quarter-mile to the weirdly wonderful **Chicken Boy** *(5558 N Figueroa St)*, a 22ft statue of a man with the head of a chicken that's evolved into one of LA's most loved landmarks. From here, head west to Santa Monica Blvd to rejoin the old route. A good place to break up the journey – and use the restrooms – is the **Hollywood Forever Cemetery** *(hollywoodforever. com)*, the final resting place of celebs ranging from Judy Garland to Chris Cornell. Don't miss the small Thai-style plot near the front, with its mosaiced monuments and its ostentation of resident peacocks.

Get back on Santa Monica Blvd, continuing through West Hollywood and Beverly Hills. After around 12 miles, you'll reach **Santa Monica** (p230), where Route 66 terminates.

BEST PLACES TO SLEEP

Wigwam Motel, San Bernardino $
One of the few surviving Wigwam Motels on Route 66, featuring 19 tepee-shaped standalone rooms plus a small pool. *(wigwammotel.com)*

Astro Pasadena Hotel, Pasadena $$
Roadside motel with 25 rooms furnished with retro interiors that go heavy on red and black hues; all come with microwaves and mini-fridges. *(astropasadenahotel.xyz)*

Pasadena Hotel & Pool, Pasadena $$
Historic 161-room property dating to 1926, with plenty of vintage charm to show for it. *(pasadenahotel.com)*

The Georgian Hotel, Santa Monica $$$
Ultra-luxe art deco property with Golden Age vibes, gorgeous rooms – some with ocean views – and a historic speakeasy. *(thegeorgian.com)*

Chicken Boy, Highland Park

EXPERIENCE ★

Watch the Sunset in Santa Monica

The final stop on Route 66, Santa Monica is a lively place to get your kicks, whether on the ride-filled pier or on the sandy shores of the Pacific Ocean.

HOW TO

Getting here: Your best bet is to drive to Santa Monica, park near the pier, and then explore on foot. Many downtown public parking structures – including the structure at 1433 2nd St – offer free parking for the first 90 minutes.

When to go: Arrive before dusk so that you can see one of Santa Monica's famously beautiful sunsets.

More info: Santa Monica Visitor Information Center *(santamonica. com; 2427 Main St)*. There's also a smaller visitor center in the same building as the Santa Monica Pier Carousel and a visitor information kiosk on Ocean Ave, next to Palisades Park. All three offer free certificates of completion to visitors who have traveled the length of Route 66.

The End of the Trail

You've made it to Santa Monica and are likely ready to complete your Route 66 journey by heading to the official end point. There's just one issue: there are three possible route ends. The most thorough approach is to visit all three.

The first (and most historically accurate) end of the route is where Lincoln and Olympic Blvds intersect; look up on the street posts to see signs marking the route's beginning and end. This is also the site of **Mel's Drive-In** (p225), a classic American diner that looks like it was plucked straight from the 1950s – some tables even have their own jukeboxes. Celebrate the end of your journey with a meal or a shake. Bonus: there's free and ample parking in the back.

From here, you're just a few minutes' drive to the intersection of Santa Monica Blvd and Ocean Ave, the second alleged end of the road. While there's little evidence to substantiate this claim (beyond a plaque dedicating the route as the Will Rogers Hwy), there is a **visitor kiosk** where you can pick up your official Route 66 completion certificate.

From here, head to the **Santa Monica Pier**, the third and final stopping point, complete with an end-of-the-route sign that's popular for selfies.

Down at the Pier

Santa Monica's most recognizable feature is its pier, thanks to

KAROLIS KAVOLELIS/SHUTTERSTOCK

HIT THE BEACH

Santa Monica's 3.5-mile stretch of sandy coastline is split into two sections: the area north of the pier and the section to the south. Northside highlights include the accessible, sensory play-focused **North Beach Playground** and the **Annenberg Community Beach House** *(adult/child $10/4)*, which features a pool, a splash pad and volleyball courts. South of the pier is the **Original Muscle Beach**, a free community workout area that's been attracting bodybuilders and gymnasts since it opened in the 1930.

EXPERIENCE

Santa Monica Pier

a massive solar-powered Ferris wheel that towers over a mix of carnival rides and games, food vendors and souvenir kiosks (including a couple of Route 66–themed vendors). Even if you aren't fond of amusement parks, or aren't dying to snap a photo at the end-of-the-route sign, it's worth dropping by to watch street performers in action. While the pier is generally noisy, things are a tad quieter at the westernmost part, where a few fishing platforms that have been used since the turn of the 20th century look over the Pacific.

CITY GUIDE:
Los Angeles

You've made it to the end of Route 66, and you've picked up your certificate and watched the sunset from the Santa Monica Pier – now what? Spend time exploring LA: glamorous, tawdry, frenetic, serene and full of world-class art, architecture, beaches, mountains, shopping and world cuisines.

WORDS BY **ANDREW BENDER**
Los Angeles–based Andrew Bender has spent more than two decades covering California

Arriving
For most drivers, LA is the end of Route 66 rather than the beginning, but to go the opposite way, here are some tips for beginning your journey.
Plane LA's main gateway is **Los Angeles International Airport** *(LAX, flylax.com)*. There are other regional airports (Hollywood/Burbank, Long Beach and Orange County), but LAX is the closest to the end (or start) of Route 66. All major car-rental agencies have LAX locations, and plenty of airport-area hotels make it easy to bed down before your journey. With a little more time and money, Santa Monica (p230) is a more charming stay at the end of the Mother Road.
Train Amtrak trains arrive at the Spanish Colonial **Union Station** *(unionstationla.com)* at Downtown LA's eastern edge. Connect to LA's Metro subway beneath the station.

HOW MUCH FOR A

Martini at Mama Shelter $17

Sandwich at Eggslut $10

Warner Bros Studio Tour $73

Getting Around
Driving As you approach on Route 66, LA's gravitational pull creates a more urban streetscape. To forge headlong into the LA scene, follow the route to Hollywood or West Hollywood.
Public transportation Most public transportation is handled by **Metro** *(metro.net)*, including subway and light rail trains, and a network of buses and bike shares. Local municipalities also offer their own bus and bike shares, including **Santa Monica** *(bigbluebus.com)* and **Pasadena** *(cityofpasadena.net/pasadena-transit)*. Purchase or download a stored-value TAP Card, available at transit stations or in the Apple Wallet and valid on all local transit systems.
Metro fares The regular fare on LA Metro is $1.75, which covers transfers to other Metro transit for up to two hours. Transfers between Metro and municipal buses cost $0.50. Metro fares are capped at $5 per day or $18 per seven days when paid with the same TAP card.
Freeway phraseology What the rest of America calls highways, expressways or interstates, LA calls 'freeways.' (And yes, freeways are free to drive.) Elsewhere people put 'I' for 'interstate' before the freeway number ('I-10', for example) or no prefix at all, but to sound like a local in LA, use 'the' before the number ('the 10').

For schedules and trip planning, go to Metro.net.

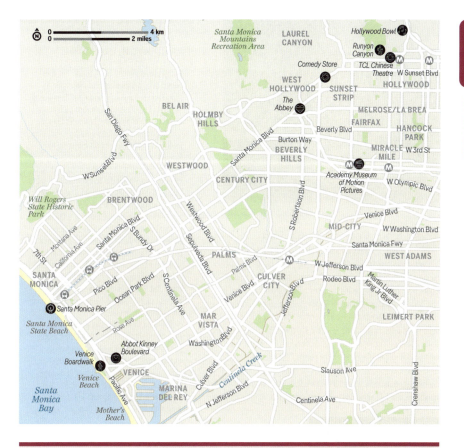

A DAY IN LOS ANGELES

Wake up easy with a coffee and a stroll, cycle or yoga class along the world-famous beachfront **boardwalk** in Venice and Santa Monica (p230). Browse street art and unique fashion along Venice's always-trendy **Abbot Kinney Boulevard**, and maybe ride **Santa Monica Pier**'s (p230) solar-powered Ferris wheel.

Explore the history and craft of filmmaking at the **Academy Museum** (p234), then continue north to gawk at the tourists gawking at the concrete hand- and footprints of screendom's biggest stars at the **TCL Chinese Theatre** (p235) in Hollywood. Extra time? Hike with the hardbodies in nearby **Runyon Canyon** (p237).

Spend a summer night with 17,499 of your besties at a concert at the **Hollywood Bowl** (p235), or head to West Hollywood to party the night away at clubs like the **Comedy Store**, or the legendary LGBTIQ+ bar **The Abbey**.

Universal Studios Hollywood

 ### Lights, Camera, Studio Tour

While **Universal Studios Hollywood** (*universalstudioshollywood.com*) grabs the spotlight, the experience is more theme park than movie studio with rides taking center stage. Alternatively, the **Warner Bros Studio Tour** (*wbstudiotour.com*) offers a fun, (mostly) authentic look behind the scenes of a working film and TV studio. The two-hour tour route changes daily based on what's shooting, but you'll get selfie ops on recreated sets like *Friends* and *The Big Bang Theory,* and peruse props, sound design, costumes, a mind-blowing collection of Batmobiles and Harry Potter memorabilia.

POP CULTURE, MEET HIGH CULTURE

Frank Lloyd Wright once said, 'Tip the world over on its side and everything loose will land in Los Angeles.' The world capital of mass entertainment also boasts attractions to blow any brainiac's mind.

LA pop culture goes way beyond Hollywood. Boutiques on Melrose Ave have been outfitting generations of punks, skaters and cool kids. Anime and manga reign in **Little Tokyo** (around 1st and San Pedro Sts in DTLA). The **Venice Boardwalk** brims with skateboarders and sidewalk artists. Baseball's **Dodgers** (*mlb.com/dodgers*), football's **Rams** (*therams.com*) and basketball's **Lakers** (*nba.com/lakers*) are all iconic teams.

LA is also home to **CalTech** (*caltech.edu*), spawning dozens of Nobel laureates; **Jet Propulsion Laboratory** (*jpl.nasa.gov*), NASA's prime research center; and **UCLA** (*ucla.edu*). Beyond the museums of the Miracle Mile (below), the 110-acre **Getty Center** (*getty.edu*), the six million rare books of the **Huntington Library**, and the cutting-edge UCLA **Hammer Museum** (*hammer.ucla.edu*), all enrich LA culture, alongside performing arts like the **Los Angeles Philharmonic** (*laphil.org*).

 ### Miracle Mile Museums

East of the intersection of Wilshire Blvd and Fairfax Ave, LA's Miracle Mile is one-stop shopping for top museums. The **Academy Museum of Motion Pictures** (*academymuseum.org*) salutes showbiz with state-of-the-art exhibitions. The **Los Angeles County Museum of Art** (*lacma.org*) shows a breadth and depth of antiquity to modernity unparalleled in the Western US. Encounter the animal stars of *Ice Age* (or at least their fossils) at the **La Brea Tar Pits** (*tarpits.org*). And the **Petersen Automotive Museum** (*petersen.org*) is an awe-inspiring look at motorized transport from concept cars to movie vehicles.

1954 Ferrari 375 MM, Petersen Automotive Museum

Stroll the Stars on Hollywood Blvd

Unless you're here for the Oscars, don't expect any actual star-sightings in Hollywood; there's even some residual pandemic-era grit. But movie glamour is a powerful force, and it shines through.

HOW TO

Getting here: Take the Metro A Line subway to Hollywood & Highland Station.

Parking: Beneath **Ovation Hollywood** (ovationhollywood.com; 6801 Hollywood Blvd).

Getting around: Hollywood is pedestrian-friendly and generally flat. Hollywood Bowl shuttles (round-trip $6) connect from Ovation Hollywood on performance nights.

Tip: Carry lots of $1 bills for selfies with costumed performers on the Walk of Fame.

It's hard not to feel starstruck on the **Hollywood Walk of Fame** (walkoffame.com). Along the sidewalks, some 2600 pink marble stars salute entertainment industry luminaries, while the hand- and footprints of the biggest stars are cast in concrete outside the **TCL Chinese Theatre** (tclchinesetheatres.com; 6925 Hollywood Blvd). The engrossing **Hollywood Museum** (thehollywoodmuseum.com; 1660 N Highland Ave) is jam-packed with props and memorabilia.

Retro movie houses on the Walk of Fame are architectural and cinematic showplaces. Blockbusters reign at TCL Chinese Theatre, live preshows accompany Disney movie magic at the **El Capitan Theatre** (elcapitantheatre.com; 6838 Hollywood Blvd), and American Cinematheque screens classics at the **Egyptian Theatre** (americancinematheque.com; 6712 Hollywood Blvd).

Summer nights belong to the **Hollywood Bowl** (hollywoodbowl.com; 2301 N Highland Ave), the 17,500-seat natural amphitheater. Programming might include Rachmaninoff, reggae or singalong *The Sound of Music*.

EXPERIENCE

Above: Hollywood Bowl; Right: TCL Chinese Theatre

LEFT: JOSEPH SOHM/SHUTTERSTOCK. RIGHT: SERGII FIGURNYI/SHUTTERSTOCK

Where to Sleep

An LA stay isn't cheap, but, hey, you get what you pay for. After your journey, staying beachside makes sense. Santa Monica (p230) and Venice offer varied lodging options plus the bike path, cooler temperatures and Metro access. Beverly Hills is synonymous with luxury, and neighboring West Hollywood has shopping, nightlife and SoCal's top LGBTIQ+ scene. Hollywood and Downtown LA hotels serve cultural institutions and nightlife, but prepare for a grunge factor.

BEST PLACES TO SLEEP

Hotel Erwin $$$
Funkified retro lodging, steps from Venice Beach. Fantastic rooftop lounge. *(hotelerwin.com)*

Beverly Hills Hotel $$$
Hollywood history lives at the 'Pink Palace,' lap of luxury since 1912. *(dorchestercollection.com/los-angeles)*

Mama Shelter $$
Playful and quirky near the heart of Hollywood. *(mamashelter.com/los-angeles)*

Hotel Figueroa $$$
A 1926 Spanish colonial look, DTLA cool. *(hotelfigueroa.com)*

Where to Eat

Dine on world cuisines and hipster vittles in DTLA, power lunch in Beverly Hills or West Hollywood, soak up showbiz energy (and martinis) in Hollywood, or enjoy easy, breezy, beachy fare in Santa Monica and Venice. And, as any Angeleno will tell you, some of the city's best eats come from strip mall storefronts and food trucks.

LA'S CUISINE SCENE

Consider the LA street dog, a decadent concoction of a bacon-wrapped hot dog grilled on a steel plate together with bell pepper, onion and jalapeño, nestled on a bun (below right).

LA cuisine spans Michelin-starred extravaganzas and diverse cultures that have staked their claims to entire neighborhoods: Chinese cuisine in the San Gabriel Valley towns of Arcadia and Monterey Park, Koreatown (below left; Mid-City LA), Thai Town (East Hollywood), Boyle Heights (LA's Mexican heart, east of Downtown), West LA's 'Tehrangeles' for Persian, and Sawtelle Japantown, just for starters.

Sample fresh, seasonal California-grown produce at irresistible farmers markets in **Santa Monica** *(Wed, Sat & Sun)* and **Hollywood** *(8am-1pm Sat)*.

BEST PLACES TO EAT & DRINK

Musso & Frank Grill $$$
Has been slaking honchos with steaks since 1919. *(mussoandfrank.com)*

Grand Central Market $
DTLA's gourmet, beaux-arts food hall. *(grandcentralmarket.com)*

Butcher's Daughter $$
Airy and vegan-friendly on buzzy Abbot Kinney Blvd. *(thebutchersdaughter.com)*

Guisados $
LA's favorite tacos, with locations around town. *(guisados.la)*

Get Outdoors in Griffith Park

With the Hollywood Hills lined with hiking trails, it's no wonder Angelenos are avid hikers. Griffith Park is king among LA's parklands.

HOW TO

Getting here: Take the Metro A Line subway to Vermont/Sunset station. From here, DASH operates the Observatory/Los Feliz shuttle bus service to Griffith Observatory.

Parking: Arrive early or pray for luck to find free parking at the observatory or its approach streets. Otherwise, park by the Greek Theatre and hike up (about 10 minutes) or take the shuttle bus up and back.

Five times the size of New York's Central Park, **Griffith Park** *(laparks.org/griffithpark)* is LA's communal backyard. It's filled with more than 4300 mountainous acres and 50-plus miles of hiking trails, a zoo, museums and performance venues.

If time is limited, visit the **Griffith Observatory** *(griffithobservatory.org; 2800 E Observatory Rd)*. It offers commanding views from Mt Hollywood across the LA Basin, plus the Hollywood Sign and hiking trails that continue uphill for even grander views. By day, take in planetarium shows or, at night, look into the universe via massive telescopes.

For tastes less outdoorsy and more cultural, the park has you covered with the impressive collection at the **Autry Museum of the American West** *(theautry.org; 4700 Western Heritage Way)* or an outdoor show at the **Greek Theatre** *(lagreektheatre.com; 2700 N Vermont Ave)*.

Can't make it to Griffith Park? From Hollywood, opt instead for chapparal-draped **Runyon Canyon**, a 130-acre park famous for its buff runners and the occasional exercising celebrity.

Above: Longhorn exhibit, Autry Museum of the American West; Right: View from Griffith Observatory

Afoot in DTLA

Downtown Los Angeles (DTLA to its friends) is the city's historic hub and now its cultural capital, studded with museums, restaurants, world-class architecture, music, sports venues and some of the city's best bars. Most of it's easily reached on foot.

Getting here: DTLA is the hub of Metro subways and light rail with multiple underground stops. The most central stop is Grand Ave Arts/Bunker Hill, which is close to most sights.

Parking: Driving can be a chore between traffic to and from DTLA, a thicket of one-way streets and expensive parking.

Getting around: To go further afield, take Metro subway or light rail, or DASH buses circulate around Downtown.

Walt Disney Concert Hall

Clad in impossibly undulating, gravity-defying steel panels, Frank Gehry's **iconic venue** *(laphil.com)* is the home base of the Los Angeles Philharmonic and hosts a full calendar of other acts from jazz to film screenings and a soul-shaking pipe organ. Can't attend a concert? Tour the architecture with a free, hour-long audio guide.

Across 1st St are the multiple venues of the **Music Center of Los Angeles County**, heading down to Grand Park and LA's iconic City Hall.

Go Broad or Go Home

The Broad *(thebroad.org)* is a must-visit for contemporary-art fans. (Local's tip: 'Broad' rhymes with 'road'.) It houses a world-class (and Insta-friendly) collection of more than 2000 postwar pieces by dozens of heavy hitters. The striking building, by Diller Scofidio + Renfro in collaboration with Gensler, is shrouded in a white lattice-like shell that lifts at the corners into the lobby. Admission is free (except during special exhibitions), but reserve a timed ticket.

To continue the adventure, the **Museum of Contemporary Art** *(moca.org)* is across the street.

Expedition to Exposition Park

A short ride from Downtown on the Metro takes you to Exposition Park, where multiple museums await. The **California Science Center** *(californiasciencecenter.org)* is home to

LEFT: STEPHANIE BRACONNIER/SHUTTERSTOCK. BELOW: LEE HARI/SHUTTERSTOCK

BARS UNDER THE STARS

Spire 73
Craft cocktails and small bites on the 73rd floor of the InterContinental, the Western Hemisphere's tallest open-air bar. *(900 Wilshire Blvd)*

Perch
City lights twinkle all around, 16 stories up a renaissance revival building in the heart of DTLA. *(perchla.com)*

Angel City Brewery
Knock back an IPA, sample tunes and enjoy food truck chow at this microbrew in a former factory in the Arts District. *(angelcitybrewery.com)*

EXPERIENCE ★

Left: The Broad; Below: Dinosaur exhibit, Natural History Museum of Los Angeles County

one of just four Space Shuttles. Get your dino on at the **Natural History Museum of Los Angeles County** *(nhm.org)* and visit the changing exhibits on African American history, arts and culture at the **California African American Museum** *(caamuseum.org)*. The **Lucas Museum of Narrative Art** *(ucasmuseum.org; 1 Lucas Plaza)*, founded by *Star Wars* creator George Lucas, is due to open in 2026. Behind it all, the **Los Angeles Memorial Coliseum** *(lacoliseum.com)* has been home to two Olympics and stands to loom large when LA hosts again in 2028.

Toolkit

First Time
242

Money
243

On the Road
244

Driving Problem-Buster
246

How to Rent More than a Car
247

Where to Stay
248

Access, Attitudes & Safety
249

Responsible Travel
250

Barstow, California (p215)
NORTHSKY FILMS/SHUTTERSTOCK

First Time

For information on arriving and airports see **Chicago** (p36) and **Los Angeles** (p232).

Visas

Visitors from 42 nations, including the UK, Australia, New Zealand, Japan and many EU countries, don't need visas for stays of less than 90 days, though they must get approval from the Electronic System for Travel Authorization (ESTA). Visitors from Canada don't need a visa or ESTA approval for stays of less than 90 days. For more, see *travel.state.gov*.

Phones & Internet

Most non-US mobile phones work fine in the US but roaming charges may be high. Check what your plan allows, especially for data as you're likely to use mapping apps a lot on Route 66. Consider a cheap eSIM card with at least 5GB of data. Free wi-fi is offered in motels, hotels, cafes and many public spots.

Health Insurance

Healthcare costs in the USA are extremely high. All travelers are advised to carry a health insurance policy valid for their US travels. Without insurance, you will be billed the full cost of any care you receive. Costs can easily rise into the thousands, especially for emergency room visits.

Smoking, Vaping & Marijuana

Most states in the US, including California and Illinois, are smoke-free in restaurants, bars and workplaces; parts of southern states such as Oklahoma and Texas are exceptions. Marijuana legality varies widely by state. Small amounts for personal use are legal in California and Illinois, but are illegal in Oklahoma, Texas and elsewhere.

TAKE PHOTO ID

You may be asked to show photo ID to buy or consume alcohol by law, even if it's obvious you are well over the legal drinking age of 21.

WHAT TO WEAR

In America just about anything goes, especially along Route 66. Unless you're planning nights out at stylish places in Chicago and LA, you can dress as casual as you like.

TIME ZONES

Route 66 crosses three time zones: Central (CT, GMT/UTC minus six hours); Mountain (MT, GMT/UTC minus seven hours); and Pacific (PT, GMT/UTC minus eight hours). Daylight saving time starts on the second Sunday in March and ends on the first Sunday in November. It's not used everywhere – use your phone to determine local time.

ELECTRICITY

Type A: 120V/60Hz

Type B: 120V/60Hz

Money

Budget

A budget of $350 to $400 per day for two people on Route 66 will not leave you feeling scrimped. In Chicago and LA, you'll likely need to budget a bit more for food and lodging; however, the rest of the road runs through mostly humble communities where residents tend to be on tight budgets themselves. Opportunities to splurge outside of large cities are few. With economizing, two people can do the road for well under $300 per day.

Methods of Payment

Contactless payment with your credit card, ATM card or phone is the way to pay at more than 90% of the establishments along the road. Gas pumps may demand a PIN for whatever card you use; when in doubt, just go inside and see the cashier.

Cash is most useful for leaving tips for servers and buying things at the more idiosyncratic shops you'll encounter. ATMs are easily found at banks and convenience stores.

HOW MUCH IS a day on Route 66?

Coffee & snacks	$20
Museum entry	$12
Souvenir	$20
Lunch at roadside diner	$30
Vintage motel room	$120
Dinner at local restaurant	$50
Gas per day	$60
Care hire per day	$60
Total (per day for two adults)	**$372**

TIPPING

Tipping is not optional; it's how service people earn their living in the US.

Bartenders
15% to 20% per round, minimum per drink $1

Housekeeping
$2 to $5 per night, left by the TV or with the provided card

Restaurant servers
20% on the total, unless a gratuity is already on the bill (try to leave cash, so the server is sure to get it)

Taxi drivers
10% to 15%, rounded up to the next dollar

Dos & Don'ts

Do let your bank know you'll be traveling.
Do check prices on an indie motel's website as they may be lower than those on major booking sites.
Do consider traveling in April, May, September or October for reduced prices and the best weather.
Don't convert the cost of your transaction into your home currency at ATMs or when making a purchase as you'll get hit with fees twice.
Don't assume winter will be cheaper.

Sales Taxes

All states have sales tax, which is not included in listed prices. Sales taxes are added when your bill is calculated and vary by state, town and region. The amount of sales tax you pay can vary wildly across states and can come as a surprise for international visitors.

On the Road

GOOD TO KNOW

Drive on the right.

55

In rural areas the speed limit ranges from 55mph to 75mph. In towns and cities, it's 25mph to 35mph.

Blood alcohol limit 0.08%

Mapping Your Journey

Most map apps, such as those from Google and Apple, allow you to download mapping data for selected areas so that it's available for use offline. It's highly recommended that you download maps when you're on wi-fi as it saves a lot of bandwidth and potential roaming fees. It also lets the app display maps, even when there's no signal.

Check Conditions

State transportation departments provide road condition information through websites and apps. Most are through the 511 system (search state name and 511), which is a nation-wide network of state sources. The Route 66 state websites are: **Arizona** azdot.gov; **California** dot.ca.gov/travel; **Illinois** gettingaroundillinois.com; **Kansas** ksdot.org; **Missouri** modot.org; **New Mexico** dot.state.nm.us; **Oklahoma** ok.gov/odot; **Texas** txdot.gov.

US Driving Laws

Seat belt use is required.
Right turns on red lights are allowed unless there's a sign prohibiting this.
Never pass a school bus with flashing lights.
Pull over for emergency vehicles with flashing lights.
Holding a phone while driving is illegal in Arizona, California, Illinois and Missouri.

HOW TO: DO ROUTE 66 ON A BIKE

Biking all 2400 miles of Route 66 is an endeavor suitable only for the most committed. Various stretches are narrow, hilly and ill-suited for cyclists. Some stretches are busy with traffic while in other areas there is no original road and the interstate alternative doesn't allow bikes. What you can do is bike short stretches and scenic country lanes.

Route 66, California

DRIVER'S LICENSE

Foreign visitors can legally drive a car in the US for up to 12 months using their home driver's license. However, an International Driving Permit (IDP) will have more credibility with US traffic police, especially if your home license doesn't have a photo or isn't in English. Always carry both.

INSURANCE

That great rental car deal won't look so good if you also spend $30 a day on insurance. Agency staff are incentivized to sell you an alphabet soup of add-on coverage. Collision Damage Waiver (CDW) and Loss Damage Waiver (LDW) are the most common. Credit cards and your own insurance may obviate the need but check carefully before you arrive at the counter.

Renting a Vehicle

Car rental is competitive in the US. You'll need a major credit card (not a debit or ATM card), be at least 25 years old and have a valid driver's license. Some companies may rent to drivers under age 25 for an additional charge. 'Unlimited mileage' is standard on contracts, but confirm it's there as the alternative for a Route 66 trip is expensive. Tax on car rental varies by state and location; always ask for the total cost, including all taxes and fees. Decline the fuel purchase option as it's only a good deal if you manage to return the vehicle empty.

Saving on Rentals

Car rental prices vary wildly. The average rate for a small car ranges from around $25 to $75 per day, or $125 to $500 per week. Discounts are offered by auto clubs, credit card companies, airlines and others. Shop around. Airports are expensive places to rent a car as contracts often include surcharges that are charged every day of your rental. Check the rates for a nearby non-airport location. Be careful about adding extra days, which may come at a premium rate, or turning in a car early, which may cancel out deeply discounted weekly rates.

DRIVING PROBLEM-BUSTER

What if my car breaks down? Call your roadside assistance service (through your auto club, credit card etc) or your car rental company (although this is becoming an extra cost option).

What if I'm stopped by the police? Remain in your vehicle unless told otherwise. Keep hands where they can be seen and make no sudden moves. Be courteous and show your ID, license and registration/rental contract as requested.

What if I'm involved in an accident? If it's safe to do so, pull over to the side of the road for minor 'fender benders' with no injuries or significant property damage, and exchange insurance and driver's license information with other drivers. Follow the instructions given to you by your car rental company and/or file a report with your insurance provider as soon as possible. For major accidents, call 911 and wait for the police and emergency services to arrive.

What if my car gets stuck? There are plenty of opportunities to drive off-road along Route 66, especially in the western states. This is never a good idea as dirt tracks can rapidly turn impassible. What looks like a small bump or rock can do significant damage to the underside of your vehicle, which may not be covered by your pricey rental insurance. After rains, unpaved roads may turn into quagmires; there are tow truck operators who make a good living rescuing foolish drivers from remote locales.

Auto repair station, Kingman, Arizona (p200)

RENT MORE THAN A CAR

HOW TO

Why rent a mere car when you can opt for something with more pizzazz like an EV, RV or a motorcycle – just be sure you get unlimited mileage!

Choosing an RV

If a recreational vehicle (RV) is your dream, sites such as *usarvrentals.com* and *cruiseamerica.com* can help. Beware: mileage is usually charged separately, there are hefty insurance costs and one-way charges can be extreme. It's essential to shop around and read the fine print. Rentals range from van-based campers to enormous custom cruisers with satellite TV, full kitchens and everything else you left at home.

RV camping and parking regulations vary widely across the regions traversed by Route 66. Always check locally before settling in for the night. However, you can always find campgrounds that welcome RVs.

Motorcycles

Many of the considerations for renting a car also apply to motorcycles, except the cost: two wheels cost more than four – often much more. A Harley touring bike can cost more than $200 a day. Companies like **Lost Adventure** *(thelostadventure.com)* can arrange for one-way rentals such as Chicago to LA. You'll need a motorcycle license in your home country or state.

Opting for an EV

Major car rental firms all rent electric vehicles, from subcompacts to luxury sedans. EVs are often priced competitively and at times are among the cheapest options. Note that renters unfamiliar with EVs have balked at the vehicle's unfamiliar driving characteristics and befuddling charging options. However, the vehicles are an undeniably green alternative to gas-based vehicles. And charging options abound along Route 66, usually at chain hotels and other businesses at nearby interstate interchanges. Be sure to familiarize yourself with an EV's operation in advance as rental companies seldom provide instructions or owner's manuals for the uninitiated.

GOING ONE WAY

With open-jaw flights (eg arrive in Chicago, leave from LA) costing little more than simple round-trips, one-way vehicle rentals would seem to be the ideal way to bridge the gap. However, drop-off charges can be high. Shop around and check for discounts from auto clubs, credit cards and other memberships like Costco. Consult discounters like *autoslash.com* to compare myriad offers at once.

Where to Stay

TOOLKIT

HOW MUCH FOR...

Route 66 motel
from $60 per night

Big city hotel
from $120 per night

Campground
from $15 per night

Vintage Motels

Motels and Route 66 have a symbiotic relationship going back decades. Built to serve auto travelers, there were once hundreds along the route (p137). Today, a few survive. Some, such as the Munger Moss Motel, Lebanon, Missouri (p74) and the Blue Swallow Motel in Tucumcari, New Mexico (p152), are Mother Road icons and are beautifully restored. Many more motels can be found on the road in all eight states.

Other Options

Chain hotels cluster around interstate interchanges. Despite different brand names, modern hotels have depressingly similar designs that vary little from brand to brand. Don't expect the kinds of landscaped grounds many motels feature. More lavish properties await in Chicago, St Louis, Tulsa, Oklahoma City, Albuquerque and LA. Campgrounds are found in and near state parks and national forests.

What to Expect

American motels and hotels all offer wi-fi. Only at the most expensive properties is this basic amenity not free. Budget and midrange places feature 'free' breakfasts. Generally, these are institutional in concept and may feature under-ripe bananas and convenience foods heavy on salt and fat. Seldom will they prevent you from enjoying breakfast at a diner. Pools are not universal but are welcome after a day on the road in summer.

HOW TO: CHOOSE A VINTAGE MOTEL

Certain vintage motels on Route 66 are classics and must be booked in advance. Others with sagging eaves, busted neon signs and weedy parking lots barely hang on. In between are motels that value every guest. Look for recent reviews on social media and always ask to see a room before committing.

Wigwam Motel, Holbrook, Arizona (p188)

Access, Attitudes & Safety

Weather
Keep track of the weather along Route 66 on your phone as there are conditions to watch for year-round. Tornados are high-profile and even inspire their own subset of tourism, but they should not be underestimated. Peak season in Texas, Oklahoma and Kansas is May and June, but they can occur at other times and hit Missouri and Illinois.

Winter storms can close roads from Illinois to Arizona. In summer, extreme heat can be deadly for both humans and cars in the Southwest and California's Mojave Desert (up to 130°F/54°C). Watch out for sudden thunderstorms with lightning and intense downpours, which flood roads.

Accessible Travel
If you have a physical disability, the USA can be an accommodating place. The Americans with Disabilities Act (ADA) requires all public buildings, private commercial buildings built after 1993 (including hotels, restaurants and museums) and public transit be wheelchair accessible. When booking a hotel or motel, ask about a disabled room, which will have features that make it fully accessible. One advantage of vintage motels is that they have parking directly in front of each room, making access easier.

Many national and state parks and recreation areas have wheelchair-accessible trails. Many also have exhibits geared to people with various sensory impairments.

Crime
For the Route 66 traveler petty theft is the biggest concern. When driving, don't pick up hitchhikers, and lock valuables in your vehicle's trunk or covered cargo area before you set out for the day (thieves watch for people locking things away in parking lots).

Women travelers won't face any unusual hazards. Solo travelers should watch their phone signals if they are venturing on remote detours.

Children
A trip on Route 66 is fun for all ages. Most attractions are geared toward the entire family and around every bend it seems like there's another wacko gift shop selling improbable novelties not found in any suburban mall (hello Uranus Fudge Factory!, p74). Natural delights abound, from Meramec Caverns (p70) to the Painted Desert (p190) and the Santa Monica Beach (p230).

Motels and hotels have rooms with two beds, which are ideal for families. Some offer rollaway beds or cribs for an extra charge. Some properties have 'kids stay free' schemes for children up to 12 or sometimes 18 years of age.

LGBTIQ+ TRAVELERS
Because of the constant influx of Route 66 tourists and the lure of operating the often offbeat and creative businesses along the road, there's acceptance of LGBTIQ+ people along the Mother Road. However, you don't have to stray too far in states like Oklahoma and Texas to find frostier attitudes.

Responsible Travel

Climate Change & Travel

It's impossible to ignore the impact we have when traveling; Lonely Planet urges all travelers to engage with their travel carbon footprint, which will mainly come from air travel. While there often isn't an alternative, travellers can look to minimize the number of flights they take, opt for newer aircrafts and use cleaner ground transport, such as trains. One proposed solution – purchasing carbon offsets – unfortunately does not cancel out the impact of individual flights. While most destinations will depend on air travel for the foreseeable future, for now, pursuing ground-based travel where possible is the best course of action.

SIGN THE GUESTBOOK

The humble guestbook sitting on a counter is more than just a quaint nicety. It's often how museums, businesses and attractions track visitors, which in turn fuels grant applications and budget requests to remain open.

The **UN Carbon Offset Calculator** shows how flying impacts a household's emissions.

The **ICAO's carbon emissions calculator** allows visitors to analyse the CO_2 generated by point-to-point journeys.

Right-Size Your Ride

Many succumb to the temptation of piloting a huge SUV or 4WD for their Route 66 adventure. Don't do it! Route 66 is not suited for burning rubber, and going offroad damages delicate ecosystems, no matter the size of your tires.

WATER

Tap water is absolutely fine to drink from one end of Route 66 to the other. In fact, many of the common national brands at the lower (yet still pricey for plain water) end of the cost spectrum are simply municipal water resold for enormous profit. Carry a refillable container or buy water once and keep refilling that container.

ISAAC LEE/GETTY IMAGES

Preserving Route 66

A patchwork of schemes in recent years have worked to preserve elements of Route 66 such as neon signs and iconic old structures such as gas stations. Many can be found at a site maintained by the **National Park Service** *(nps.gov/subjects/travel route66/visit.htm)*. The National Trust for Historic Preservation is leading a campaign to get the Mother Road declared a **National Historic Trail** *(savingplaces. org/preserve-route-66)*. This will pave the way for more preservation funding.

Indigenous Nations

Route 66 passes near and through significant lands of more than 25 tribal nations. These cultures and heritage are evident as you travel the Mother Road. While some roadside attractions in the Southwest popular in Route 66's heyday perpetuate wildly inaccurate stereotypes about Native peoples in these regions, there are increasingly more authentic, respectful opportunities for non-indigenous peoples to engage with and learn from Native peoples. The **American Indian Alaska Native Tourism Association** *(aianta.org/american-indianexperiences -along-route-66)* has a list of experiences that provide insight into or support Native communities. It also has a free downloadable guidebook *(route66news. com/wp-content/uploads/2016/04/ route66-native-americans-min.pdf)* with loads of information about the various nations, including maps. Also worth checking out is *navajoguide.com,* an information-packed website covering travel in Navajo Nation created by George Joe, who wrote That Ain't Us (p164).

California Route 66 Museum, Victorville (p224)

STAY TRUE TO THE ETHOS OF ROUTE 66

Go local. It may seem obvious, but we all get so inured to the idea of national chains that we patronize them for shopping or as a matter of habit and because they offer ease. The whole point of touring Route 66 is to enjoy a more authentic and idiosyncratic adventure, so take the pledge: Always local! (And your support is vital to the businesses that give Route 66 its character.)

Stay local. Ignore the bland chain hotels clustered at interstate interchanges. On awakening, few can tell if they're in a generic Hampton Inn or a bland La Quinta, each offering 'free' waffles more akin to Styrofoam. Meanwhile, characterful, locally owned motels – where you can pull right up to your room – can be found all along Route 66, from Lebanon, Missouri to Flagstaff, Arizona and beyond. Often, they have histories closely linked to the Mother Road.

Eat local. Don't go through that drive-through and get a bag of food you'll forget before you're done. Local favorites serving regional food are found in nearly every town and are an ideal first introduction to a region. And almost every place has a favored spot for morning coffee.

Index

Map pages **000**

A

accessible travel 249
accommodations 137, 248, *see also* vintage motels, *individual routes*
Adrian, TX 138
Albuquerque, NM 21, 172, 173, 174-7, 179, **175**
Albuquerque to Lupton 168-81, **170-1**, *see also* Glenrio to Albuquerque, Lupton to Topock
  accommodations 170, 179
  food 170, 173, 175
  highlights 170-1
Amarillo, TX 13, 21, 127, 130, 132-4, 135-6
Amboy, CA 210-11
Arcadia, OK 110
architecture 10-11, 43
  Albuquerque, NM 174, 176
  Flagstaff, AZ 193
  Laguna Pueblo, NM 172
  Los Angeles, CA 238
  Painted Desert, AZ 191
  Palm Springs, CA 226
  Pasadena, CA 228
  Santa Fe, NM 160
  Tulsa, OK 96
  Winslow, AZ 188
Arizona 184-201, **186-7**
  Ash Fork 196
  Cool Springs Station 198-9
  Flagstaff 189, 192, 193, 199
  Grand Canyon Caverns 196-7
  Grand Canyon National Park 194-5
  Hackberry 198
  Kingman 198, 200
  Lupton 188
  Meteor Crater 192
  Oatman 199, 201
  Painted Desert 188, 190-1
  Seligman 182-3, 196, 199
  Topock 201
  Truxton 197-8
  Valentine 198
  Williams 189, 192, 196
Winona 192
Winslow 188-9, 199
art galleries & installations
  Affeldt Mion Museum, AZ 189
  Art Institute of Chicago, IL 39
  Broad, The, CA 238
  Cloud Gate, IL 41
  Cuba murals, MO 72
  Elmer's Bottle Tree Ranch, CA 224
  Flagstaff murals, AZ 193
  Gallup murals, NM 180
  Georgia O'Keeffe Museum, NM 158
  Larry Baggett's Trail of Tears Memorial, MO 73
  Liberty Sculpture Park, CA 214
  Los Angeles County Museum of Art, CA 234
  Museum of Contemporary Art, CA 238
  National Hispanic Cultural Center, NM 177
  New Mexico Museum of Art, NM 160
  Palm Springs Art Museum, CA 226
  Philbrook Museum of Art, OK 97
  St Louis Art Museum, MO 68
Ash Fork, AZ 196
Atlanta, IL 13, 52
Auburn, IL 57

B

Bagdad Cafe 10, 120-1, 212, 215
Barstow, CA 211, 212, 215
Barstow to Santa Monica 220-31, **222-3**, *see also* Los Angeles, Needles to Barstow
  accommodations 222, 229
  food 222, 225, 227
  highlights 222-3
baseball 42, 234
Baxter Springs, KS 90
beaches 231
Bernalillo, NM 163
Better Call Saul 177
Black Americans & Route 66 100-3, 110
Blueberry Hill 69
Blues Brothers 50
Bluewater, NM 179
books 24
Breaking Bad 177
bridges
  Brush Creek Bridge, KS 90
  Chain of Rocks Bridge, IL 56, 59
  Lake Overholser Bridge, OK 114
  McKinley Bridge, IL 58
  Pony Bridge, OK 29, 116
  Pryor Creek Bridge, OK 94
  Rio Puerco Bridge, NM 172
  Route 66 Gasconade Bridge, MO 74
  Trails Arch Bridge, CA 210
  Walnut Canyon Bridge, AZ 192
budget 36, 232, 243, 245
burros 198, 199, 201

C

Cadillac Ranch, TX 24, 136, 138
California 206-17, 220-31, **208-9**, **222-3**
  Amboy 210-11
  Barstow 211, 212, 215
  Calico Ghost Town Regional Park 212, 215, 216-17
  Fenner 210
  Goffs 210
  Joshua Tree National Park 212, 213
  Los Angeles 232-9
  Ludlow 211
  Needles 210, 211, 212
  Newberry Springs 212, 215
  Oro Grande 224
  Palm Springs 226-7, 228, **227**
  Pasadena 225, 228, 229
  San Bernardino 225, 228, 229
  Santa Monica 225, 229, 230-1, **231**
  Victorville 224-5
  Yermo 211, 212, 214, 215, 216-17
car rental 245, 247
carbon offset calulators 250
Cars 10, 61, 90, 108, 117, 119, 120, 126, 138, 183, 196, 197
Carthage, MO 78
Catoosa, OK 94-5

caves
  Fantastic Caverns, MO 77
  Grand Canyon Caverns, AZ 196-7
  Meramec Caverns, MO 13, 70-1
cell phones 242
cemeteries
  Calico Ghost Town, CA 216
  Hollywood Forever Cemetery, CA 229
  Oak Ridge Cemetery, IL 55
Chandler, OK 108, 110
Chelsea, OK 94
Chicago 36-43, 48-50, **37**
  accommodations 40
  food 21, 40, 48-9
  itineraries 37
  transport 36
Chicago to St Louis 44-59, **46-7**, see also Chicago, St Louis to Joplin
  accommodations 46, 51
  food 49
  highlights 46-7
children, travel with 249
chukars 217
Claremore, OK 94
climate change 250
Clinton, OK 116
clothing 242
Colorado River, AZ 201
comedy clubs 38
Continental Divide 178-9
Conway, MO 74
Conway, TX 127, 130
Cool Springs Station, AZ 198-9
costs 36, 232, 243, 245
COVID-19 218-19
crime 249
Cuba, MO 71-2
Cuervo, NM 154
cycling 59, 244

Davis, Bette 71-2
Delgadillo, Angel 119, 182-3, 196
diners 18, 20, 28-9
  Emma Jean's Holland Burger Café, CA 225
  Lou Mitchell's, IL 48-9
  Ludlow Café, CA 211
  Mel's Drive-In, CA 230
  MidPoint Cafe, TX 138
  Mr D'z Route 66 Diner, AZ 200
  Rock Cafe, OK 108, 111

disabilities, travelers with 249
documentaries 121, see also films
drive-in theaters
  66 Drive-In Theatre, MO 79
  Cozy Dog Drive In, IL 52, 58
  Dog House Drive In, NM 177
  Rt 66 Skyview Drive-In, IL 56
drive-through restaurants 29
driver's licenses 245
Dust Bowl 27-8, 118, 131
Dwight, IL 50-1

electric vehicles 247
electricity 242
El Malpais National Monument, NM 178
El Reno, OK 114-16
Elk City, OK 116
Erick, OK 116-17
events, see festivals & events

family travel 249
Fenner, CA 210
festivals & events 76-7, 176
films 10-11, 120-1, 166, see also individual films
Flagstaff, AZ 189, 192, 193, 199
food 18-21, see also diners, individual routes
  Arizona cuisine 201
  barbecue 20, 130
  chicken fried steaks 20, 93, 135
  fried chicken 18, 50
  frozen custard 18
  fudge 24, 74
  horseshoe sandwiches 55
  hot dogs 40, 53, 200, 236
  ice cream 50, 66, 79, 196, 228
  New Mexican cuisine 161
  onion burgers 115
  pizza 40
  toasted ravioli 18
Foyil, OK 94
Funks Grove Pure Maple Sirup, IL 52

Galena, KS 90
Galena to Tulsa 86-99, **88-9**, see also St Louis to Joplin, Tulsa to Texola

accommodations 88, 96, 99
food 88, 93, 97
highlights 88-9
Gallup, NM 166, 179-80
Gateway Arch, MO 66
Gehry, Frank 41, 238
Gillespie, IL 57
Girard, IL 57
Glenrio to Albuquerque 148-63, **150-1**, see also Albuquerque to Lupton, Texola to Glenrio
  accommodations 150, 157
  food 150, 153, 159
  highlights 150-1
Glenrio, TX 138
Glorieta Pass, NM 157
Goffs, CA 210
Grand Canyon National Park, AZ 194-5
Grants, NM 178
Grapes of Wrath, The 11, 27, 118, 121
Gray Summit, MO 70
Great Depression, the 27-8, 118
Green Book 100-3
Groom, TX 127
guestbooks 250
Guthrie, Woody 96

Hackberry, AZ 198
health insurance 242
Hemingway, Ernest 178
highlights 13, 17
  Arizona 186-7
  California 208-9, 222-3
  Illinois 46-7
  Kansas 88-9
  Missouri 64-5
  New Mexico 150-1, 170-1
  Oklahoma 88-9, 106-7
  Texas 124
hiking
  Grand Canyon, AZ 194-5
  Gray Summit, MO 70
  Joshua Tree National Park, CA 213
  Palm Springs, CA 226
  Palo Duro Canyon, TX 128-9
  Rio Grande Nature Center State Park, NM 175
  Runyon Canyon, CA 237
  Santa Fe, NM 159
  Wildcat Bluff Nature Center, TX 132

historical sites & markers
  Andy Payne statue, KS 94
  Battle of Carthage State Historic Site, MO 78
  Battle of Virden, IL 57
  Cahokia Mounds State Historic Site, IL 56
  Centennial Land Run Monument, OK 112
  Fort Reno, OK 116
  La Brea Tar Pits, CA 234
  La Cieneguilla Petroglyph Site, NM 159
  Lincoln Home National Historic Site, IL 54
  Mela Leger historical marker, NM 154
  Mother Jones Monument, IL 56
  Pecos Pueblo, NM 156
  Puerco Pueblo, AZ 191
  site of original McDonald's, CA 225
  Wilson's Creek National Battlefield, MO 78
history 26-9
  birthplace of Route 66 77
  Black Americans & Route 66 100-3, 110
  boarding school abuses 198
  Bonnie & Clyde 79
  decommissioning of Route 66 29
  Dust Bowl 27-8, 118, 131
  evolution of motels 137
  Federal-Aid Highway Act 28, 29
  first-person accounts 164-7, 182-3, 202-3, 218-19
  Great Chicago Fire 38
  Great Depression, the 27-8, 118
  Green Book 100-3
  Homestead Act of 1862 131
  impact of interstates 165, 182-3, 197
  Indian Removal Act of 1830 73
  Kansas mining strikes 91
  Oklahoma City bombing 112
  post-WWII 28-9
  Santa Fe Trail 156
  Times Beach scandal 70, 71
  Trail of Tears 72-3
  Tulsa Race Massacre 98
Hollywood Walk of Fame, CA 235

Illinois 36-59, **46-7**
  Atlanta 52
  Auburn 57
  Cahokia Mounds State Historic Site 56
  Chain of Rocks Bridge 56, 59
  Chatham 53
  Chicago 36-43, 48-50, **37**
  Dwight 50-1
  Funks Grove Pure Maple Sirup 52
  Gillespie 57
  Girard 57
  Joliet 50
  Litchfield 53, 56
  McKinley Bridge 58
  Mt Olive 56
  Nilwood 57
  Pontiac 51-2
  Springfield 52-3, 54-5
  Thayer 57
  Virden 57
  Wilmington 50
insurance 242, 245
Isleta, NM 172

Jerome, MO 72
Joliet, IL 50
Joplin, MO 79

Kansas 90-1, **88-9**
  Baxter Springs 90
  Galena 90
Kewa Pueblo, NM 163
Killers of the Flower Moon 98, 108, 109
Kingman, AZ 198, 200

L

La Bajada Mesa, NM 163
La Ventana Arch, NM 178
Laguna Pueblo, NM 172-3
Lange, Dorothea 118
Las Vegas, NM 156
Lebanon, MO 74
Leger, Mela 154
LGBTIQ+ travelers 227, 249
Lincoln, Abraham 54-5
Litchfield, IL 49, 53, 56

Los Alamos, NM 161
Los Angeles, CA 21, 232-9, **233**
  accommodations 236
  food 236
  itineraries 233
  transport 232
Los Lunas, NM 172
Ludlow, CA 211
Lupton, AZ 188
Lupton, NM 181
Lupton to Topock 184-201, **186-7**, *see also* Albuquerque to Lupton, Needles to Barstow
  accommodations 186, 199
  food 186, 189, 201
  highlights 186-7
Luther, OK 110

M

Madrid, NM 162
Manhattan Project 161
Manuelito, NM 180-1
maps 244
marijuana 242
McCartys, NM 173, 178
McLean, TX 126
Meramec Caverns, MO 13, 70-1
mesas 16, 152, 154, 178, 191
Mesita, NM 172
Meteor Crater, AZ 192
Miami, OK 93
Missouri 62-79, **64-5**
  Carterville 79
  Carthage 78-9
  Cuba 71-2
  Jerome 72
  Joplin 79
  Lebanon 74
  Meramec Caverns 13, 70-1
  Pacific 70
  Route 66 Gasconade Bridge 74
  Route 66 State Park 67
  Shaw Nature Reserve 70
  Springfield 75-7
  St Louis 21, 66-7, 68-9, **69**
  Uranus 74
  Webb City 79
  Wilson's Creek National Battlefield 78
mobile phones 242
money 243
Montoya, NM 152-3
Moriarty, NM 155

motorcycles 247
Mt Olive, IL 56
Muffler Men 13, 23, 24, 56
　Atlanta, IL 52
　Gallup, NM 180
　museums 52
　Tulsa, OK 99
　Wilmington, IL 50
　YouTube series 24
museums, *see also* Route 66 museums
　100th Meridian Museum, OK 117
　Academy Museum of Motion Pictures, CA 234
　Albuquerque Museum, NM 174
　American Giants Museum, IL 52
　American International Rattlesnake Museum, NM 174
　American Quarter Horse Hall of Fame & Museum, TX 132
　Autry Museum of the American West, CA 237
　Baxter Springs Heritage Center & Museum, KS 90
　California African American Museum, CA 239
　California Science Center, CA 238
　City Museum, St Louis, MO 68
　Civil War Museum, MO 78
　Claremore Museum of History, OK 94
　First Americans Museum, OK 112
　Getty Center, CA 234
　Gilcrease Museum, OK 96-7
　Goffs Schoolhouse, CA 210
　Greenwood Rising, OK 98
　Hammer Museum, CA 234
　Hollywood Museum, CA 235
　Indian Pueblo Cultural Center, NM 174
　Jack Sisemore RV Museum, TX 132
　Joplin History & Mineral Museum, MO 79
　Kingman Railroad Museum, AZ 200
　Lewis Antique Auto & Toy Museum, NM 155
　Lincoln Presidential Library & Museum, IL 54
　Lucas Museum of Narrative Art, CA 239
　Madrid Old Coal Town Museum, NM 162
　Missouri History Museum, MO 68
　Museum of Indian Arts & Culture, NM 158
　Museum of Transportation, MO 66
　National Cowboy & Western Heritage Museum, OK 112
　National Museum of Nuclear Science & History, NM 174
　National Route 66 Museum, OK 116
　Natural History Museum of Los Angeles County, CA 239
　New Mexico Mining Museum, NM 178
　Oklahoma City National Memorial & Museum, OK 112
　Oklahoma History Center, OK 112
　Osage Nation Museum, OK 109
　Petersen Automotive Museum, Los Angeles, CA 234
　Rex Museum, NM 179-80
　Route 66 Interpretive Center, OK 108
　St Louis Science Center, MO 68
　Tinkertown Museum, NM 162
　Turquoise Museum, NM 174
　Western America Railroad Museum, CA 215
　Will Rogers Memorial Museum, OK 94
　Woody Guthrie Center, OK 96
　Yavapai Geology Museum, AZ 195
music 60-1

national & state parks
　Cerrillos Hills State Park, NM 162
　El Malpais National Monument, NM 178
　Gateway Arch, MO 66
　Grand Canyon National Park, AZ 194-5
　Joshua Tree National Park, CA 212, 213
　Manhattan Project National Historical Park, NM 163
　Mt San Jacinto State Park, CA 226
　Osage Hills State Park, OK 109
　Palo Duro Canyon State Park, TX 128
　Pecos National Historical Park, NM 156
　Petrified Forest National Park, AZ 188, 190-1
　Rio Grande Nature Center State Park, NM 175
Navajo culture 164-7
Needles, CA 210, 211, 212
Needles to Barstow 206-17, **208-9**, *see also* Barstow to Santa Monica, Lupton to Topock
　accommodations 208, 212
　food 208, 211
　highlights 208-9
neon signs 80-3
　66 Bowl, OK 110
　Berghoff Restaurant, IL 48
　Blue Swallow Motel, NM 152, 157
　Comet II Drive In & Restaurant, NM 154
　De Anza Motor Lodge, NM 176
　Dell Rhea's Chicken Basket, IL 50
　Lincoln Motel, OK 108
　Meadow Gold, OK 95
　Munger Moss Motel, MO 74
　Route 66 drive-thru neon sign, NM 178
　Route 66 Neon Sign Park, OK 99
　Roy's Motel & Café, CA 211
　Sands Motel, NM 178
　Skyliner Motel, OK 108
　TeePee Curios, NM 152
　Tewa Lodge, NM 176
　West Theatre, NM 178
New Mexico 148-63, 168-81, **150-1**, **170-1**
　Albuquerque 121, 72, 173, 174-7, 179, **175**
　Bernalillo 163
　Bluewater 179
　Cuervo 154
　El Malpais National Monument 178
　Gallup 166, 179-80
　Glorieta Pass 157
　Grants 178
　Isleta 172
　Kewa Pueblo 163
　Laguna Pueblo 172-3
　Las Vegas 156
　Los Alamos 161
　Los Lunas 172
　Lupton 181
　Madrid 162
　Manuelito 180-1
　McCartys 173, 178
　Mesita 172
　Montoya 152-3
　Moriarty 155
　Pecos Valley 156
　San Jon 152
　Santa Fe 153, 157-1, **159**
　Santa Rosa 154
　Tucumcari 152
　Zuni Pueblo 181
Newberry Springs, CA 212, 215
Nilwood, IL 57
nomenclature 26-7, 75

Oatman, AZ 199, 201
Oklahoma 92-9, 104-19, **93-4**, **106-7**
　Arcadia 110
　Catoosa 94-5
　Chandler 108, 110
　Chelsea 94
　Claremore 94
　Clinton 116
　El Reno 114-16
　Elk City 116
　Erick 116-17
　Foyil 94
　Luther 110
　Miami 93
　Oklahoma City 21, 111-13, 114, **113**
　Osage County 108-9
　Pony Bridge 116
　Sapulpa 108
　Stroud 108
　Texola 118
　Tulsa 93, 95-9, **97**
　Vinita 13, 93
original stretches of Route 66
　Chatham, IL 53
　Conway, TX 127, 130
　Miami, OK 92
　Springfield, IL 57
Oro Grande, CA 224
Osage County 108-9
Osage Nation 108-9
Owens Thompson, Florence 118

Pacific, MO 70
Painted Desert, AZ 188, 190-1
Palm Springs, CA 226-7, 228, **227**
Palo Duro Canyon, TX 128-9
Palomas, NM 152
parks & gardens
　Birthplace of Route 66 Park, MO 76
　California Botanical Garden, CA 228
　Cholla Cactus Garden, Joshua Tree National Park, CA 213
　Forest Park, MO 68
　Grant Park, IL 48
　Griffith Park, CA 237
　Guthrie Green, OK 96

　John Hope Franklin Reconciliation Park, OK 98
　Joseph H. Williams Tallgrass Prairie Preserve, OK 109
　Lurie Garden, IL 41
　Millennium Park, IL 41
　Park Lake Historic District, NM 154
　Shaw Nature Reserve, MO 70
　Standin' On the Corner Park, AZ 189
Pasadena, CA 225, 228, 229
Pawhuska, OK 109
Payne, Andy 94
Pecos Valley, NM 156
photo ID 242
planning 8-25, 30-1, 241-51
　Arizona 186-7
　budget 36, 243, 243, 245
　California 208-9, 222-3
　car rentals 245
　clothing 242
　documentation 242
　Illinois 46-7
　insurance 242, 245
　Kansas 88-9
　Missouri 64-5
　money matters 243
　New Mexico 150-1, 170-1
　Oklahoma 88-9, 106-7
　road laws 244
　RV rentals 247
　Texas 124
playlists 61
podcasts 11, 109
ponderosa pines 192
Pontiac, IL 51-2
preservation organizations 251
Pritzker Pavilion, IL 41
pueblos 181

resources 117, 244
responsible travel 164-7, 250-1
Riggs, Lynn 94
Riverwalk, IL 43
roadside attractions 22-5, *see also* Muffler Men
　Blue Whale of Catoosa, OK 94-5
　Cadillac Ranch, TX 24, 136, 138
　Calico Ghost Town Regional Park, CA 212, 215, 216-17
　Chicken Boy, CA 229
　Chief Yellowhorse, NM 181

　Gemini Giant, IL 50
　Jack Rabbit Trading Post, AZ 188
　Leaning Water Tower, TX 127
　Road Runner's Retreat, CA 210
　Rock-A-Hoola Waterpark, CA 215
　Rocky the Route 66 Snake, CA 210
　Round Barn, OK 110
　Sandhills Curiosity Shop, OK 117
　Slug Bug Ranch, TX 136
　Wigwam Motels 23
Rogers, Will 95
Route 66 completion certificates 230
Route 66 museums
　Ash Fork Route 66 Museum, AZ 196
　California Route 66 Museum, CA 224
　Devil's Rope Museum & Route 66 Museum, TX 126
　Oklahoma Route 66 Museum 116
　Red Cedar Inn Museum & Visitor Center, MO 70
　Route 66 Association of Illinois Hall of Fame & Museum, Pontiac 51
　Route 66 Museum, AZ 200
　Route 66 Museum & Research Center, MO 74
　Route 66 State Park, MO 67
Route 66 (television series) 28, 121
routes 30-1, *see also individual routes*
Russell, Harley 24
RVs 247

sales taxes 243
San Bernardino, CA 225, 228, 229
San Jon, NM 152
Santa Fe, NM 153, 157-61, **159**
Santa Monica, CA 225, 229, 230-1, **231**
Santa Rosa, NM 154
Sapulpa, OK 108
scenic train rides 195
Seligman, AZ 182-3, 196, 199
Shamrock, TX 126, 130
Slug Bug Ranch, TX 136
smoking 242
solo travelers 249
speed limits 244
Springfield, IL 49, 51, 52, 54-5
Springfield, MO 29, 67, 75-7
St Louis, MO 21, 66-7, 68-9, **69**
St Louis to Joplin 62-79, **64-5**, *see also* Chicago to St Louis, Galena to Tulsa

accommodations 64, 72
food 66, 67, 69
highlights 64-5
Stroud, OK 108

taxes 243
Texas 122-39, **124-5**
  Adrian 138
  Amarillo 127, 130, 132-4, 135-6
  Cadillac Ranch 24, 136, 138
  Conway 127, 130
  Glenrio 138
  Groom 127
  McLean 126
  Palo Duro Canyon State Park 128-9
  Shamrock 126, 130
  Slug Bug Ranch 136
  Vega 138
Texola, OK 118
Texola to Glenrio 122-39, **124-5**, see also Glenrio to Albuquerque, Tulsa to Texola
  accommodations 124, 130
  food 124, 127, 129, 133, 161
  highlights 124-5
Thayer, IL 57
theme parks
  Universal Studios Hollywood, CA 234
  Warner Bros Studio Tour, CA 234
  Wonderland Amusement Park, TX 133
Threatt, Allen 110
time zones 242
tipping 243
Topock, AZ 201
Trail of Tears 72-3
train travel 189
travel alerts 244
travel insurance 242
travel seasons 16, 31, 249
travel to/from USA 36, 232
tribal nations 166, 251

Troup, Bobby 28, 61, 197
Truxton, AZ 197-8
Tucumcari, NM 13, 152
Tulsa, OK 93, 95-9, **97**
Tulsa to Texola 104-19, **106-7**, see also Galena to Tulsa, Texola to Glenrio
  accommodations 106, 114
  food 106, 109, 111, 113, 115
  highlights 106-7
Turquoise Trail, NM 162

Uranus, MO 24, 74

Valentine, AZ 198
vaping 242
Vega, TX 138
Venice Boardwalk, CA 234
Victorville, CA 224-5
Vinita, OK 13, 93
vintage gas stations 11, 28-9, 140-5
  Ambler's Texaco Station, IL 50-1
  Cucamonga Service Station, CA 228
  Gary's Gay Parita Sinclair Station, MO 78
  Hackberry General Store, AZ 198
  Lucille's Service Station, OK 116
  Phillips Gas Station, McLean, TX 126
  Soulsby Service Station, IL 56
  Spencer Station, MO 78
  Threatt Filling Station, OK 110
  Tower Station, TX 126
  Westfall Phillips 66 Station, OK 110
vintage motels 28-9, 137, 248
  Astro Pasadena Hotel, CA 229
  Aztec Motel & Creative Space, AZ 196, 199
  Best Western Route 66 Rail Haven, MO 76
  Blue Swallow Motel, NM 152, 157

Boots Court Motel, MO 78
El Trovatore Motel, AZ 200
Historic Route 66 Motel, AZ 196
Historic Route 66 Motel, NM 152
Lincoln Motel, OK 108
Luna Lodge, NM 176
Motel DuBeau Travelers Inn, AZ 199
Motel Safari, NM 152
Munger Moss Motel, MO 72, 74
Roadrunner Lodge, NM 152
Shamrock Country Inn, TX 130
Skylark, The Palm Springs, CA 226
Skyliner Motel, OK 108
Wigwam Motel, AZ 188
Wigwam Motel, CA 229
Virden, IL 57
visas 242
visitor centers
  Litchfield Museum & Route 66 Welcome Center, IL 53
  Route 66 Springfield Visitor Center, MO 76
  Route 66 Visitors Center, KS 90
  Texas Route 66 Visitor Center, TX 132

Waldmire, Bob 58
Walt Disney Concert Hall 238
water 250
weather 244, 249
Webb City, MO 79
Williams, AZ 29, 189, 192, 196
Winona, AZ 192
Winslow, AZ 13, 188-9, 199
Wright, Frank Lloyd 43
Wrigley Field, Chicago, IL 42

Yermo, CA 211, 212, 214, 215, 216-17

Zuni Pueblo, NM 181

THIS BOOK

Destination Editor
James Smart

Production Editor
Lauren O'Connell

Assisting Editor
Anne Mulvaney

Book Designer
Fergal Condon

Cartographer
Daniela Machová, Katerina Pavkova

Cover Illustration
Guy Shield

Illustrated Map
James Gulliver Hancock

Product Development
Anne Mason, James Smart,
Marc Backwell, Katerina Pavkova

Series Development Leadership
Darren O'Connell, Piers Pickard, Chris Zeiher

Thanks
Sofie Anderson, Esti Fernandez, Sandie Kestell, Dan Moore, Sarah Stocking, Melissa Yeager

Paper in this book is certified against the Forest Stewardship Council™ standards. FSC™ promotes environmentally responsible, socially beneficial and economically viable management of the world's forests.

Published by Lonely Planet Global Limited
CRN 554153
1st edition – Sep 2025
ISBN 9781837586653
© Lonely Planet 2025 Photographs © as indicated 2025
10 9 8 7 6 5 4 3 2 1
Printed in China

All rights reserved. No part of this publication may be copied, stored in a retrieval system, or transmitted in any form by any means, electronic, mechanical, recording or otherwise, except brief extracts for the purpose of review, and no part of this publication may be sold or hired, without the written permission of the publisher. Lonely Planet and the Lonely Planet logo are trademarks of Lonely Planet and are registered in the US Patent and Trademark Office and in other countries. Lonely Planet does not allow its name or logo to be appropriated by commercial establishments, such as retailers, restaurants or hotels. Please let us know of any misuses: lonelyplanet.com/legal/intellectual-property.

Mapping data sources:
©Lonely Planet, ©OpenStreetMap, ©Natural Earth, ©GEBCO, ©Esri, ©NASA Earth Observatory, ©USGS-ASTER and the GIS User Community